PALETTE KNIFE PAINTING
In Acrylics

PROJECTS, TECHNIQUES & INSPIRATION TO GET YOU STARTED

TIM FISHER

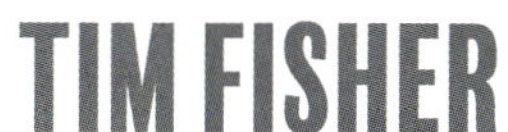

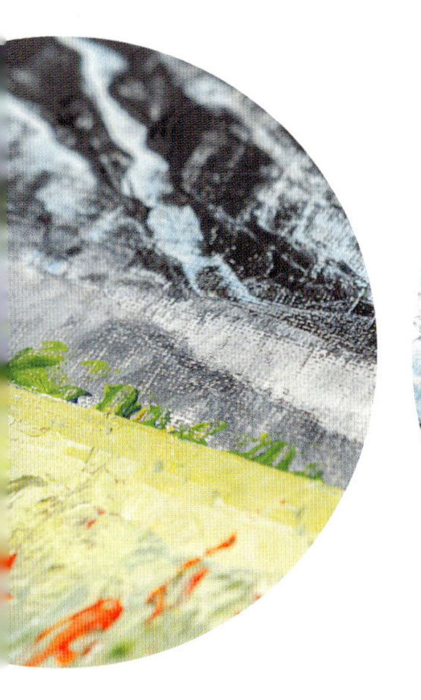

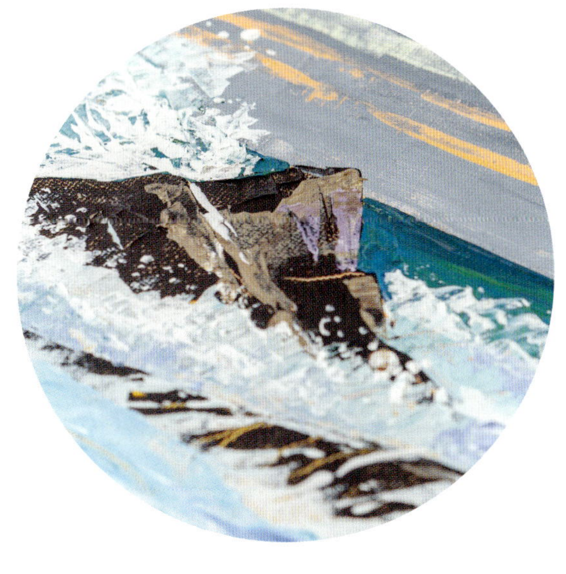

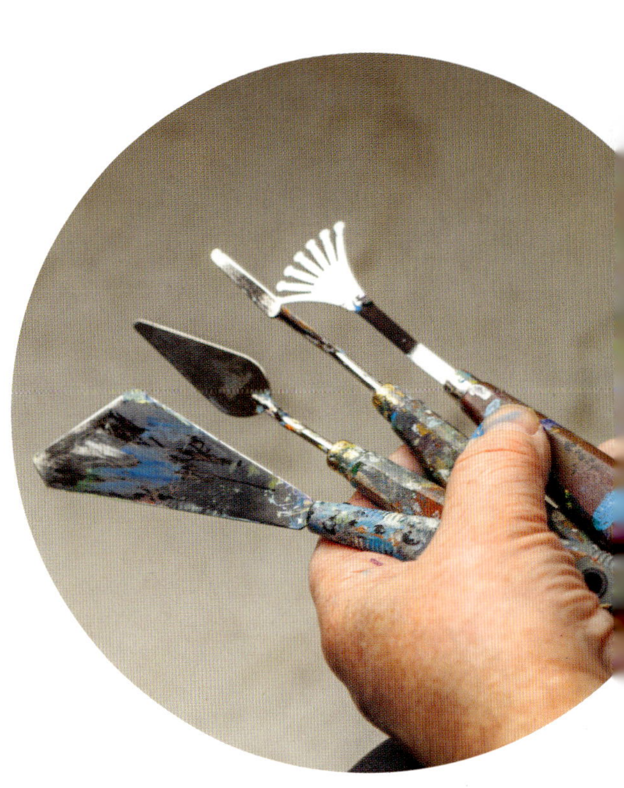

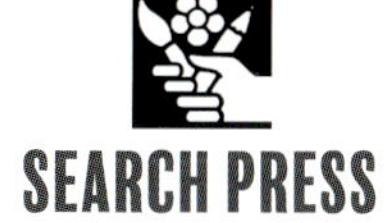

SEARCH PRESS

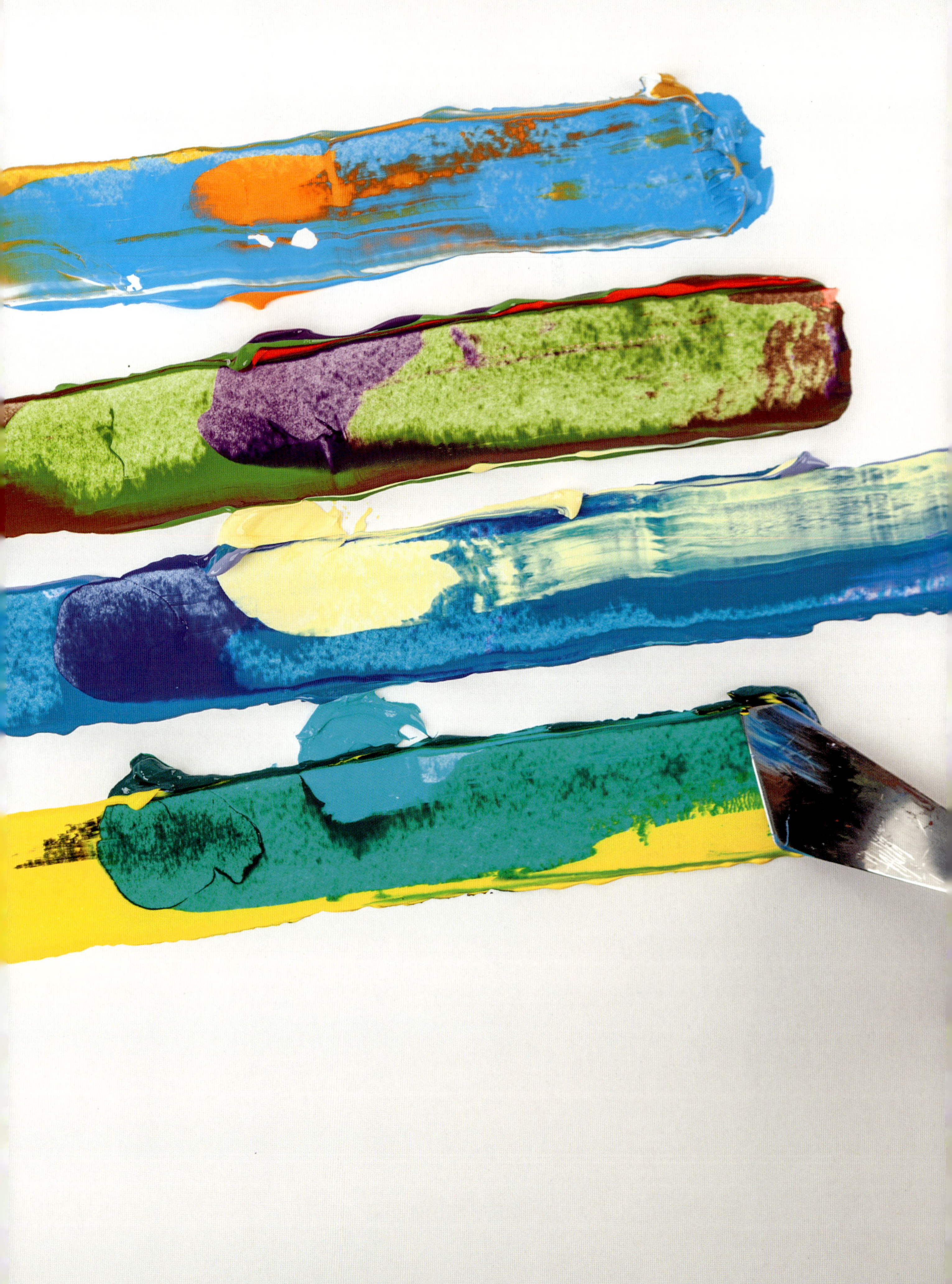

PALETTE KNIFE PAINTING
In Acrylics

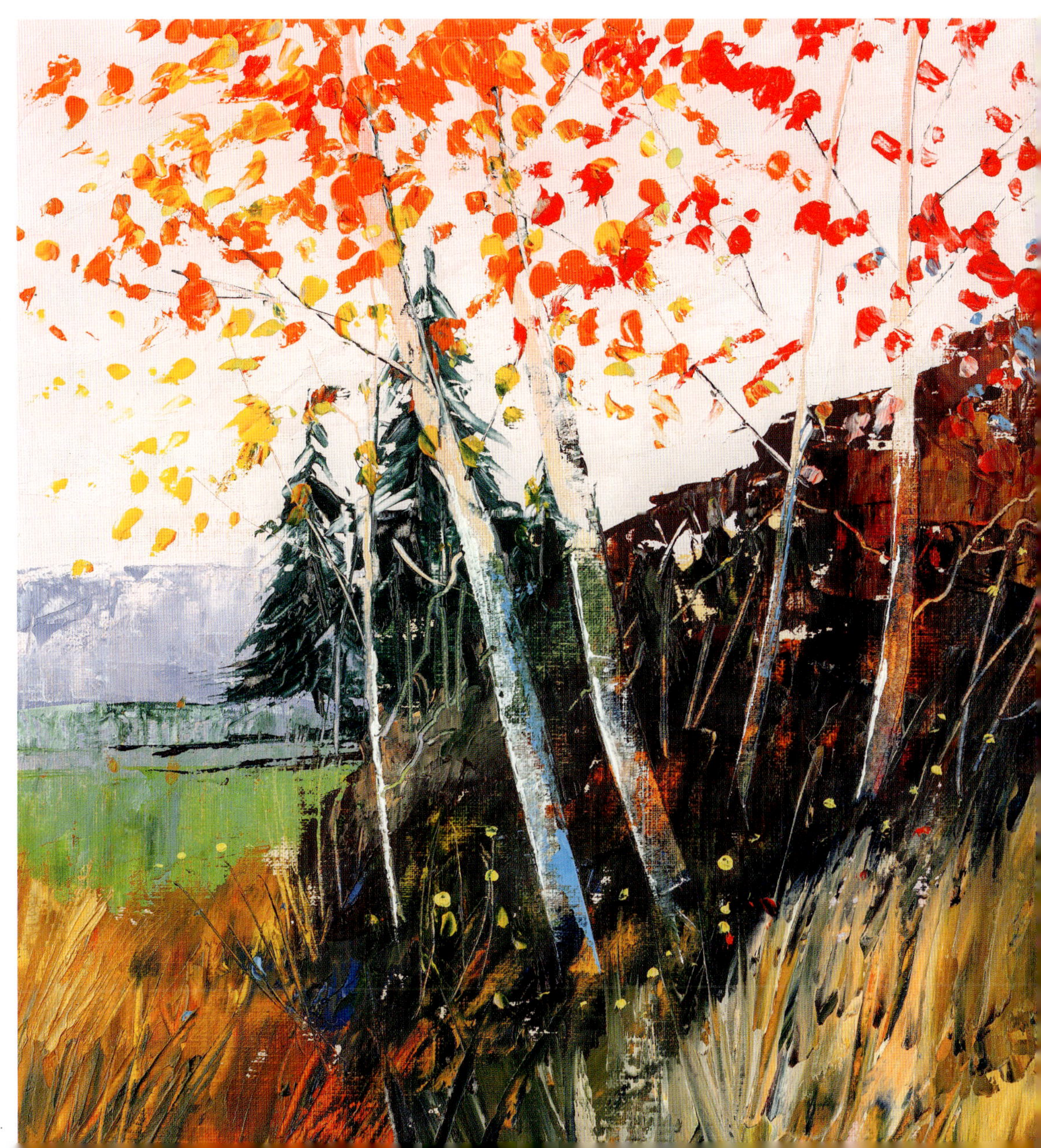

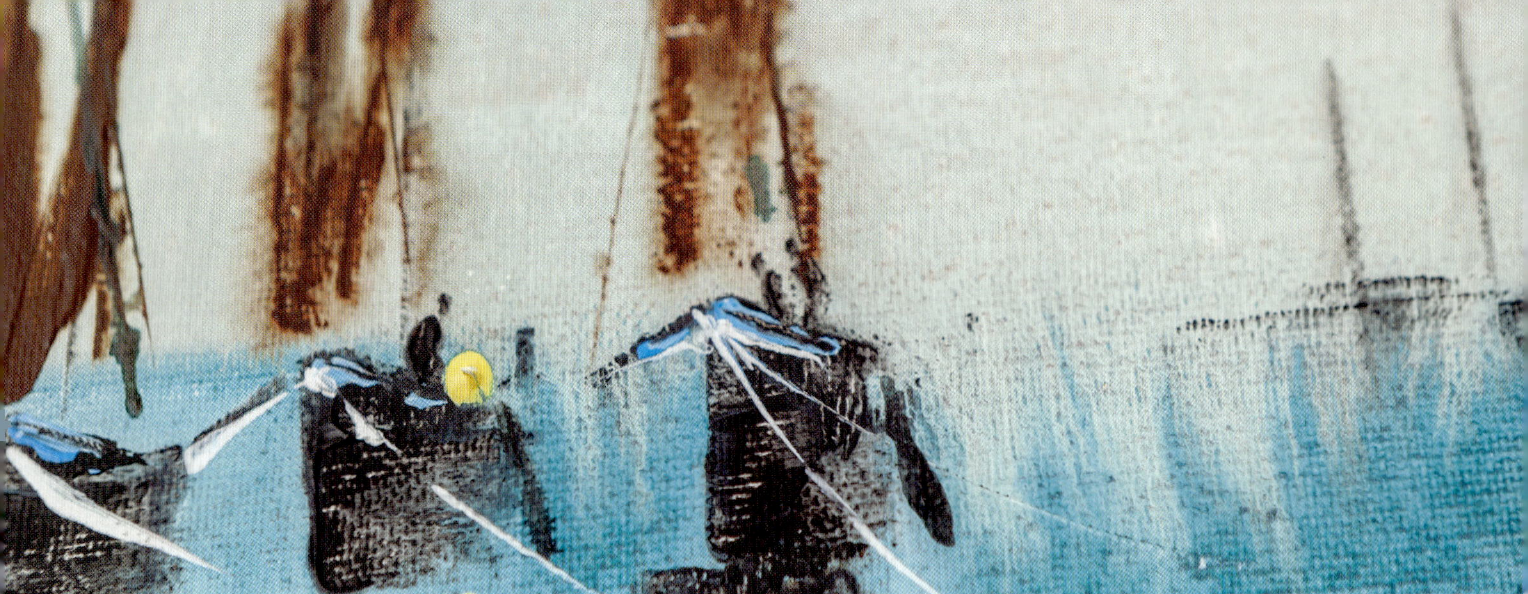

Acknowledgements

I would like to thank Jason at Global Art Supplies for his continuing help and advice and for supplying the art materials used. My thanks also go to everyone at Search Press and especially to Katie and Beth for helping to turn my ideas into something tangible. Thanks to Mark for doing a brilliant job on the photography, and a special thanks to Debbie Dickens for allowing me to use one of her photos to create a painting.

Most of all, a huge thank you to my wife Louise for all the support given during the process of developing the artwork for this book.

Dedication

To my wife and inspiration, with love…
Louise.

First published in 2023
Search Press Limited
Wellwood, North Farm Road,
Tunbridge Wells, Kent TN2 3DR

Text copyright © Tim Fisher, 2023

Photographs by Mark Davison for Search Press Studios, except for page 114 by Tim Fisher.
Photographs and design copyright © Search Press Ltd. 2023

ISBN: 978-1-78221-969-9
ebook ISBN: 978-1-78126-961-9

Suppliers

If you have difficulty in obtaining any of the materials and equipment mentioned in this book, then please visit the Search Press website for details of suppliers:
www.searchpress.com

You are invited to visit the author's:
Website: www.timfisherartist.co.uk
Instagram: @timfisherartist
Facebook: @tim.fisherartist
Twitter: @timfisherartist

Publishers' note

All the step-by-step photographs in this book feature the author, Tim Fisher, demonstrating how to paint with palette knives in acrylics. No models have been used.

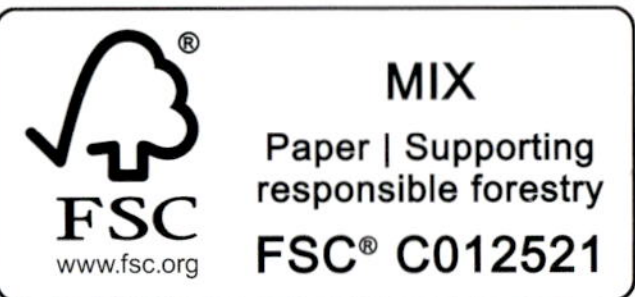

CONTENTS

Introduction

My interest in painting with a palette knife began even before picking one up, let alone using it.

In my youth I was greatly attracted to the work of one artist, Sir John Kyffin Williams OBE, RA. There was something about those wonderful renditions of the Welsh landscape and farmlands with their chunky textured skies and simple cottages that really inspired me to paint.

Using a brush didn't seem to be able to reproduce the textures I admired, and it was only by observing a fellow artist using a knife with acrylics to create wonderful textures that I was inspired to try the same. The advantage of the acrylic medium is that it is fast drying and textured layers can be quickly built up on the painting surface. Now I could produce layer upon layer, without the paint blending together.

For those who desire to become more competent in their painting abilities, the palette knife offers a great opportunity to do just this. Something of a blunt instrument as opposed to using a brush, the painting knife, when mastered, can open up a whole universe of possibilities for creative work. This is especially so when combined with acrylic media and the occasional brushstroke. The use of these instruments also opens up opportunities to add various outside elements to your artwork. This gives greater scope to communicate a message or an idea. This can be done through the addition of collage or other found materials. A good example is the lobster project on pages 84–91. Applying the acrylic paint thickly with the edge of a knife creates an almost seamless interface between the applied materials and the painting medium.

Knives allow you to create a vast range of painting styles, from thick impasto to smooth textured, calm or out of focus subjects. This book helps to unlock the techniques of how to create a range of marks using a variety of knives. Step-by-step, each chapter of the book will cover a different subject, helping to build and develop new skills, which will help you to become proficient when handling a painting knife.

I hope you enjoy using this book to discover new techniques whether you are a beginner, or want to experience new techniques with acrylic and knife.

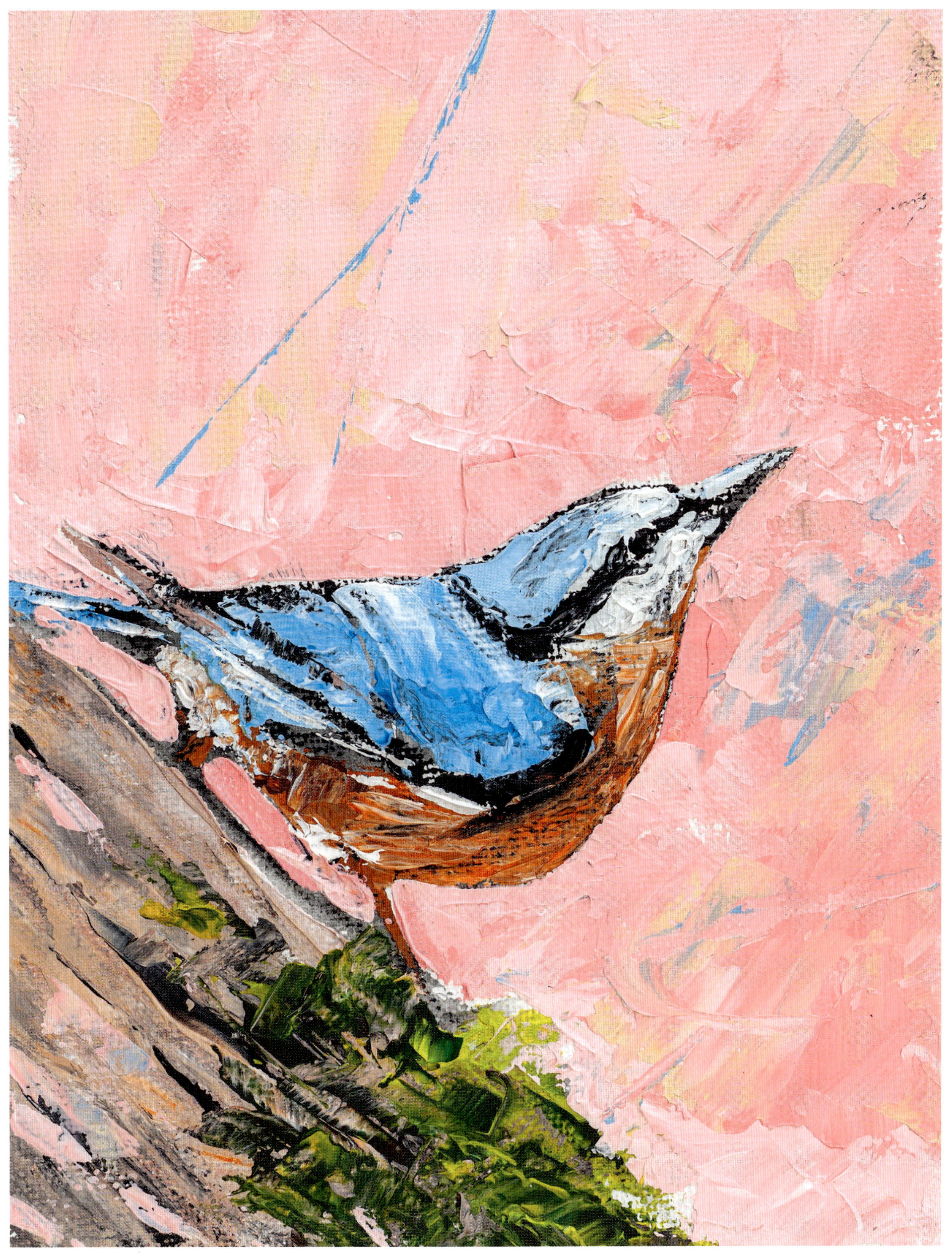

Nuthatch

12.5 × 18cm (5 × 7in)

A brief history of the palette knife

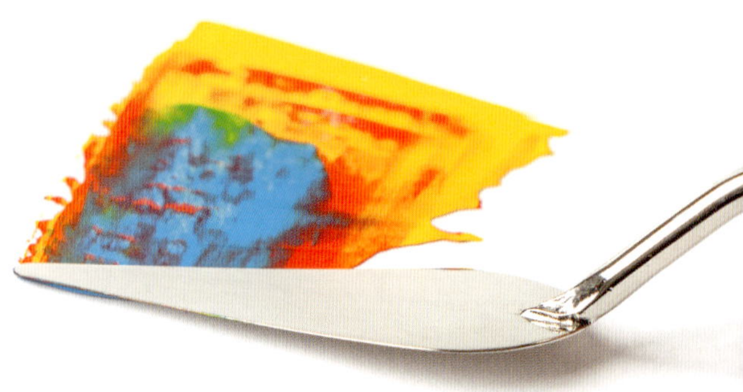

The palette knife is a blunt tool featuring a dull-edged flexible steel blade; its original purpose was to mix oil paint upon the artist's palette.

Early references to palette knives appear in the 1600s. Elaborate palettes of pre-mixed tints became fashionable during this period, containing fully developed gradations of **tints and colours. This would allow the artist to concentrate on shape and form upon the canvas.** This is probably how the palette knife came into being, most likely adapted from a putty knife. Some artists would spend hours preparing their mixtures and so the need for a tool with a flexible blade evolved. As use of the knife as a painting tool became more common, the instrument evolved into a small flexible blade that was often trowel-shaped with a cranked handle.

The cranked handle made the knife more comfortable to hold and kept the knuckles out of the way to prevent any smudging. The changing shape of the blade gave the artist more flexibility of technique when applying paint and allowed them to create entire artworks just with a knife.

Artists such as Rembrandt soon learned that by applying paint directly to the canvas with the knife, an array of edges with interesting textures and marbling could be produced.

However, it is difficult to credit one artist with creating the miniature trowel shape, though Constable, Hawthorne and Courbet are all associated with its invention. Most of the post-Impressionist artists, such as Cézanne, Pissarro, Chagall and van Gogh used a palette knife, but combined it with brushes, which was a common thing to do.

When using a palette knife, it is possible to paint layer upon layer without having the paint blend together. Delightful broken colour effects can be achieved using this method which are not possible when using a brush alone.

The trowel-shaped knife is still in manufacture and has many variants, some with rounded edges, curves and teardrop shapes. This allows for more flexible movement when applying paint.

To this day, palette knives with straight handles are still used, as well as a huge range of crank-handled painting knives. You can purchase cheaper plastic knives, but, depending on the techniques you have chosen and the effect you want to achieve, they may not work as effectively as the ones made from stainless steel or other metals.

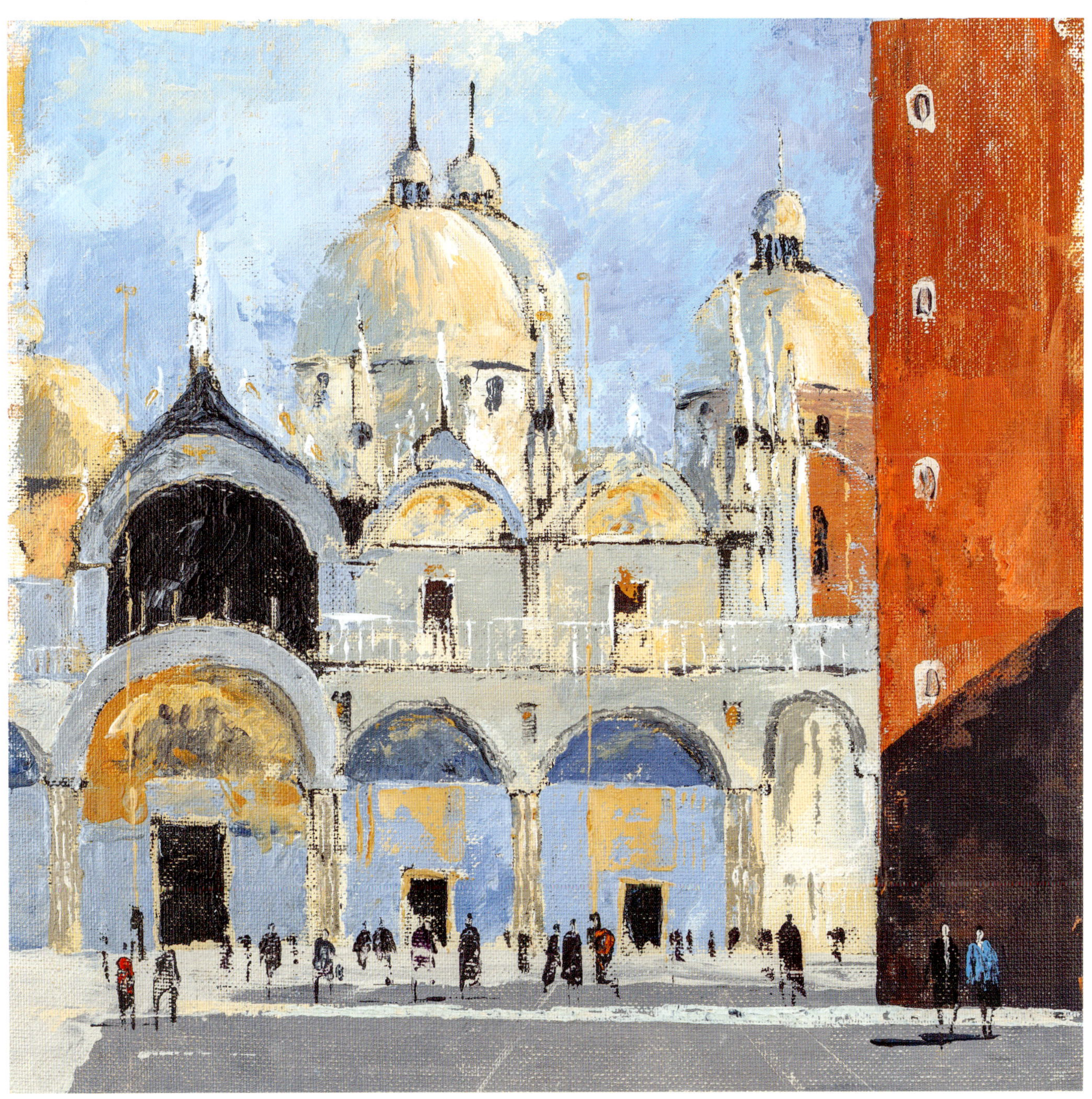

St Mark's Square, Venice

30.5 × 30.5cm (12 × 12in)

Tools

The knife allows the user to apply not just mixed but clean slabs of colour to the painting surface. Acrylic paint can be applied directly over wet or dry layers of paint. Experience will dictate the shape of knife that suits your working methods. Over the years I have settled for the combination of shapes shown below. Some I have modified from an existing shape to suit a particular painting application.

THE KNIVES

The **RGM 6** is a teardrop-shaped knife and the one I use most frequently. The shape allows for great dexterity when applying paint.

The **RGM 41** is smaller, measuring just 3.5cm (1⅜in) in length, and I use it as my 'tight corners' knife. It's very useful when tackling difficult areas within a detailed subject.

The **Conda No. 3** has a crown-shaped head that has earned it the title of the '**King**'. The multi-pronged springy tip is great for spattering diluted paint onto the painting surface, or for making abstract marks.

The bull nose is a modified **RGM 41**. I've taken a pair of tin snips and removed the tip, removing any rough spots with fine emery paper. The square tip allows me to produce specific shapes such as rectangular windows in buildings.

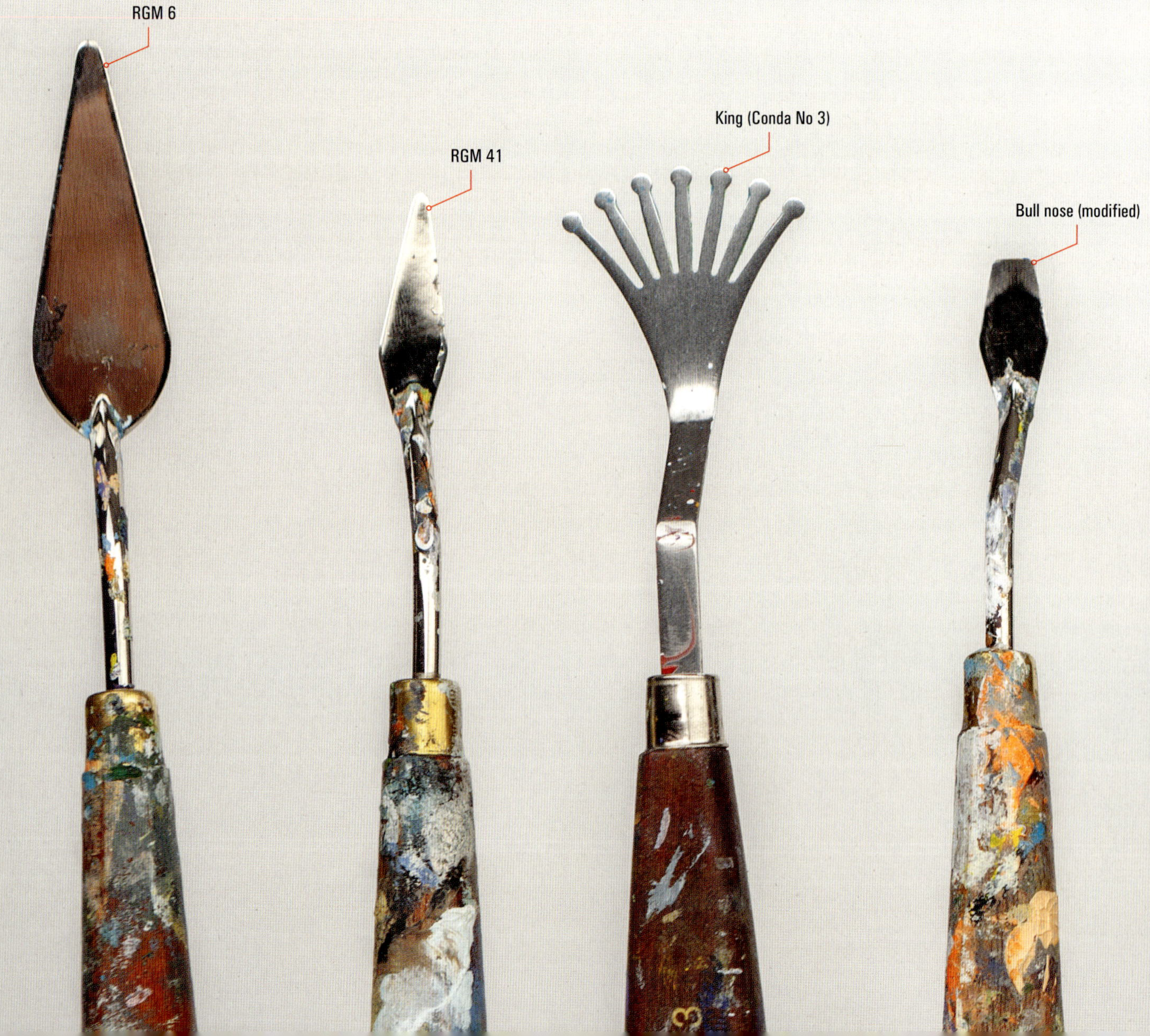

The small round is a modified **RGM 6**. After cutting down, it is now approximately 1cm (⅜in) round. I use this to represent summer foliage or flowerheads.

For larger leaf detail I use the large round, again fashioned from an **RGM 6** to a size approximately 2.5cm (1in) long. The **RGM Pastrello 38** has its own unique shape, which allows me to make very fine lines representing a wide variety of subjects from twigs and branches to sailing ship masts.

The last knife is the straight-handled **RGM 109**. This knife is great for representing skies. Large swatches of paint can be applied and blended in broad strokes. Specific shapes can be created which are ideal when describing buildings.

See page 38 for details on caring for your knives.

RGM KNIVES

RGM takes its name from Rosa Gastaldo Mario, who founded the company in 1961. The knives are made from steel and tempered to create a balance of flexibility and strength. They have now become synonymous with quality around the world.

In later years RGM collaborated with the artist Franco Pastrello to produce a new line of palette knives. This range of thin flexible blades has been designed specially for detail work.

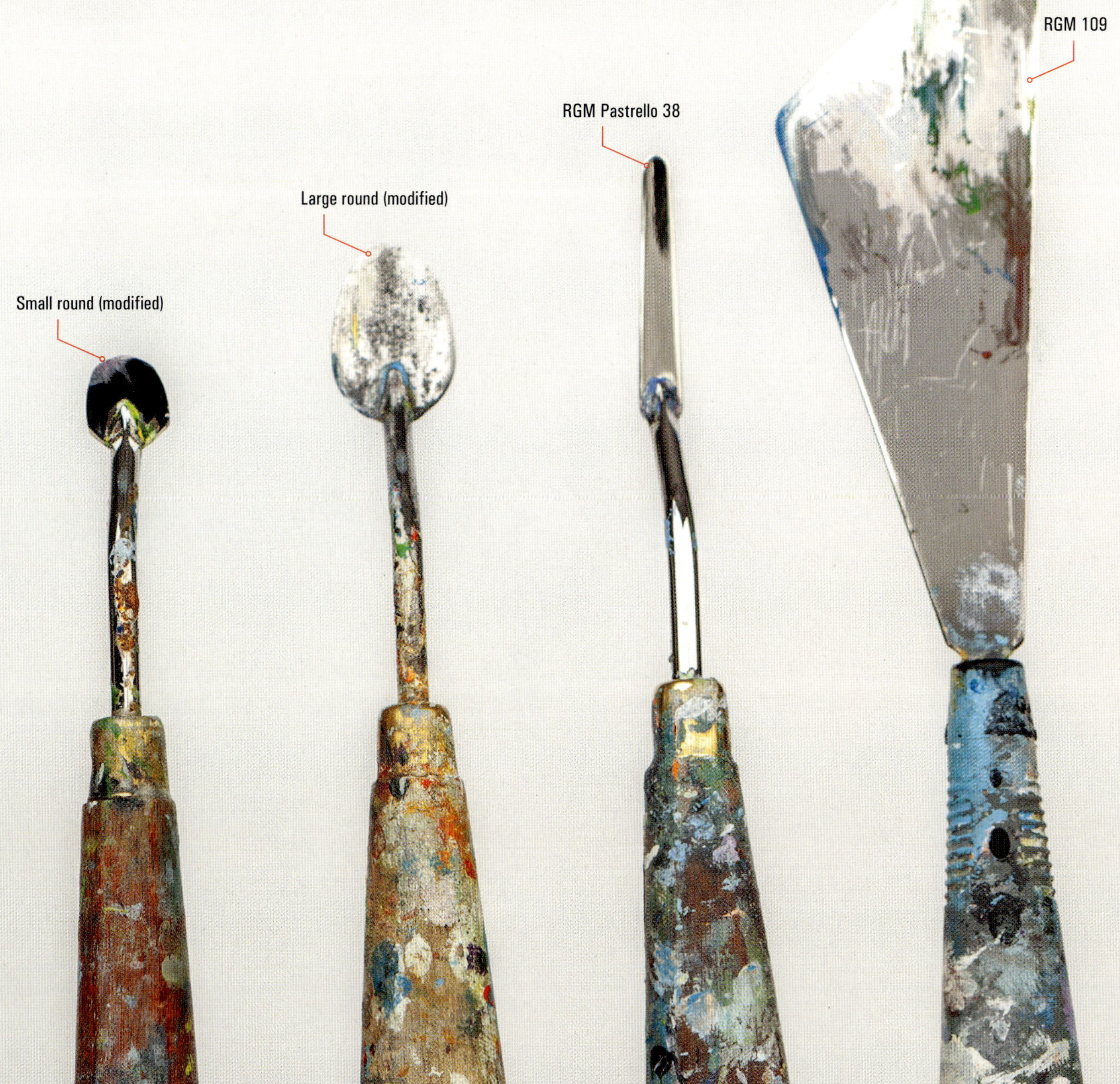

Materials

These pouches of acrylic paint have the perfect consistency for palette knife use. The style of container offers a number of benefits. There is less waste, as it's possible to extract almost all of the paint from the pouch, and the airtight design reduces the likelihood of paint going off.

THE PAINTS

Throughout this book I use primarily Sennelier, or Golden, paints; other makes are available.

Sennelier Abstract acrylic is a high-quality, heavy-body paint which is manufactured in France. There are currently 36 satin finish, 12 high gloss, six iridescent and six fluorescent colours to choose from. They are supplied in a unique strong flexible pouch which is comfortable to hold and use. The fill is airtight, preventing any bubbles from drying out the paint. The transparent window allows for easy identification of the colour within. The paint has a pigment-rich, creamy consistency, which makes handling, mixing and applying the colour with a knife so much easier. The consistency of the paint allows you to hold peaks and retain the knife marks when sculpting the painting surface. The paint has excellent covering power and can be easily applied to a multitude of surfaces, making it a very popular choice for the palette knife artist.

Sennelier also manufactures a set of eight different shaped painting tips designed to fit the nozzle. This allows creative, expressive painting directly from the pouch and combines ideally with palette knife painting.

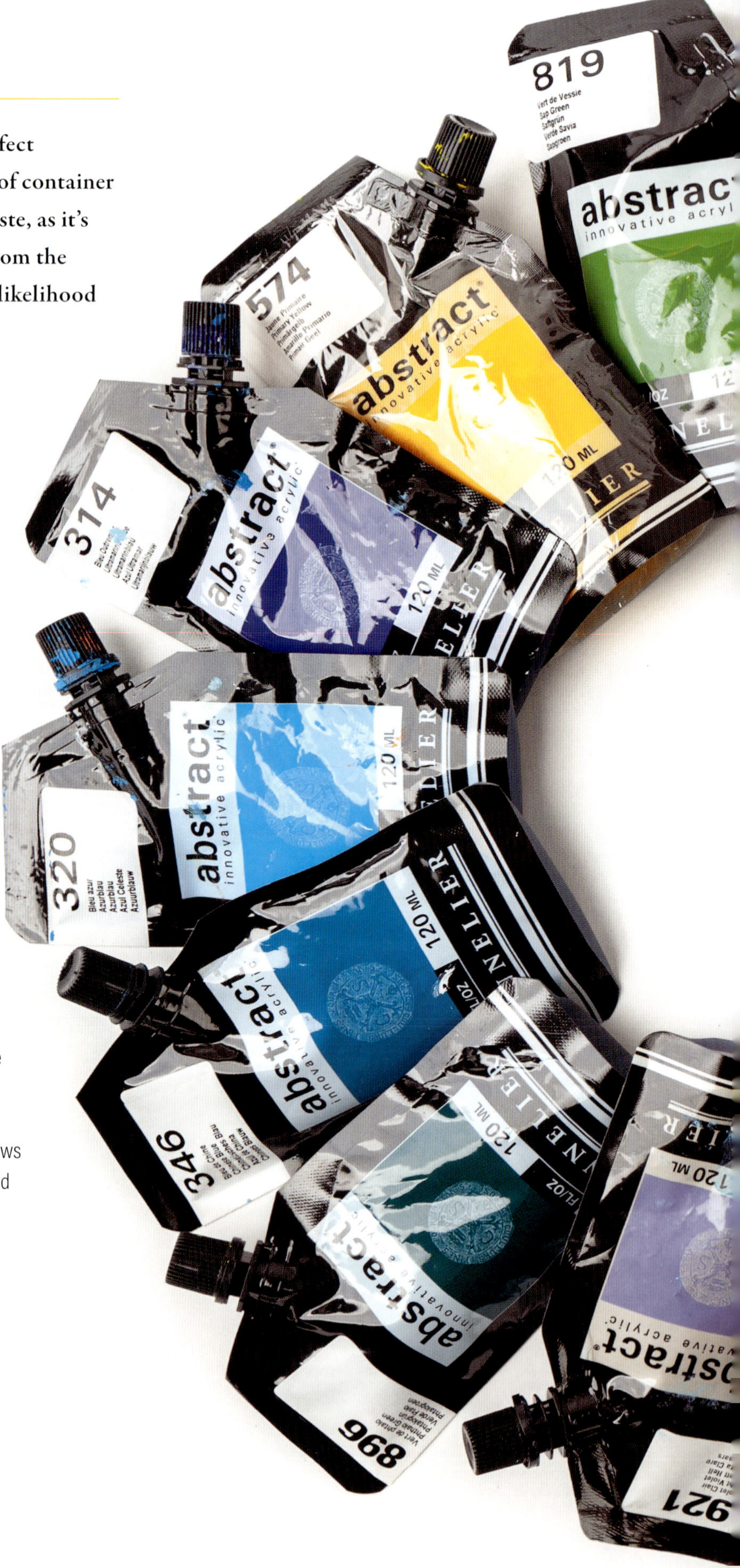

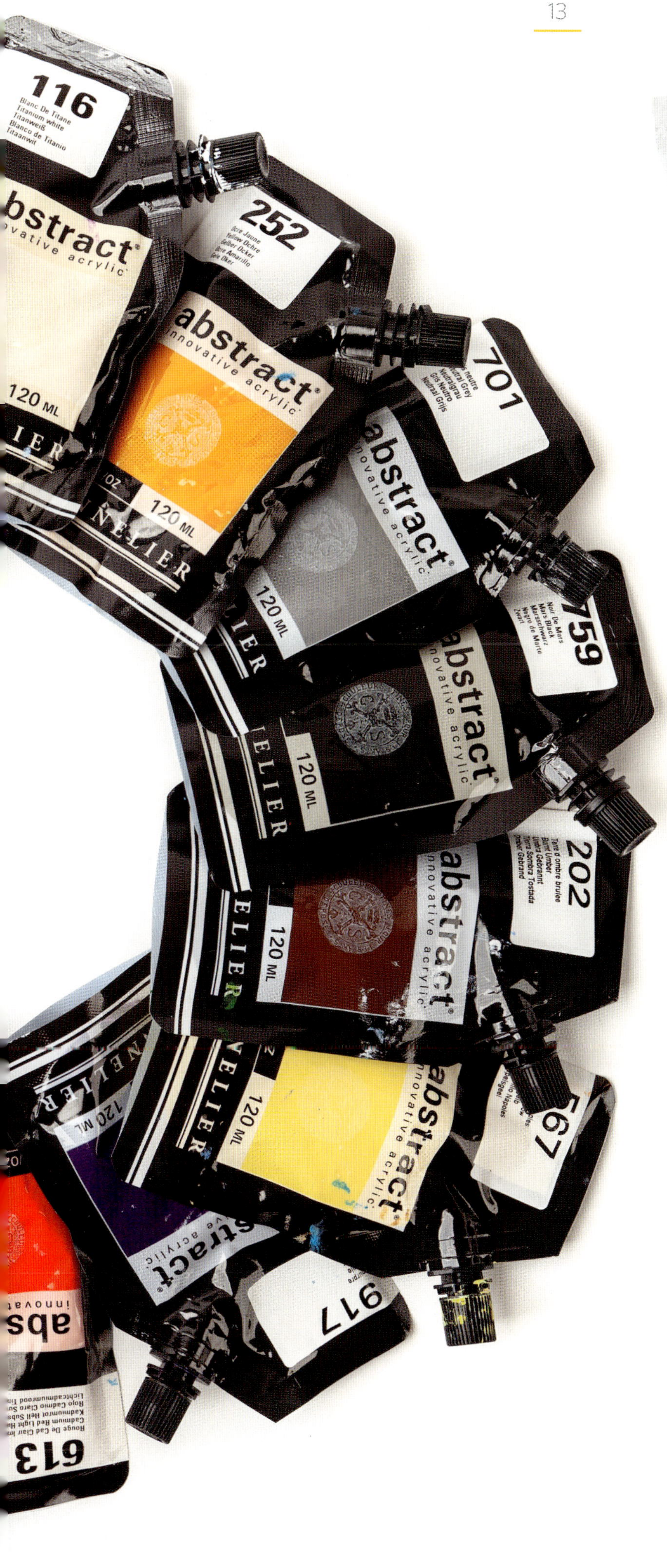

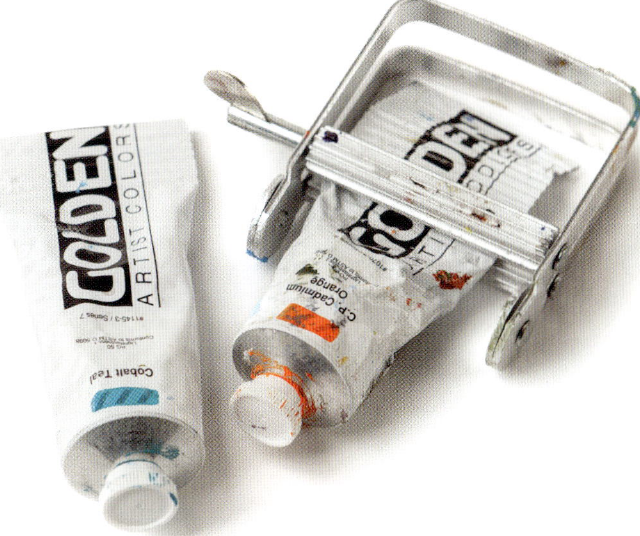

Paint tubes and squeezer.
I occasionally use acrylic contained in traditional tubes.
To extract all the paint, I use a squeezer. This clamps the end
of the tube between serrated rollers and removes all the
paint from the tube.

My palette

With acrylics, there is a large choice of modern colours and tints available today. I still use some traditional classic colours, but have extended the range I use with some more interesting pigments, which have shaped my colour palette as you see it today.

Titanium white is a bright white with an almost bluish appearance. It is quite opaque and will rapidly lighten other colours when mixed together and is excellent for adding highlights.

Yellow ochre is an opaque, warm yellow with good covering power and will create muted tints when mixed with other colours.

Azure blue is a cool colour I use as an alternative to cerulean blue. It is great when featured in skies and will generate bright, clean greens when mixed with primary yellow.

Cadmium orange is one of the few colours I use that is manufactured by Golden. It has a thick buttery consistency and is highly pigmented. It is a warm, bright colour and is indispensable when a pure orange is needed.

Cadmium red light hue looks similar to cadmium red but is made from other pigments. I find this a good low-cost alternative when a lot of red is required.

Burnt umber is a dark opaque colour that is a good alternative to black when darker colour mixes are required and gives them a slightly warmer appearance.

Sap green is a warm deep green which can offer some relief when more muted shades are needed.

Purple is a powerful violet colour. Undiluted this can be used as a deep black, or mixed with other colours to create subtle shadow tones.

Light violet is made from a slightly different combination of pigments; the addition of a small amount of blue gives an arresting shade when applied directly to the paint surface.

Chinese blue is a greenish blue. It is a powerful colour and should be used in moderation. A range of vivid greens can be achieved when mixed with primary yellow.

Ultramarine blue is a warm blue, biased towards purple. The red tinge can result in some disappointing greens when mixed with yellow, though some lovely violets can be created when added to red.

Naples yellow is a very useful pigment, especially when added to skies to create a flash of yellow on the lower horizon.

Mars black is strong and dense – it must be used sparingly when mixed with other colours as it will quickly dominate. Superb dark greens can be achieved when mixed with a bright yellow.

Primary yellow is a bright, clean pure yellow. It mixes well with other colours and is an excellent alternative to cadmium yellow.

Finally, **cobalt teal** is one of my favourite colours from Golden; it looks fantastic on its own or can be used to make a selection of light greens.

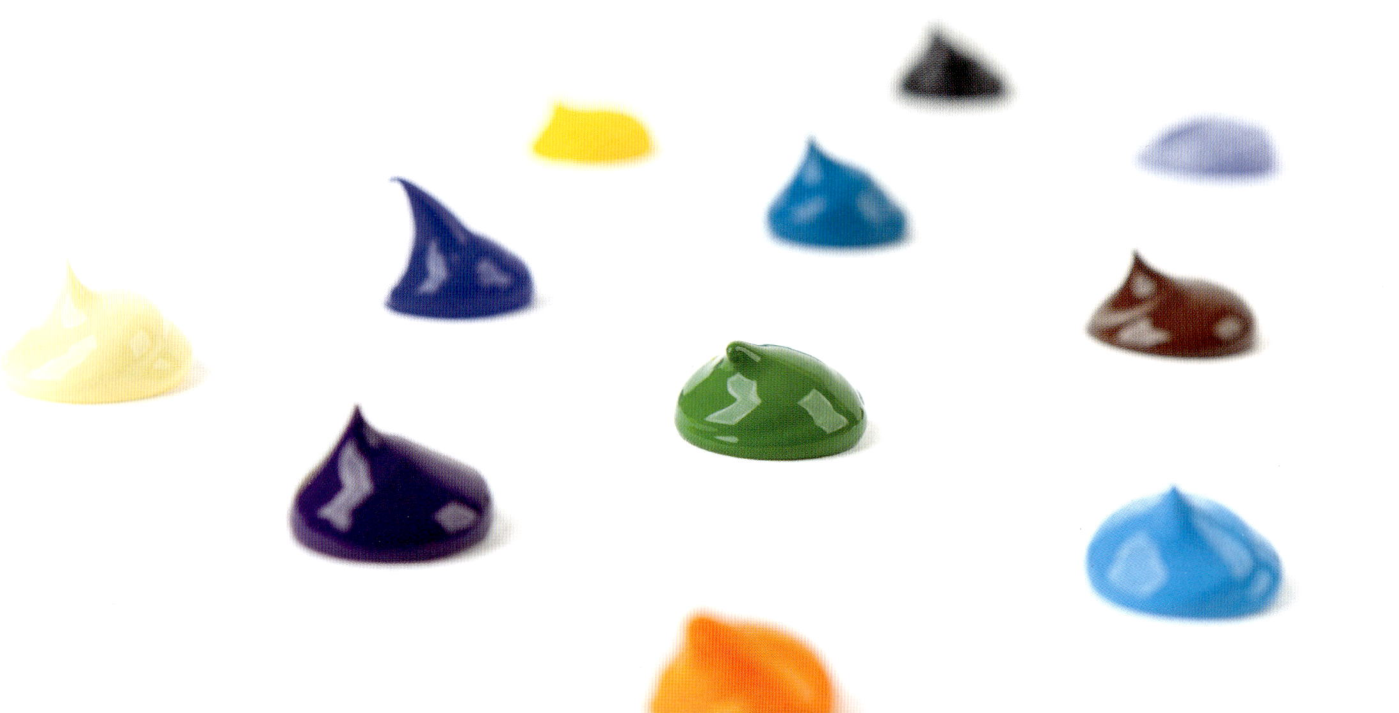

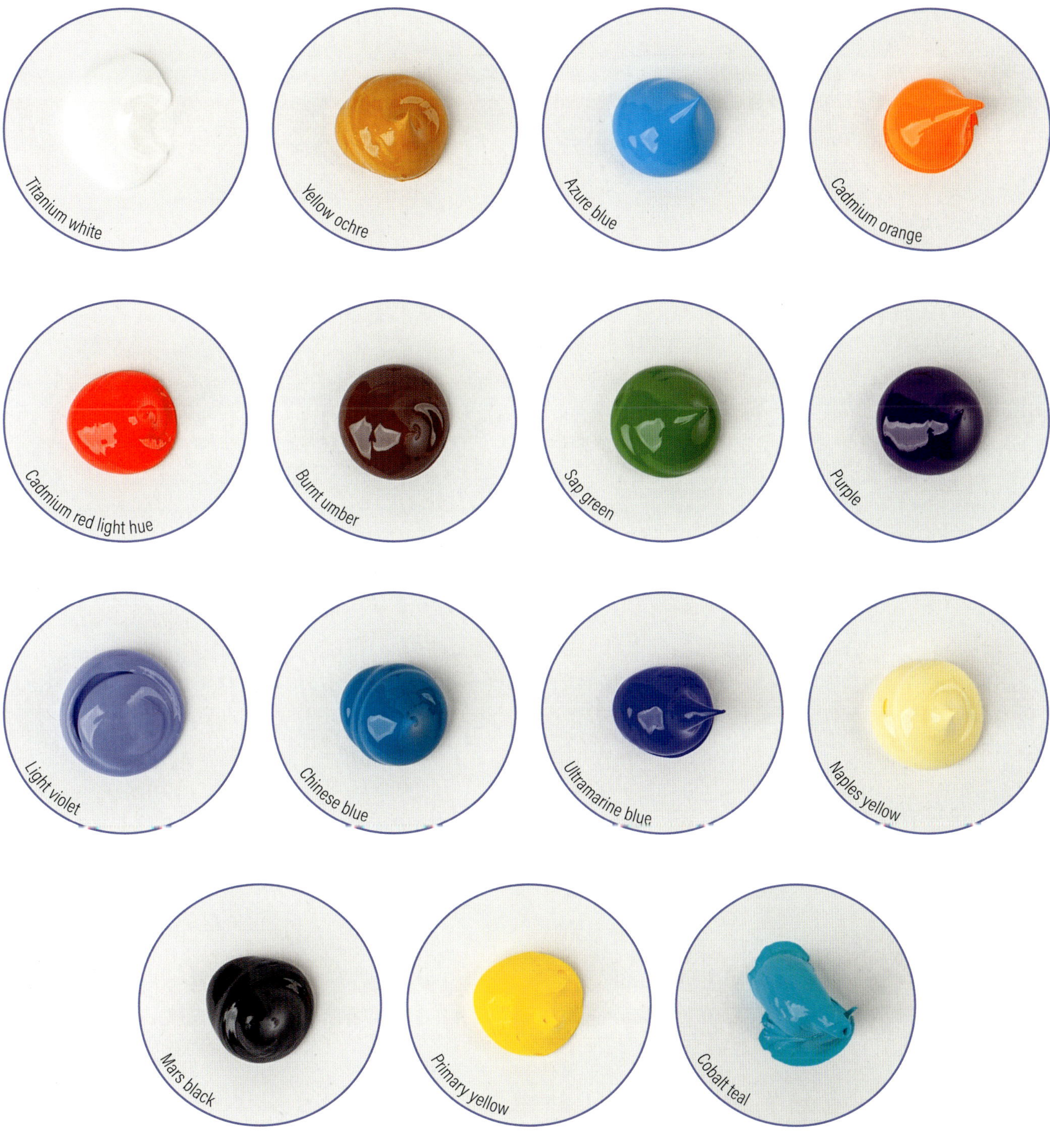

Titanium white
Yellow ochre
Azure blue
Cadmium orange
Cadmium red light hue
Burnt umber
Sap green
Purple
Light violet
Chinese blue
Ultramarine blue
Naples yellow
Mars black
Primary yellow
Cobalt teal

Additives and mediums

My experimental nature is attracted to a range of different additives and mediums that will help me to achieve painterly effects and therefore enhance any artwork I produce. To get the full benefit of these additives, they must be thoroughly mixed into the pigment.

Gloss glazing liquid (1) keeps the acrylic paint workable for longer periods of time, creating greater colour depth to the work. Use **nail polish remover (2)** that contains acetone to clean and remove any dried-on acrylic paint from the palette knife before use. **Mod Podge® (3)** is a glue and sealer used for sticking down subjects cut from paper when designing a mixed media painting. **Crackle paste (4)** is added to colour: as the paint dries, the surface forms a *craquelure*, which adds texture to the painting. **Heavy gel gloss (5)** is mixed into paint to add a sculpted effect to the work or to be used as an adhesive for heavier bits of collage.

The disposable cup contains **Liquitex pouring medium (6)** and azure blue acrylic paint. This allows the paint to be thinned without affecting its quality. A **lollipop stick (7)** is used for mixing pigments with this medium. A **syringe (8)** can be used to add water precisely, to further improve paint performance.

Lastly, **marble dust (9)** picked up by a paint-loaded knife can produce broken textures on the painting's surface.

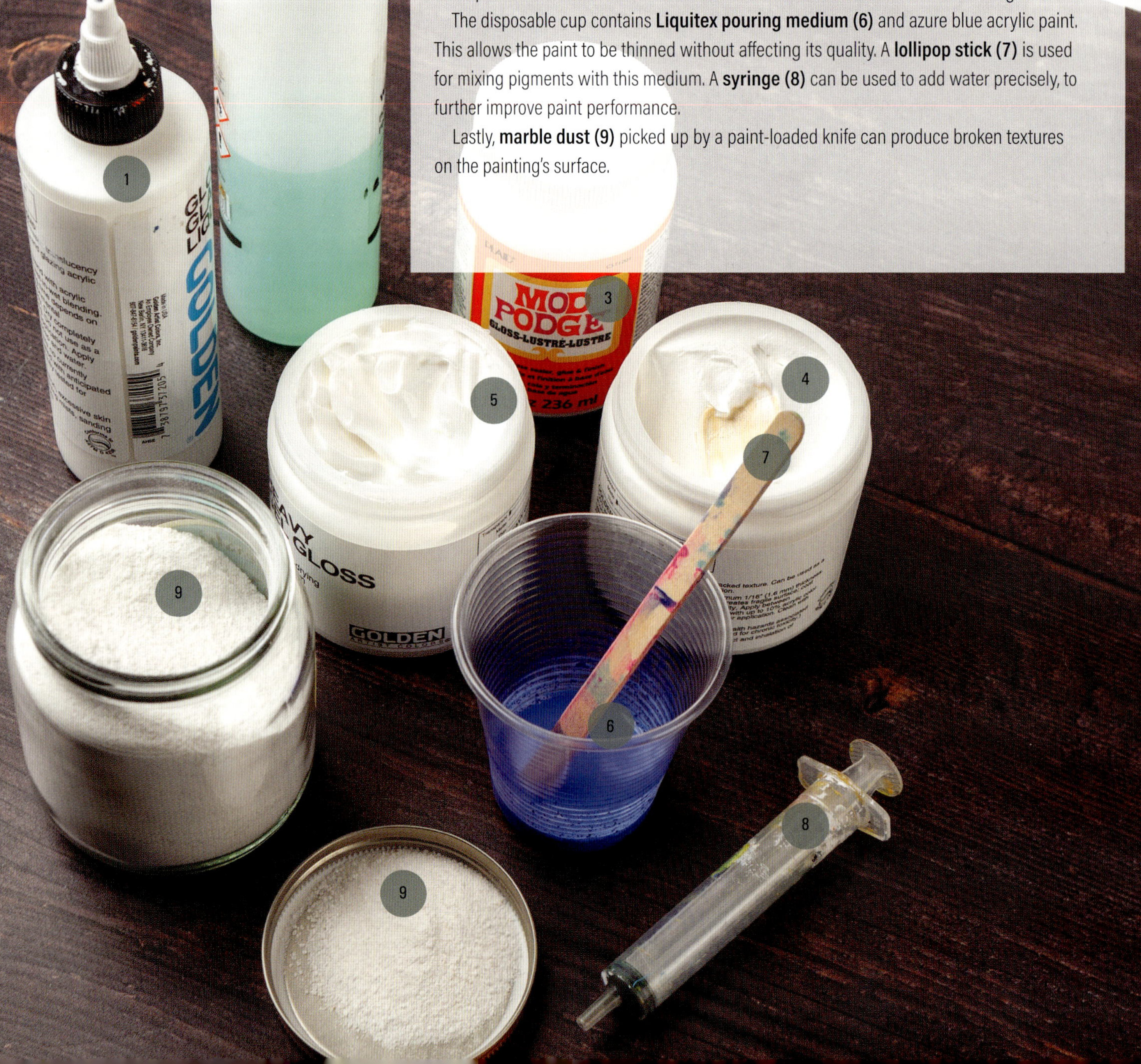

Surfaces

Working on a flat surface will often produce the best results when using a knife. My preference is to use medium canvas-covered board available from most good art shops. I find that it's most economical to buy in A1-size sheets (59.4 x 84.1cm/23⅜ x 33⅛in) and cut these down to the required size.

Medium-grain textured canvas has some of the best surface characteristics, which can profoundly affect how applied paint appears to the viewer. I also like to work on a stretched canvas surface of the same grade, which has a satisfying spring to it when applying paint. Offcuts of mount card from a picture framer are a low-cost option when practising some of the strokes described later in this book. Other flat surfaces such as MDF or plywood can be used, though these must be prepared, or primed, with a good-quality gesso before use.

Other items

My studio contains a number of items that are instrumental in producing a good palette knife painting; here, I show you just a selection of the things I have bought, found and scrounged over the years. Not all of these are used at once, though they can be brought out as and when required.

It is essential to have a flat mixing area when using palette knives. A4-paper size (21 × 29.7cm/8¼ × 11¾in) **disposable palettes (1)** are about the right size. I also have a couple of **homemade palettes (2)**, cut down to 42 × 30cm (16½ × 11¾in) from Dibond composite sign-making sheets. These are easy to clean by soaking in warm soapy water, using a **sponge scourer (3)** and then applying a final wipe with nail polish remover.

Masking tape, and the wider **Eurotape (4)**, can be used to secure panels to a painting board.

Coloured foldback clips (5) indicate the contents of partly used pouches of paint (see pages 12–13, and 20–21).

A **two-compartment water pot (6)** helps to keep brushes clean. Dirty palette knives can also be plunged in to prevent paint drying.

I've layered sheets of **kitchen paper** together **(7)** and held them in place with a clip, for cleaning the blades of the knives. These can be torn off to reveal a clean surface for wiping.

Black **permanent marker pens**, a **carbon pencil** and a couple of Neocolor II **water-soluble wax pastels**, one black and one light grey **(8)** are useful for making bold marks prior to painting. The paler coloured pastel is used if I'm working on a surface with a dark tint.

A **ruler (9)** provides a straight edge, which is handy when adding a horizon line to seascapes.

I use **wet wipes (10)** to keep my hands clean when working.

Finally, there is **an assortment of found objects (11)** discovered while combing our local beaches, which I use in collage (see pages 84–93).

BRUSHES

I have just a few **flat synthetic brushes (12).** Most have a slanted, chisel edge and are useful when producing highly detailed work. Care has to be taken when combining brushes with knifework as each has a distinctly different mark.

It is important to keep the brushes clean when using acrylic. Wash thoroughly in water and dry on kitchen towel or plunge them into the water pot to be cleaned later on.

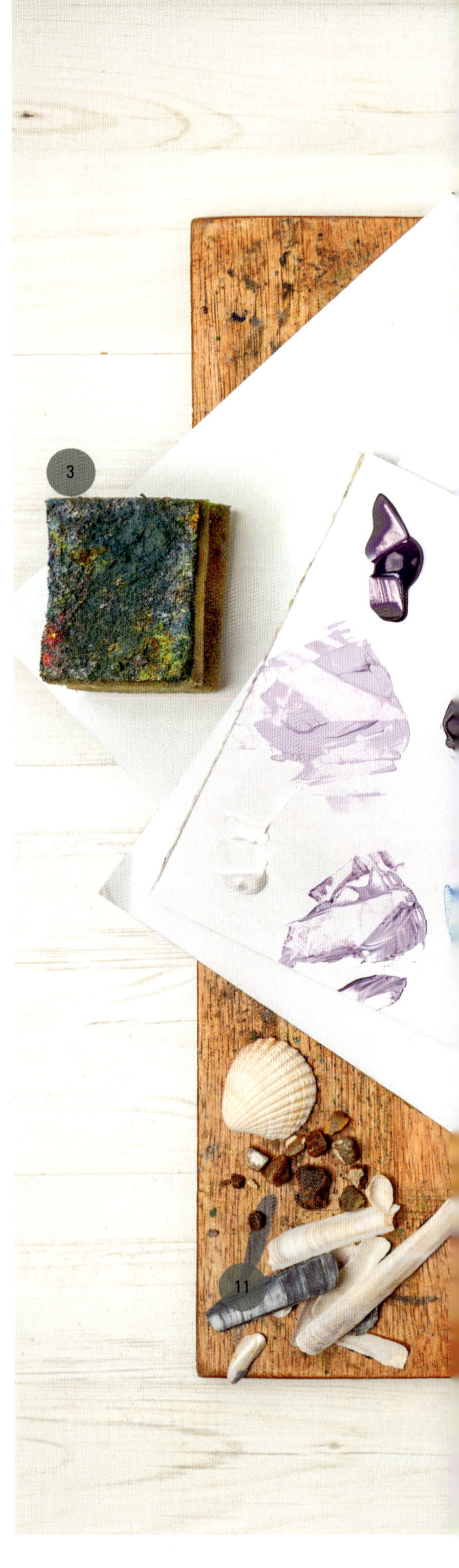

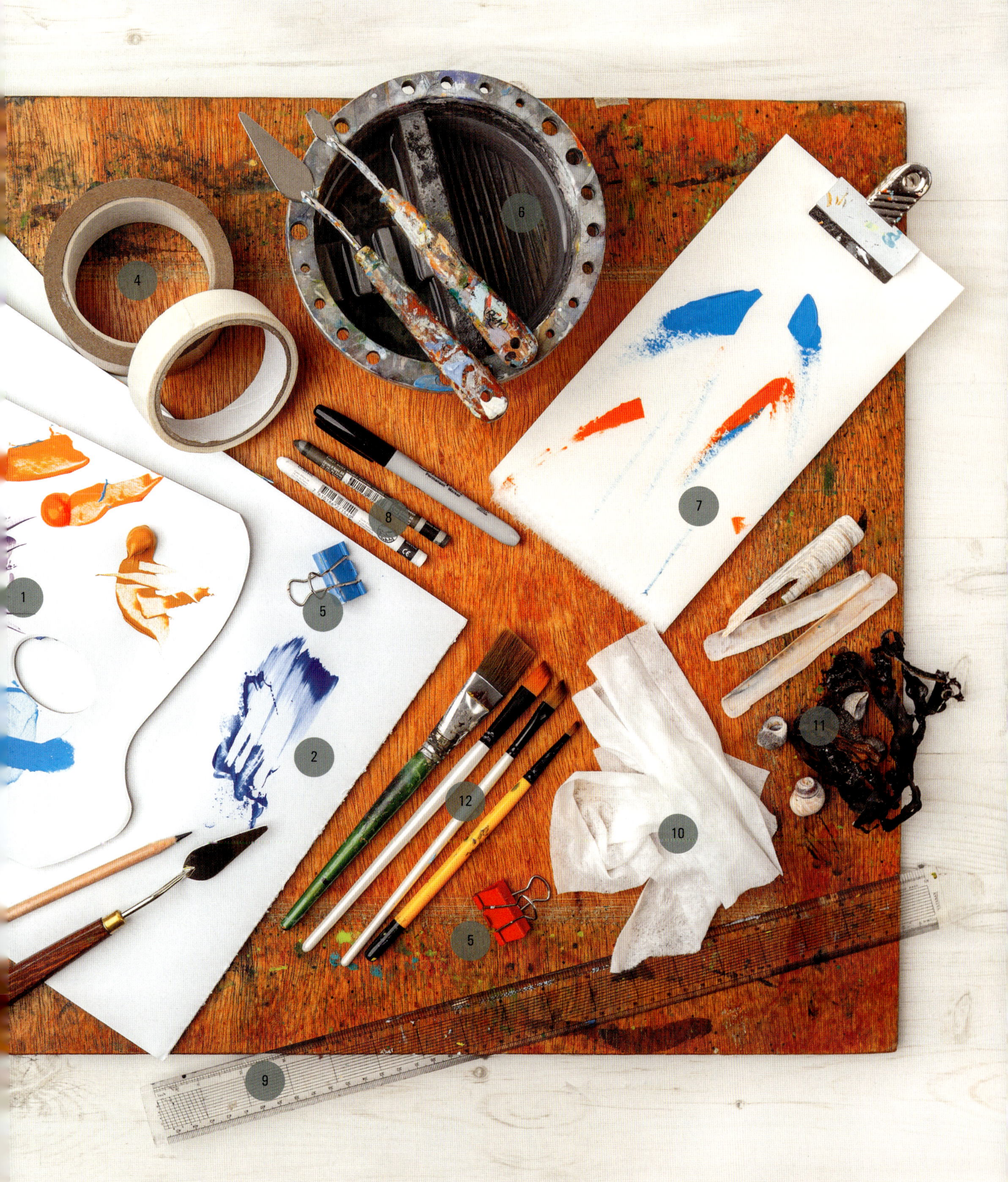

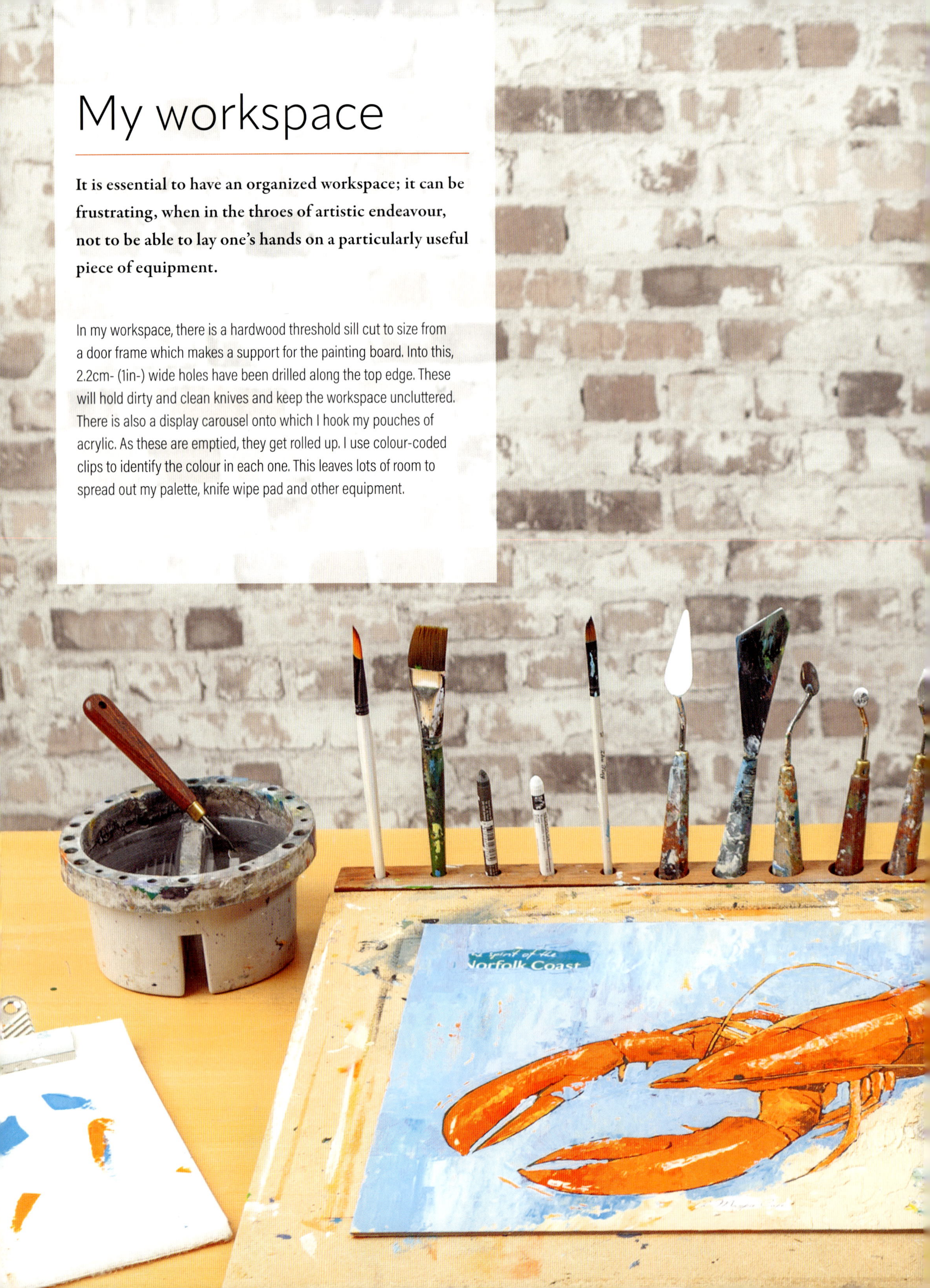

My workspace

It is essential to have an organized workspace; it can be frustrating, when in the throes of artistic endeavour, not to be able to lay one's hands on a particularly useful piece of equipment.

In my workspace, there is a hardwood threshold sill cut to size from a door frame which makes a support for the painting board. Into this, 2.2cm- (1in-) wide holes have been drilled along the top edge. These will hold dirty and clean knives and keep the workspace uncluttered. There is also a display carousel onto which I hook my pouches of acrylic. As these are emptied, they get rolled up. I use colour-coded clips to identify the colour in each one. This leaves lots of room to spread out my palette, knife wipe pad and other equipment.

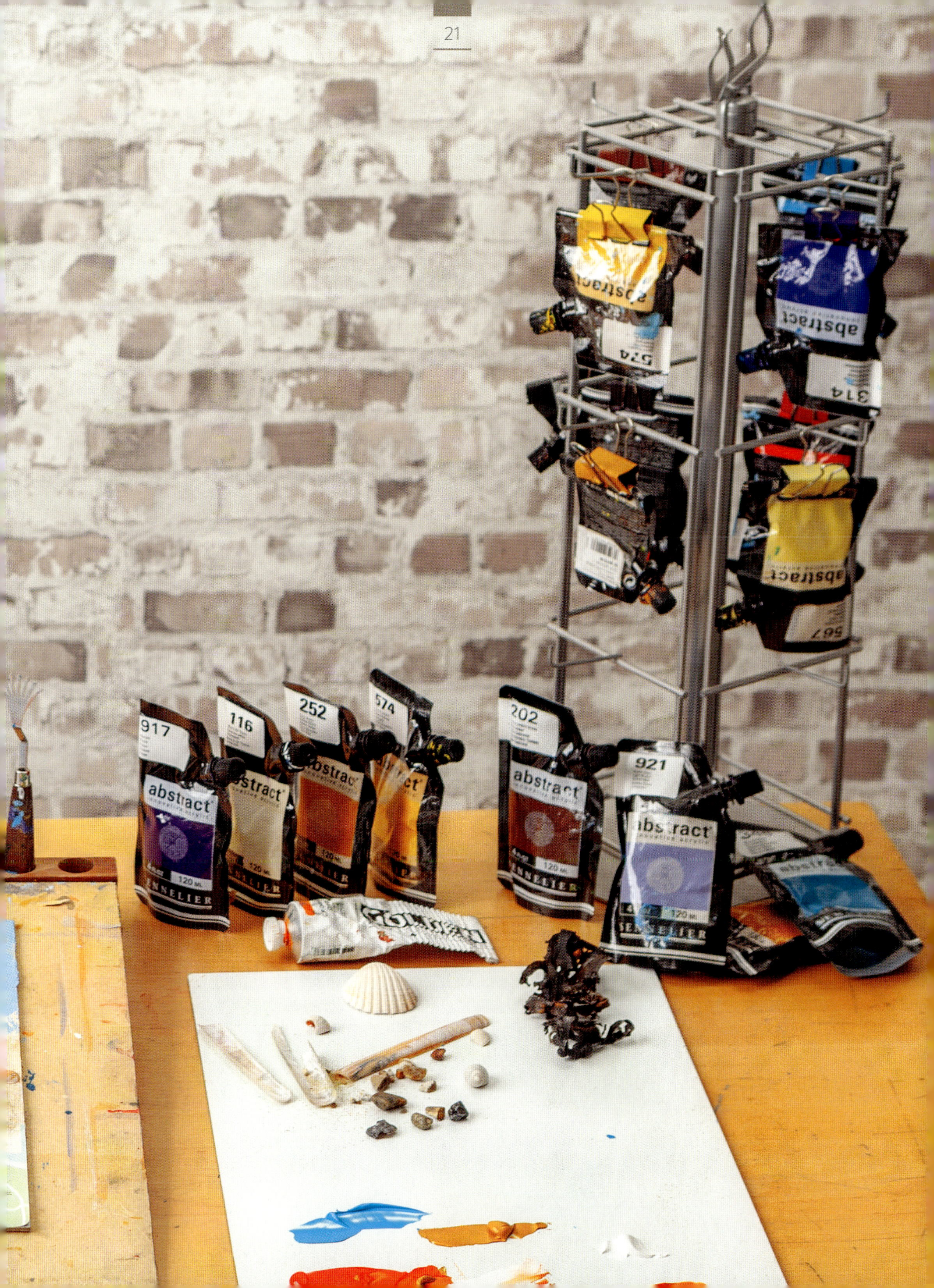

Basic techniques

This chapter helps to give a thorough understanding of the essential features and functions of the different types of palette knife. Within this section I have tried to cover most of the techniques that need to be understood when handling acrylics. The chapter starts with some very basic techniques, which form the core of any painting you may wish to tackle. It then progresses to more specialized mark-making with the specially shaped blades.

HOLDING THE KNIFE

A FLAT-HANDLED PALETTE KNIFE

The straight-handled knife with the large angled blade has evolved from the original straight-handled mixing blade and possibly the putty knife. The shape allows for a wide variety of broad flat strokes to be made with a choice of two edges on the front of the blade.

I naturally curl my fingers around the knife handle. With a straight handle, the knife is held off the surface at a slightly greater angle to prevent the hand coming into contact with the wet painting surface. To paint with a more acute angle, a less secure grip is used to hold the sides of the handle and the index finger of the other hand is sometimes required for extra support.

A CRANK-HANDLED PALETTE KNIFE

The crank-handled knife is the more common design used today. Available in a wide variety of shapes, the teardrop is the most useful form and after becoming comfortable with its use, a wide variety of shapes and patterns can be created.

The crank-handled design is something that has been developed over the years to provide a more comfortable grip and keep the hands away from the paint, though it is sometimes necessary to adopt the less secure side grip for some painting applications.

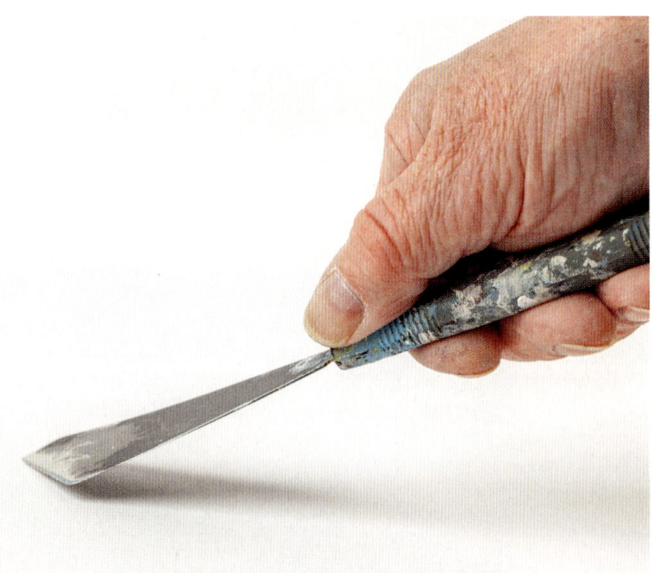

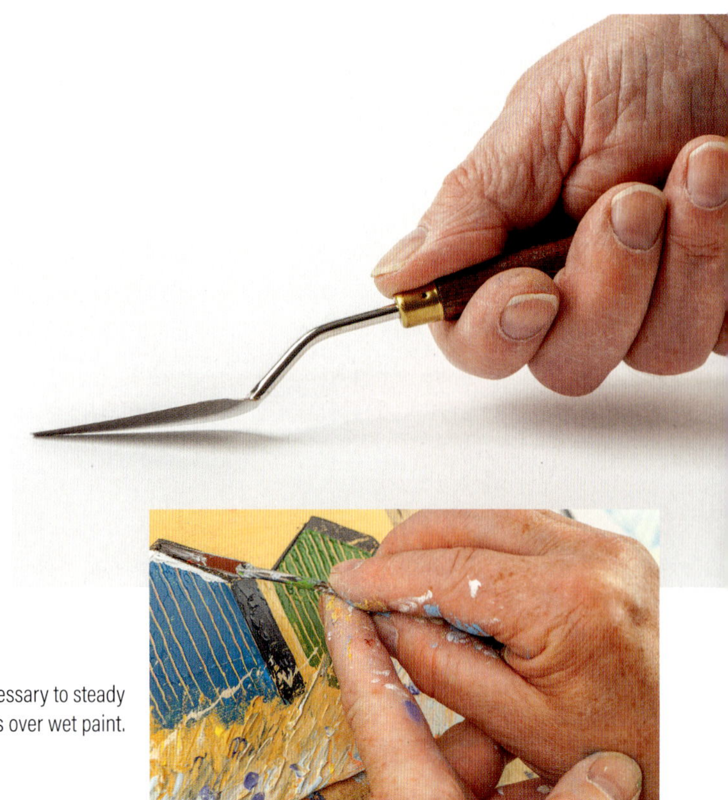

Sometimes a two-handed grip is necessary to steady the knife when accessing difficult areas over wet paint.

LOADING THE KNIFE AND MAKING A STROKE

Loading paint along the wide edge of the blade is the same operation for nearly all shapes of palette knife.

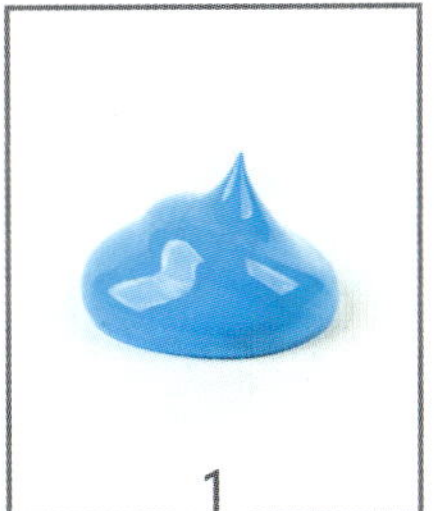

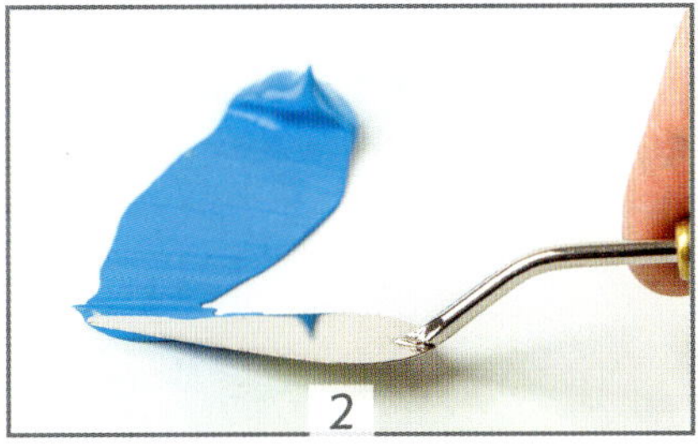

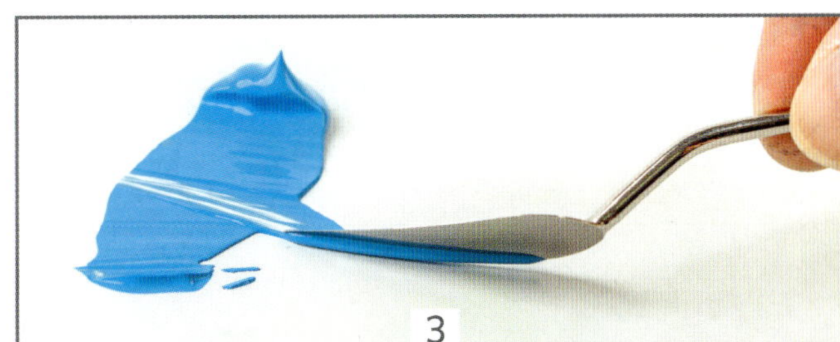

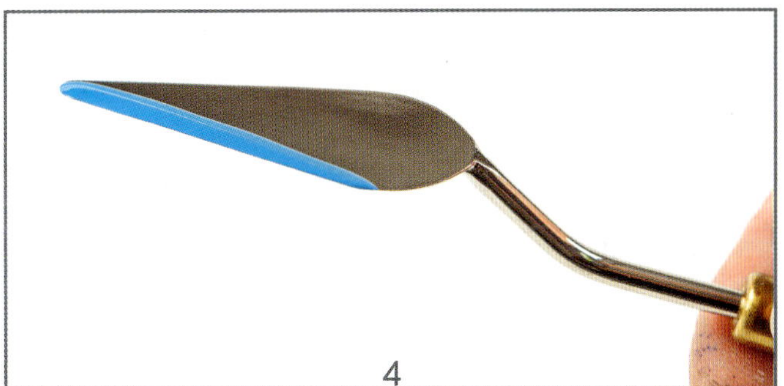

1 Squeeze a small amount of paint out onto the palette.

2 Spread the paint out thinly, holding the knife at a shallow angle.

3 Holding the knife at a slightly steeper angle, after cleaning, pull the blade down and slightly sideways through the paint.

4 Looking at the base of the knife, there should be a fine, even roll of paint on the blade.

THE SWEEP

Before making a mark, place the blade gently on the painting surface and held at an angle. Starting with 1, as the blade progresses over the surface to 4, turn the top edge towards the canvas in a smooth action which will trap the paint between the contact point and the surface. 5 shows the knife running out of paint as the stroke is concluded.

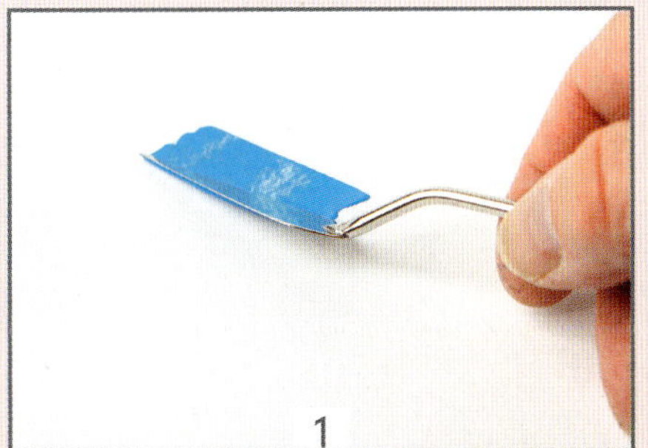

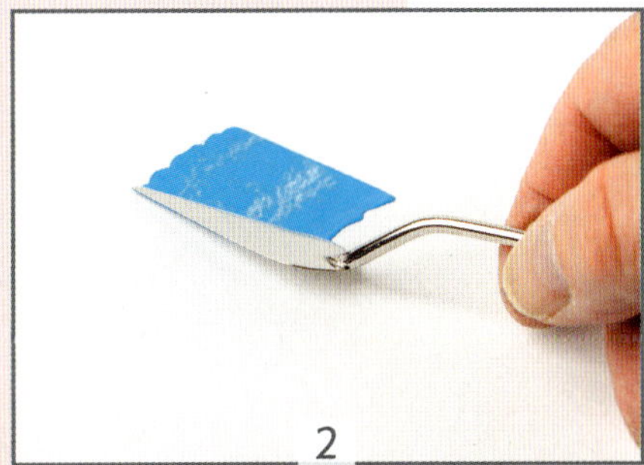

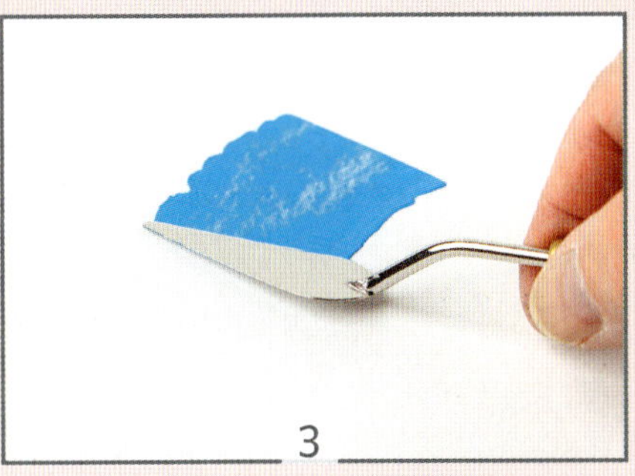

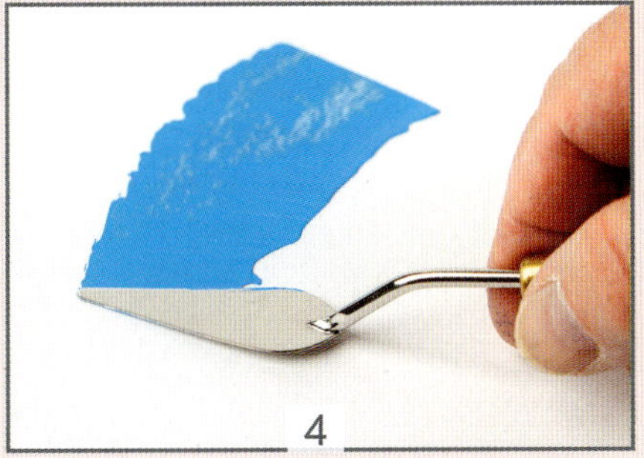

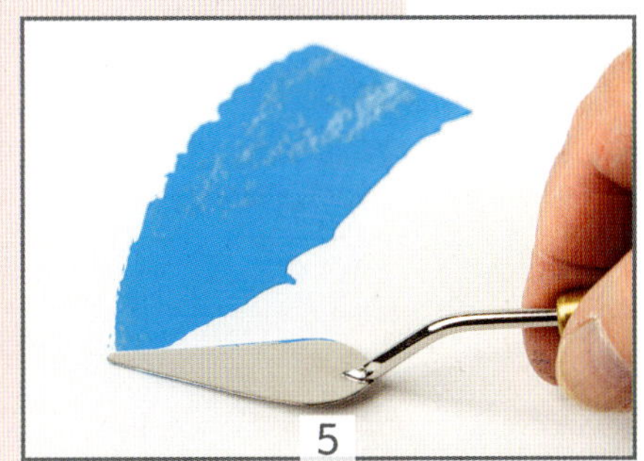

WORKING WITH THE SHAPES OF THE KNIVES: MARK-MAKING

Sometimes it's necessary to select different knife shapes to achieve a particular mark-making technique. Most knifework comprises a few specific marks, and these are some basic marks and gestures that are worth understanding. It's always best to experiment and explore different knife shapes to see what types of mark can be achieved.

USING THE VERSATILE RGM 6 KNIFE

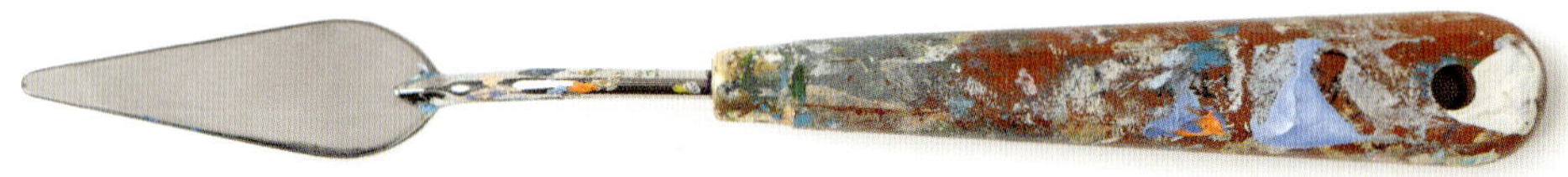

This is one of the knives I most commonly use. Below, I describe some of the wide range of strokes that can be achieved using this instrument.

This knife has developed from the traditional trowel shape. Made from flexible spring steel, the corners at the back of the blade have evolved into rounded edges, which allow for a greater flexibility of movement. The knife is suitable for mixing colours on the palette and for applying paint to the painting surface in a wide variety of styles.

1. Single-colour broad stroke

The simplest mark to be made is the single-colour broad stroke as described on page 23. This is the process of applying colour onto a relatively smooth surface. A large proportion of my paintings are produced using this stroke. It is used for quickly applying large areas of colour such as skies and foregrounds onto the painting surface.

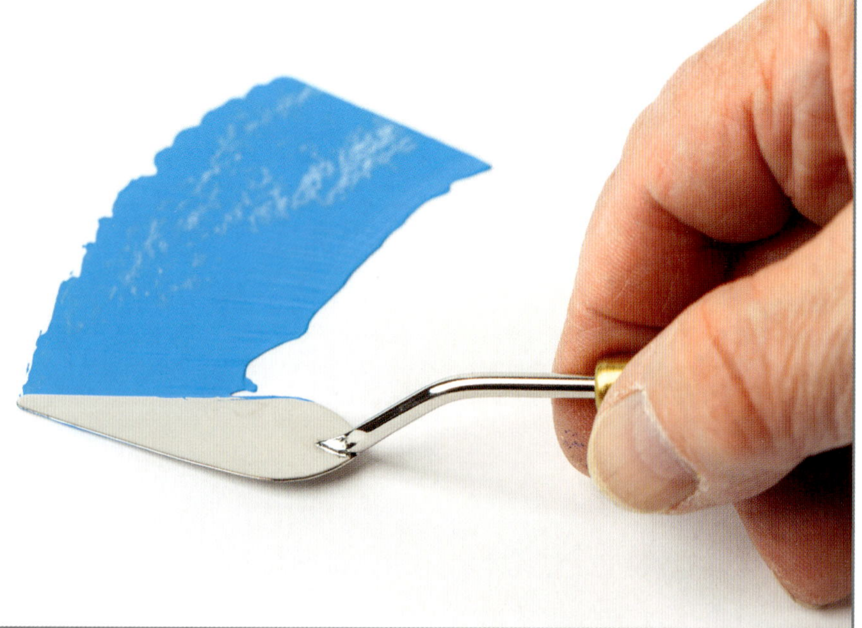

2. Stacking multiple colours

Layers of colour can be picked up using the broad-stroke method. The knife can be loaded with several different colours that have been spread out on the palette. This technique is known as 'stacking'. When the colours are swept across the surface, an interesting marbled effect can be produced. I use this technique where colours are required to blend on the surface such as in grassy foregrounds.

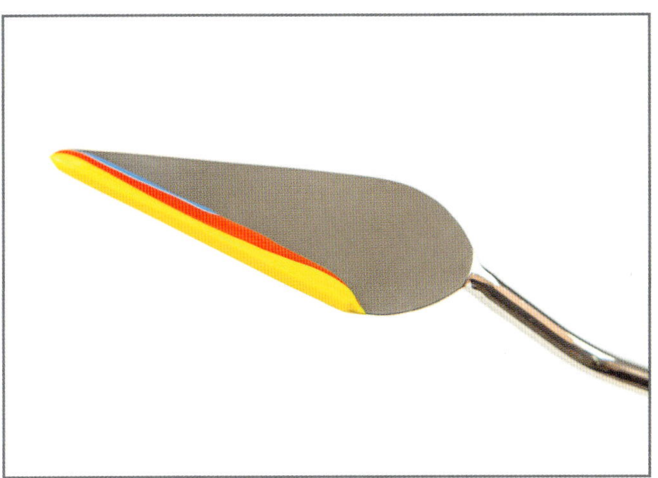

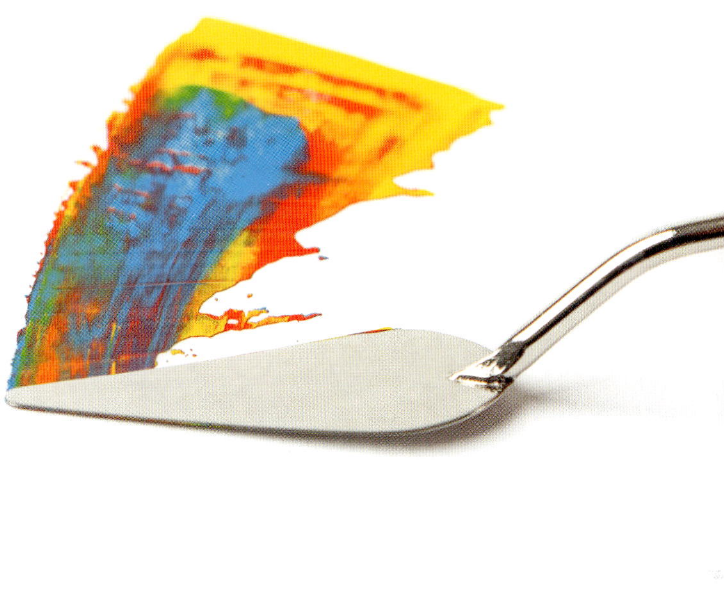

3. Buttons

A button is a simple mark that is achieved by picking up a small amount of paint on the tip of the knife and then 'touching' the point onto the painting surface. This method comes in really handy when portraying flower meadows where little dots of colour are required to represent the blooms.

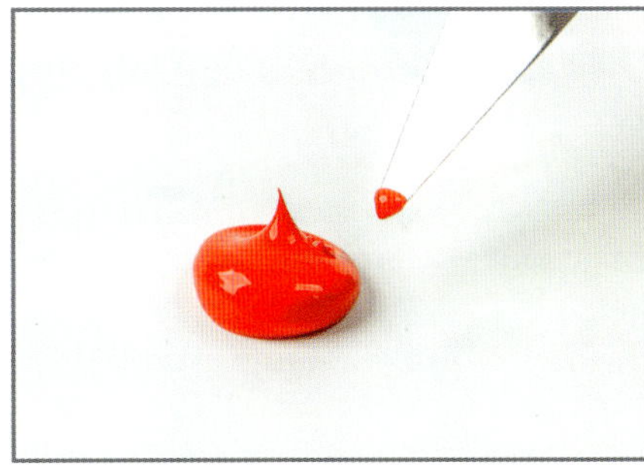

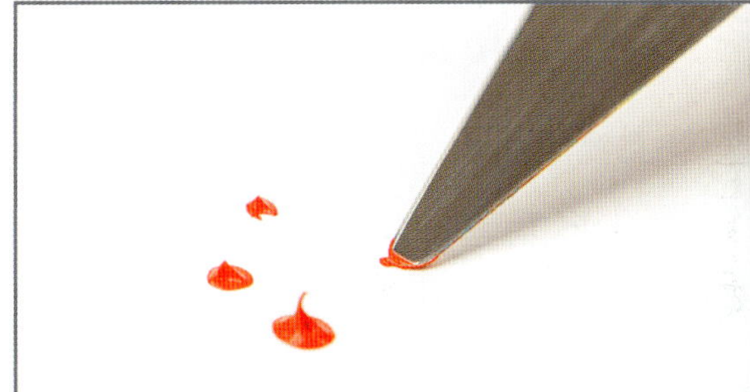

4. Single-colour fine stroke

There is often the requirement to add fine lines into a painting. To achieve this, the knife is loaded in the same way as for the sweep. It is then dragged across or down the surface in a straight line. Starting with the knife at an acute angle, the top edge of the knife is turned towards the painting surface as you progress. This method takes a little bit of practice but is very satisfying once you get the hang of it.

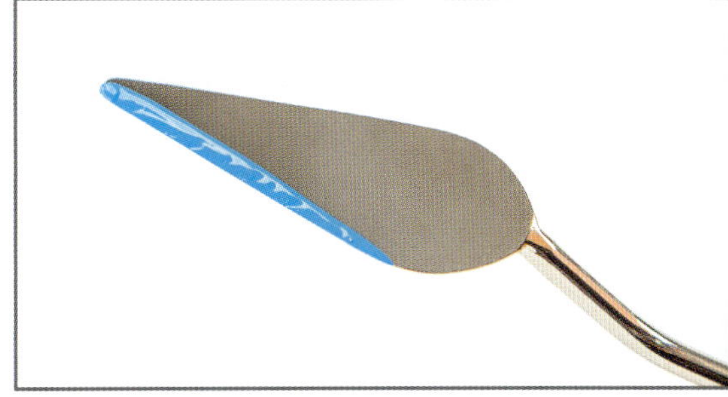

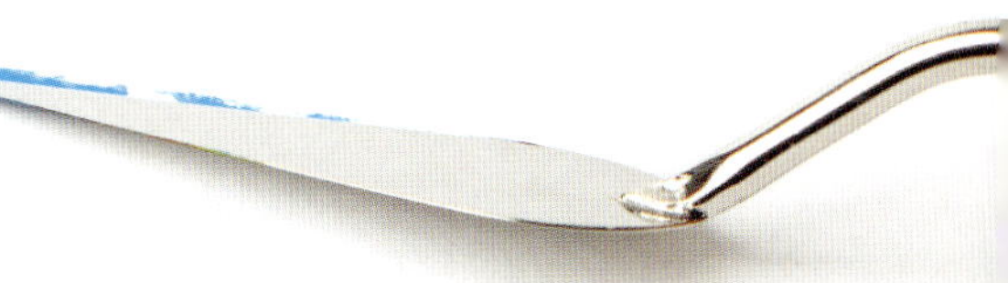

5. Heavy textures

This technique takes advantage of the properties of a heavy-body acrylic paint, such as the Sennelier Abstract and Golden paints that I use.

I apply the paint thickly with the knife and, once dry, the thick paint remains as texture. This method creates marks that are richer in colour and intensity.

One of the beauties of knifework is that textured sculpted effects can be achieved. I particularly like using this method when painting stormy seas. Heavy gel gloss medium can be added to the paint mix to enhance this effect.

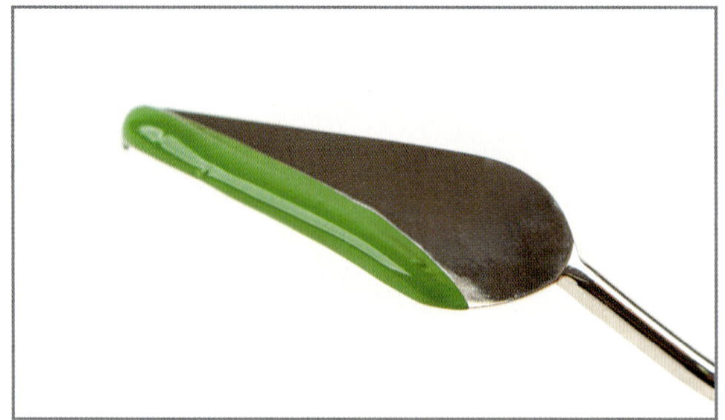

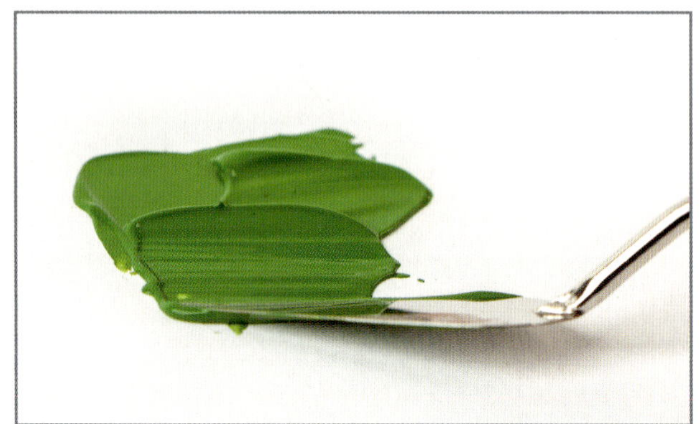

6. Making marks in wet paint

Making marks into the wet paint can add an extra dimension to the work. The method is the same as applying the single colour fine stroke but this time dragged through wet paint.

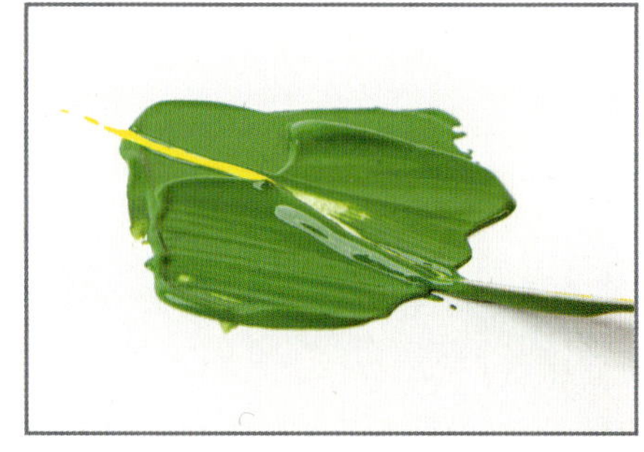

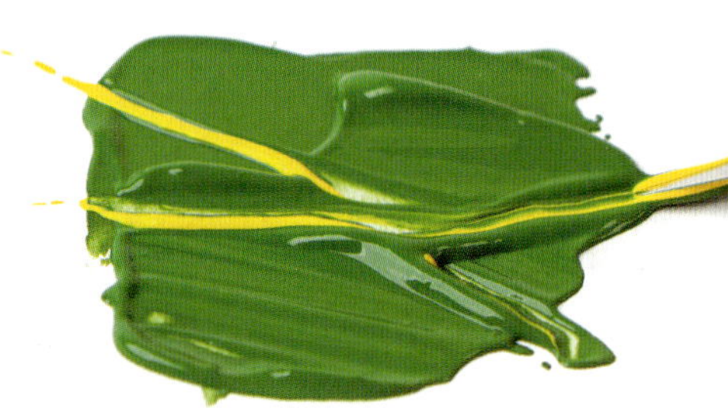

7. Touching knife edges for straight lines

A fine sliver of paint is loaded onto the edge of the blade as described on page 23 (loading the knife) for the single colour stroke. The blade is gently touched onto a smooth painting surface to deposit a thin straight line. If you add a series of these lines, the mark will become progressively fainter, which could suggest a line of fenceposts disappearing into the distance.

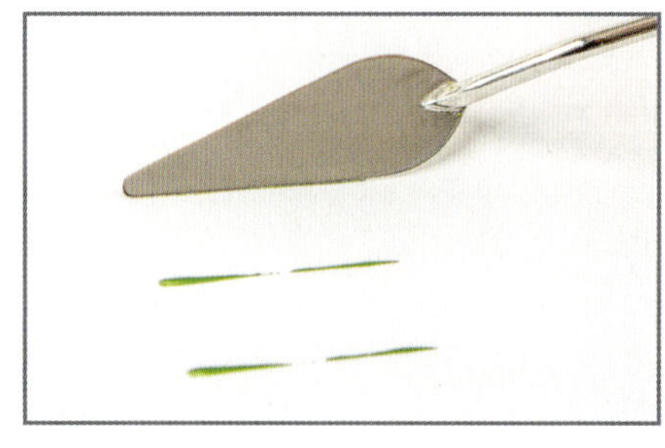

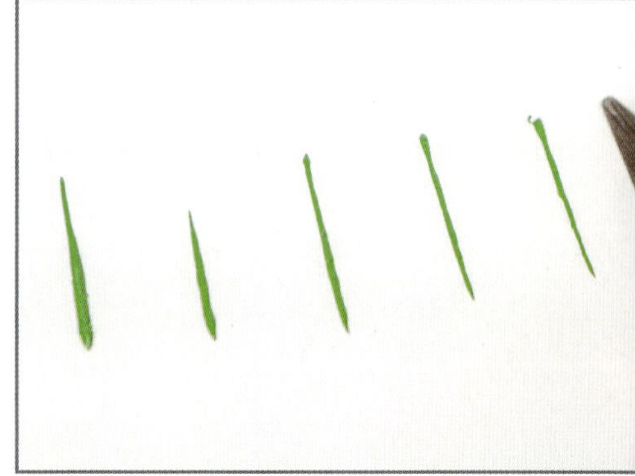

8. Dragging for broken textures

I often use this technique to suggest broken textures in a landscape. Paint is loaded onto the tip of the knife and dragged horizontally across the painting surface. This deposits a broken texture onto the painting.

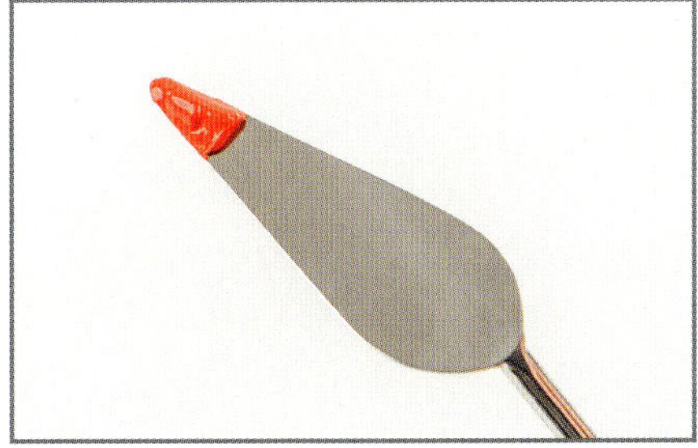

Loading the paint...

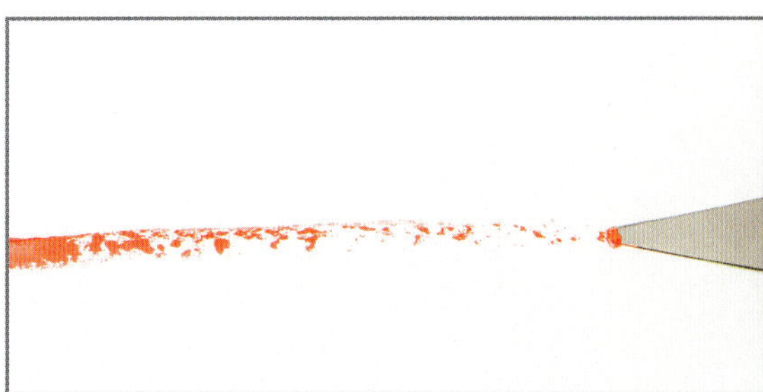

Applying the paint.

9. Blending colours and edges

Acrylic colours can be easily blended whilst still wet. This mixable period can be extended by adding Gloss glazing medium, or by spraying the surface with an atomizer and clean water. Where two colour edges meet, use a clean knife and 'wibble' it from side to side to blend the colours (see page 29 for more on 'wibble').

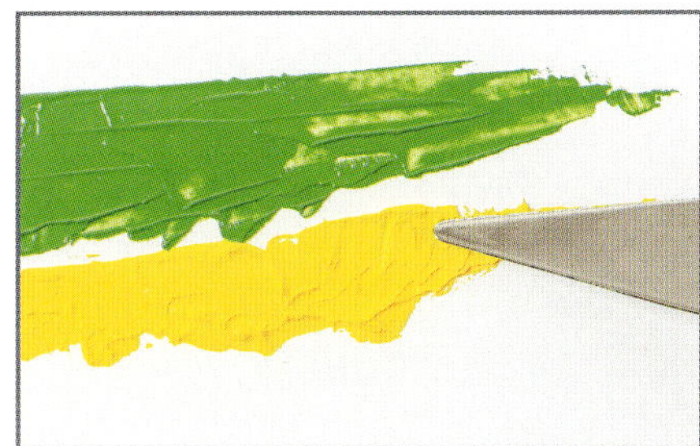

The separate colours...

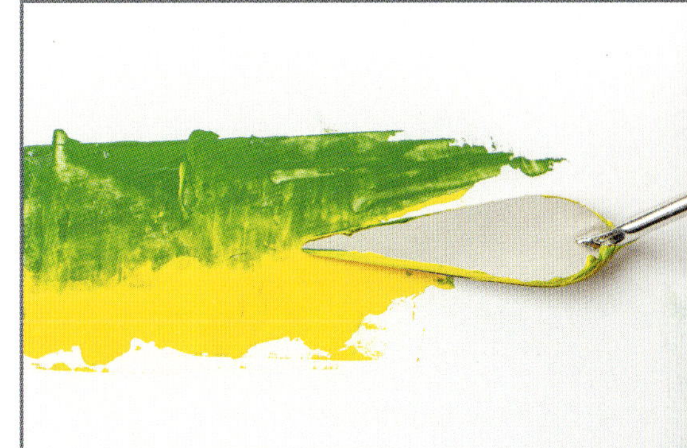

Blending the colours.

10. Scraping out/sgraffito

This method is used to reveal hidden colours below layers of paint. To explore this, spread a layer of bright colour and allow to dry. Then apply a layer of a contrasting colour using the sweep method (see page 23). Using the tip of a clean knife, scrape lines into the wet paint revealing the dry colour below.

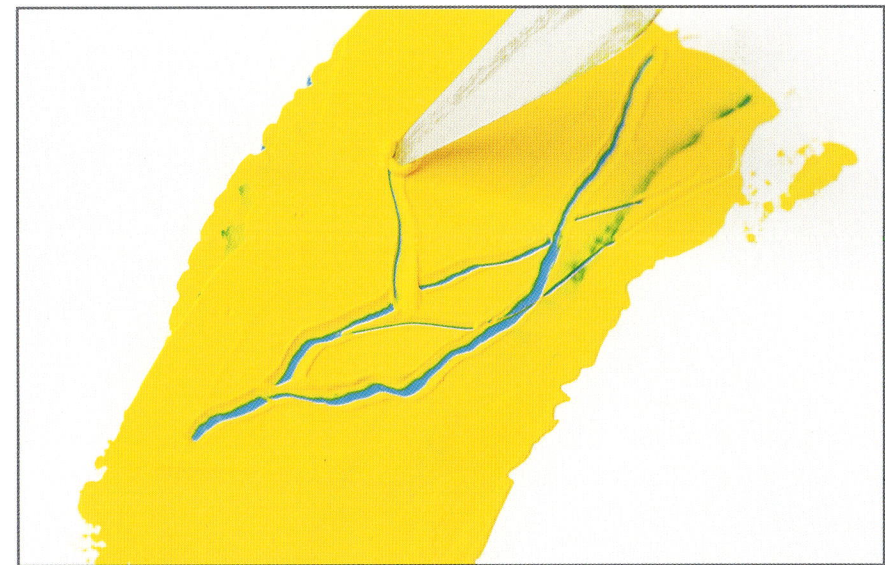

11. Stamps

To add a series of random dots to a painting I sometimes use the stamp method. Pick up some paint with a fingertip and dot randomly onto the base of a clean knife. Touch the knife onto the painting surface to deposit the marks. Further dots can be added by cleaning the blade and repeating the process.

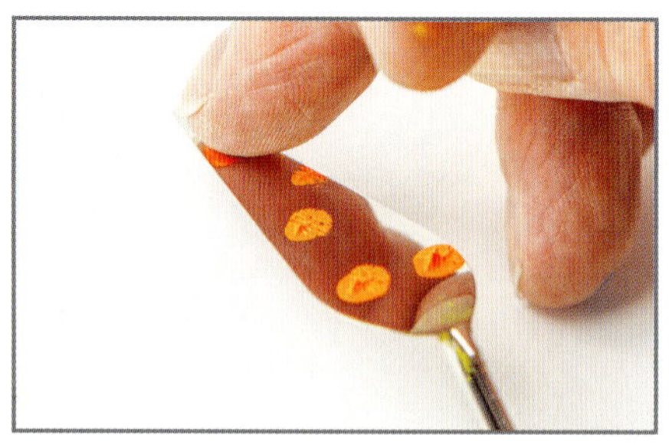
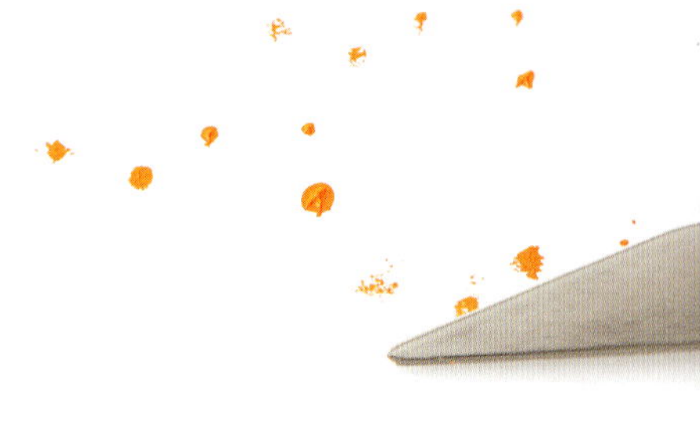

12. Cutting around complex shapes

This often becomes a crucial method to use when painting with knives. A good exercise is to draw a complex shape and then accurately apply paint around it. You will quickly learn which side of the blade to load the knife and how to only partially load paint along the length of the blade to get into tight spaces.

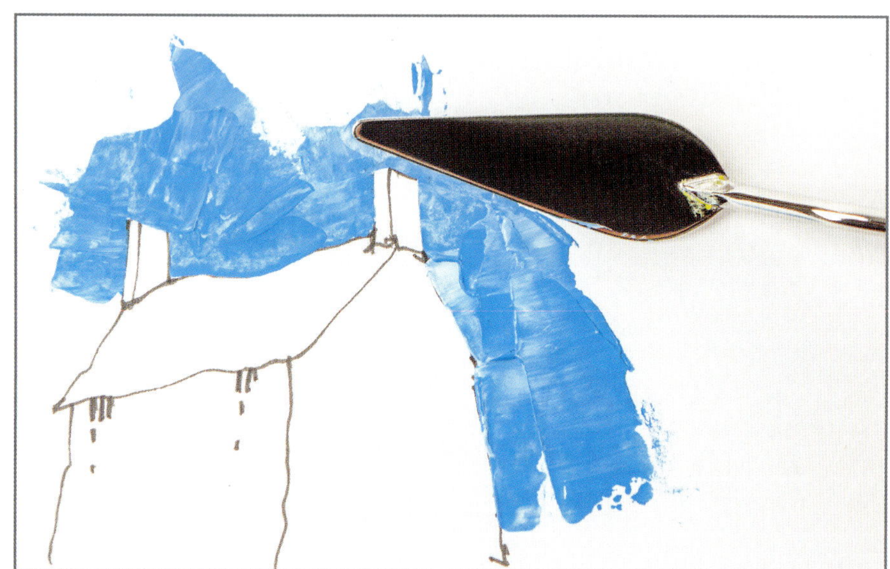

13. Flicking

This technique is useful for adding long thin fibrous marks onto the painting. I often use it to describe foreground grasses. A button-sized amount of paint is added to the tip of the knife; the tip is gently bent back and released to 'flick' pigment across the painting surface. With practice, it can be found that changing the position of the knife in relation to the painting surface can produce a wide variety of marks.

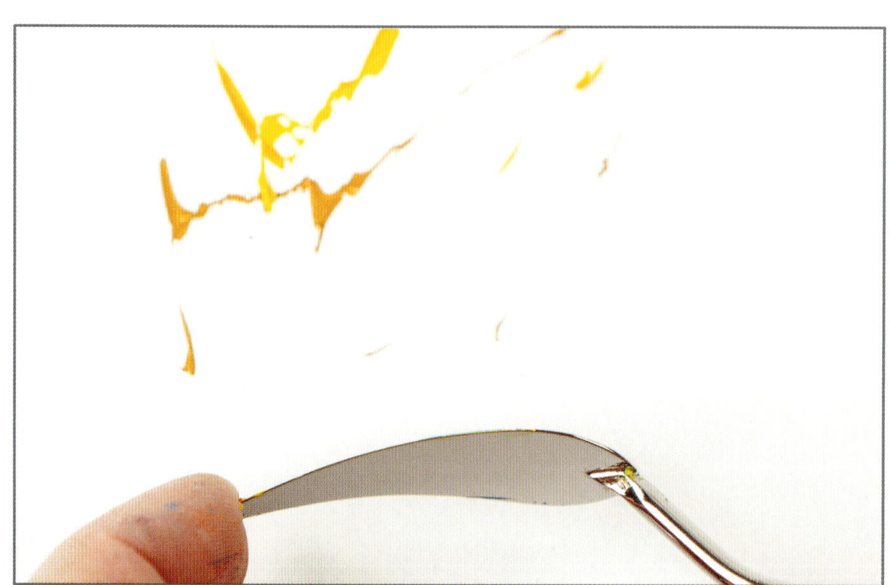

14. Wibble

In this example I have added azure blue and primary yellow to one side of the blade and cadmium orange to the other side. The knife is then turned and mixed on the painting surface. I call this method 'wibble'. It is the action of rocking the blade and at the same time moving from left to right to mix and agitate paint as it is being placed onto the painting surface.

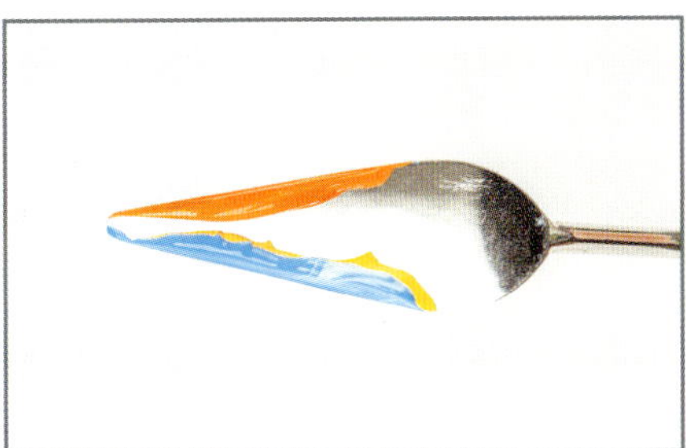
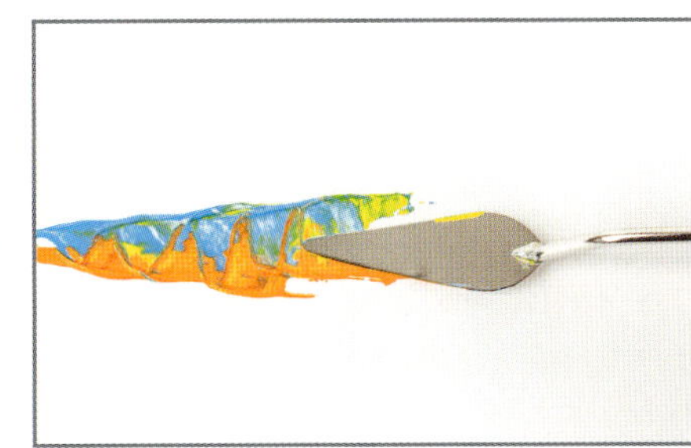
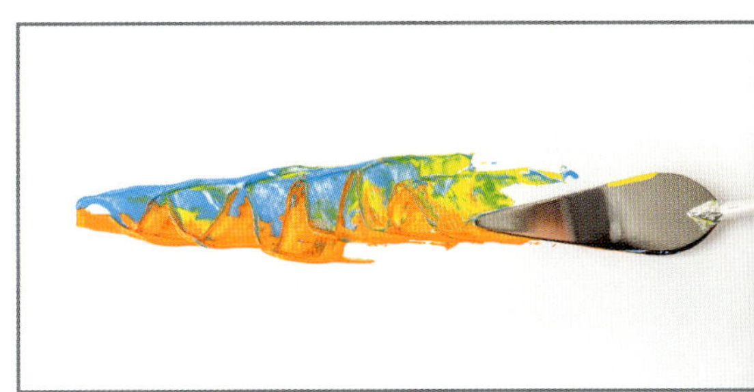

15. Splat

The splat is a method for creating interesting shapes on the painting surface. The knife is loaded with paint on the tip, then turned to face the painting. Holding the knife approximately 1cm (⅜in) from the surface, gently bend back the blade and allow the tip to come forcefully into contact with the surface. I have used the marks produced here to suggest cornflowers and other blooms.

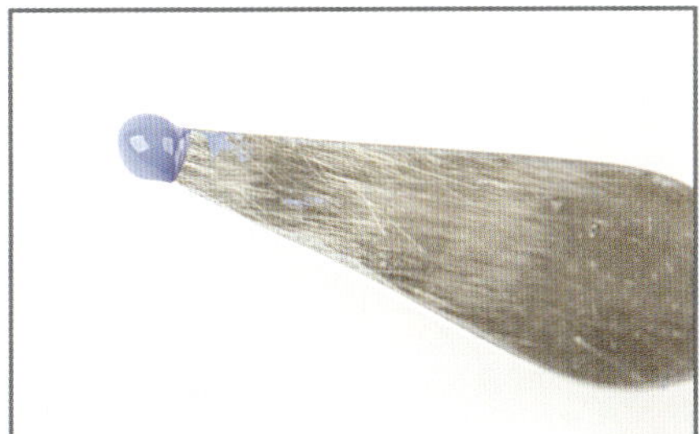
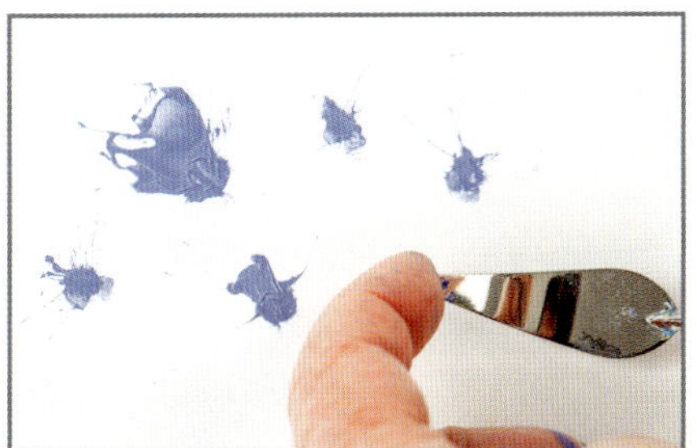

16. Rotation

This is a technique for producing circular or semi-circular marks. Partially load paint along the edge of the blade. I usually start at the heel of the knife (see page 38) and build different colours finishing at the tip. Hold the knife against the painting surface and rotate the wrist. There is a limit as to how far you can go, so the knife must be lifted and replaced on the surface to start a fresh part of the curve.

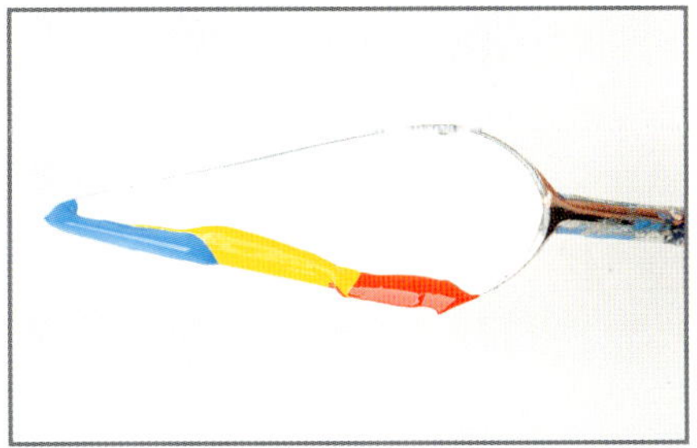
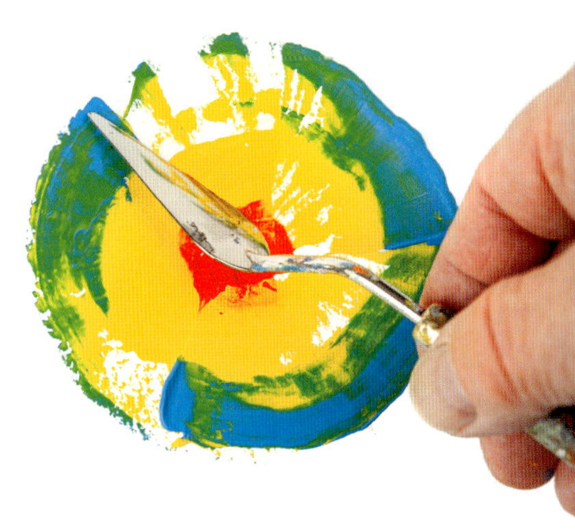

17. Painting figures

When creating figures, it's worth doing some sketches to get to understand proportion. Fitting eight head lengths into the body is usually a recommended standard for figure drawing.

I usually create my people using a small amount of paint on the tip of the knife, starting with the head and working down the body. If colour needs to be added, this is best done with a colour change as the figure is created.

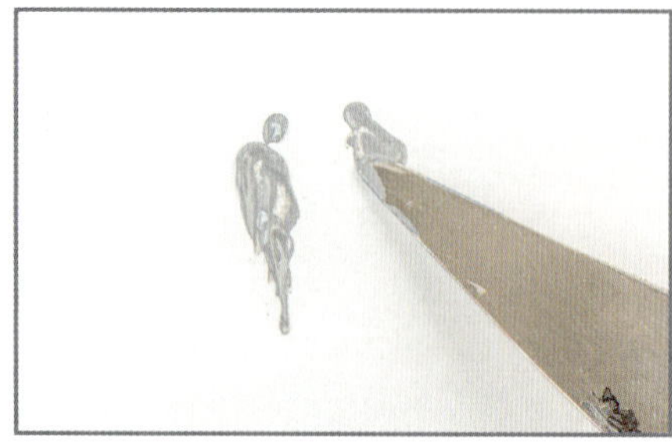
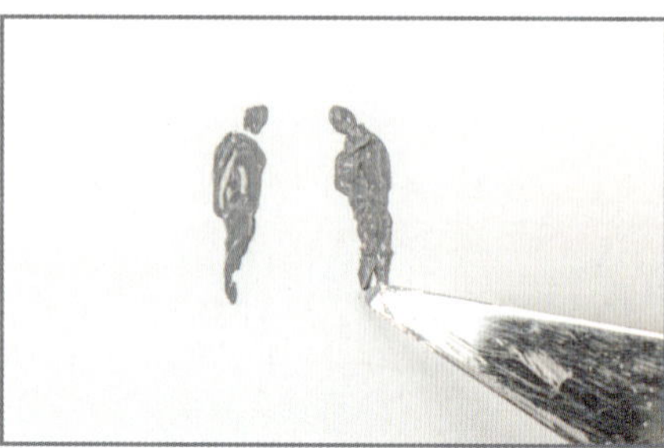
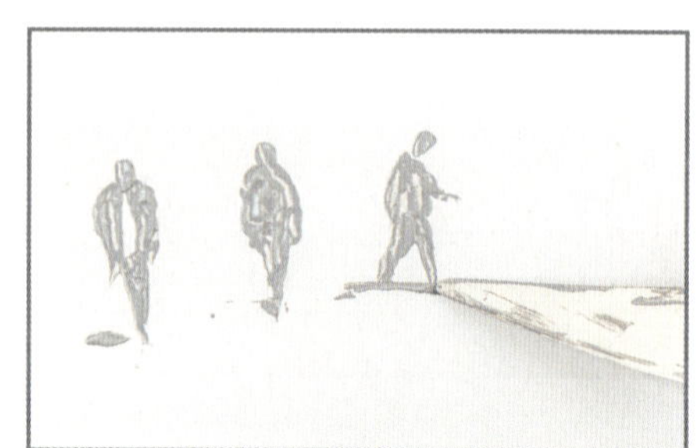

18. Covering errors with thick paint

One of the beauties of working with a knife is its covering power. Even transparent colours such as yellows or oranges will cover and conceal other darker colours when applied with a blade. The technique is the same as the single colour broad stroke (see page 24). If more coverage is required, add a slightly larger roll of paint onto the blade edge.

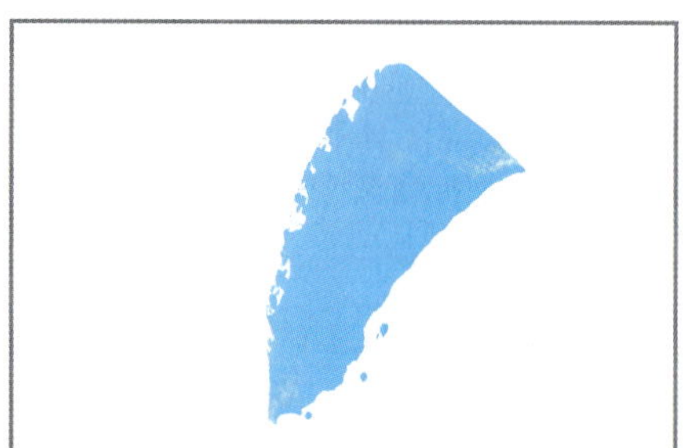

Before...

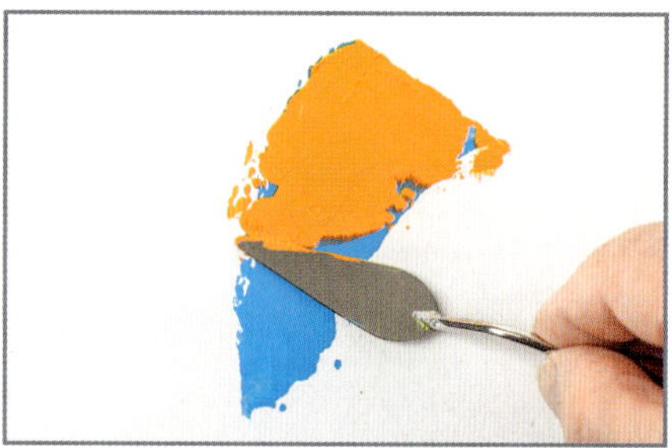

During...

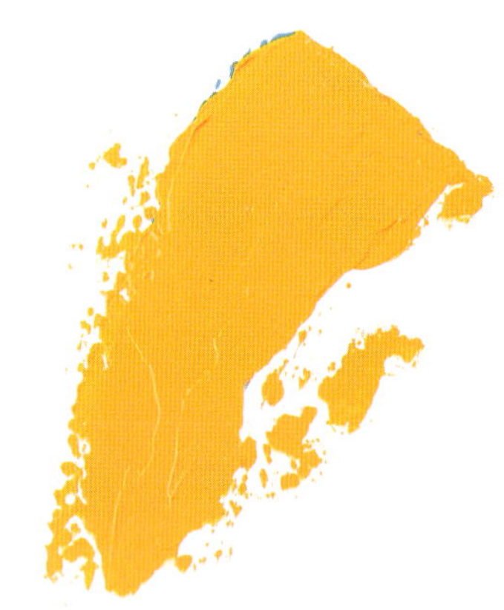

After!

19. Wet-into-wet scumble

(as used in *Barges on the Blackwater*; see pages 98–103)

This is a new technique I have developed, myself. A roll of paint on the edge of the knife is added to a very wet surface of colour. The knife acts as a squeegee, pushing the wet paint aside and allowing the roll of paint to stick to the surface with a slight bleed. Some inspiring atmospheric effects can be achieved when using this method.

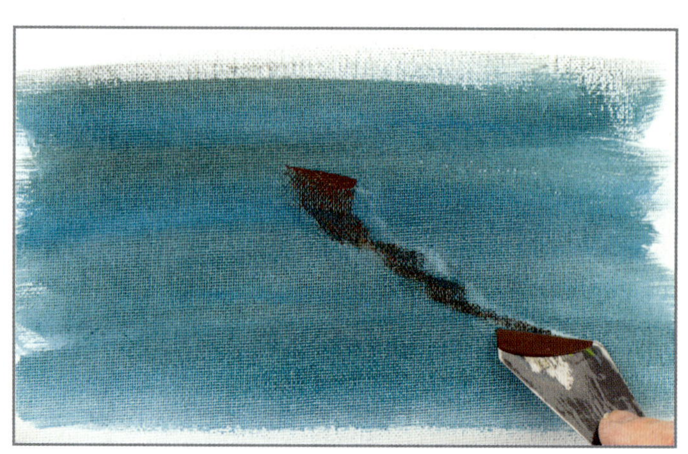

USING THE RGM 109 KNIFE

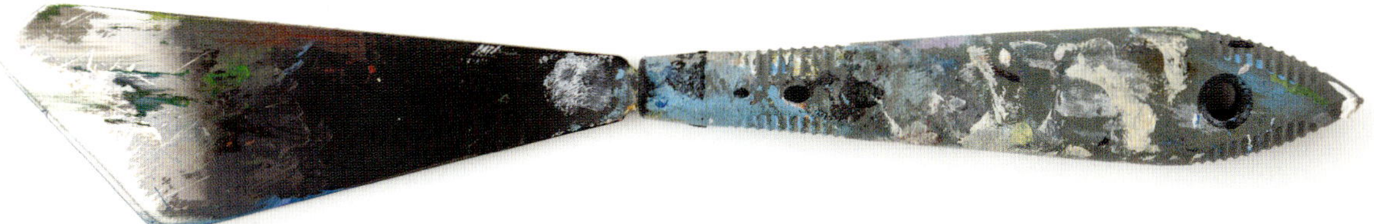

This knife is one of the few I use that doesn't have a crank handle, and it's the one I use most frequently. The shape at the front offers the choice to make a broad or narrow mark. I find this blade is very useful when layering skies or creating building shapes.

20. Dry scumble

As well as being able to produce a large variety of the marks already demonstrated, it is also possible to scumble with this knife. This process involves allowing the knife to run out of paint, revealing the texture of the canvas surface. This is a very useful technique that can be used to describe the edge of a tree canopy, or for creating softer marks within a landscape painting.

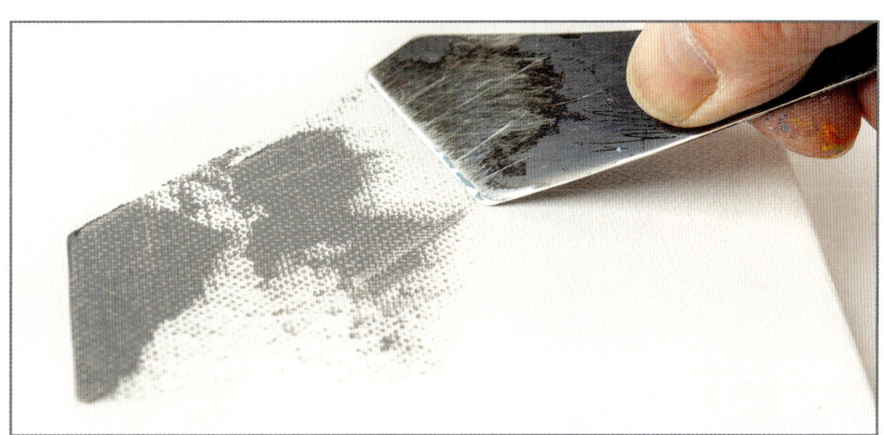

21. Piggybacking/reversing the mark

It's quite important to work quickly when applying acrylics to prevent the paint drying. The broad blade of the RGM 109 allows you to do this.

Apply a slightly larger roll of paint to the knife and pull the blade across the painting surface. Add more paint and pull in the reverse direction, slightly overlapping or piggybacking the strokes. When doing this, add a little more pressure than normal, which will tend to flatten out the paint and create a flat, uniform surface, allowing further knifework to be carried out later. The wet paint should blend as this is done.

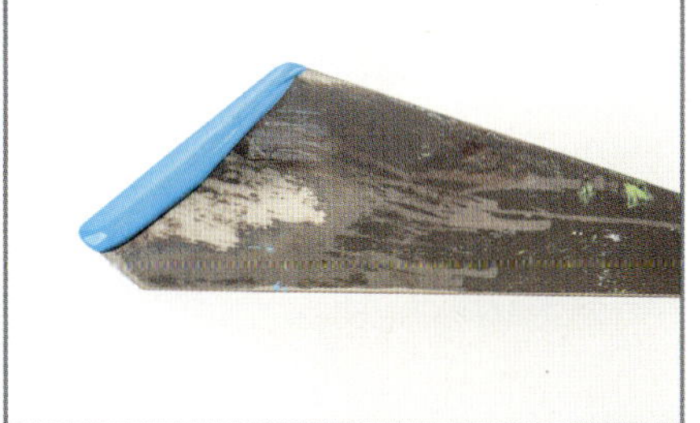

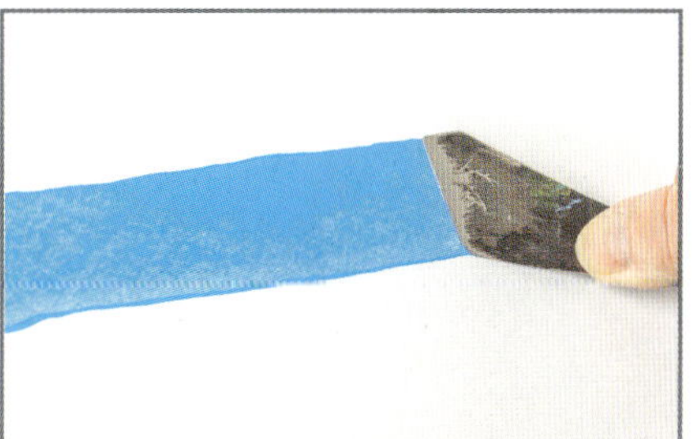

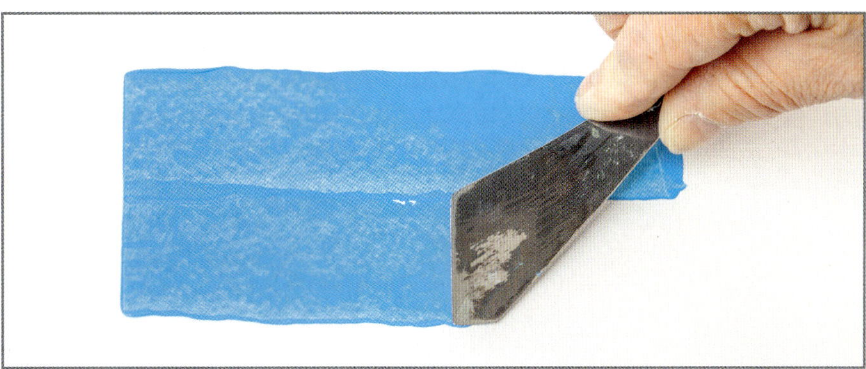

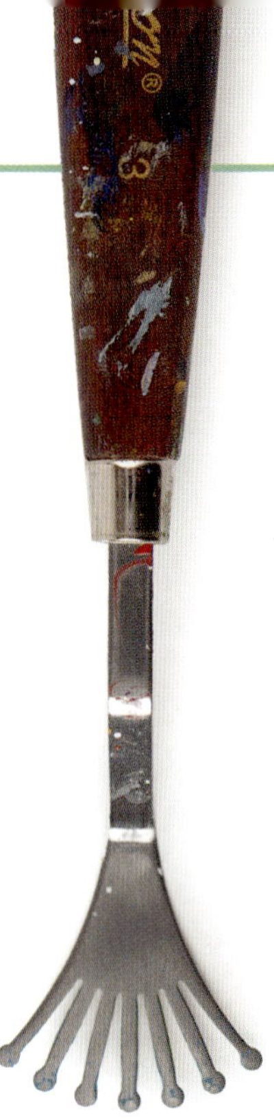

USING THE KING KNIFE

This knife has a unique crown shape with a springy steel tip and is one of the few specialist tools for making creative marks. The multi-pronged tip allows the user to create a wide variety of spatter effects for subjects such as flower meadows or seascapes.

22. ...with fluid acrylic for spatter

Mix a small amount of paint with pouring medium in a disposable cup. Add a little water if necessary using a plastic pipette or syringe until the paint has a runny consistency resembling single pouring cream. Dip the prongs into the mix, then bend slightly and flick the ends over the painting surface to create a spatter effect. For a different end result, try having more than one colour to dip into.

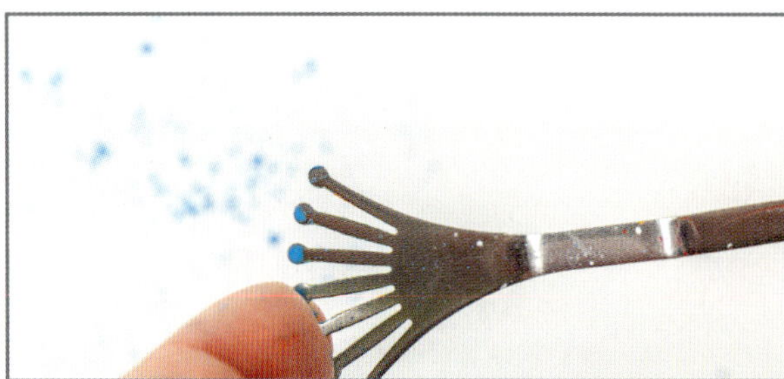

23. Dragging the paint on the surface

Another technique is to apply a thick layer of paint using another knife, then drag the clean tips of the King through the paint. Further marks can be achieved by selecting which of the prongs come into contact with the paint surface.

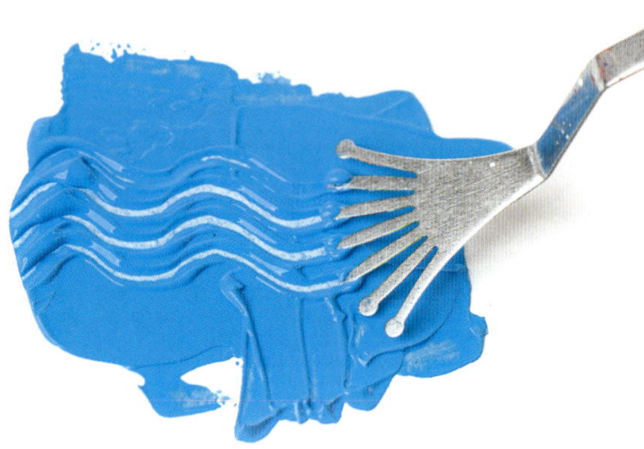

USING THE RGM 41 KNIFE

The RGM 41 is a smaller version of the standard palette knife trowel shape. The short edge of the blade makes working with it much easier when cutting around demanding shapes. It's also very useful when tackling small areas within a detailed subject.

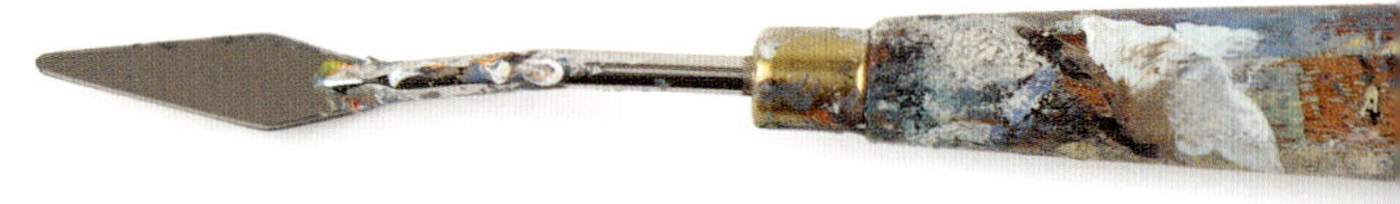

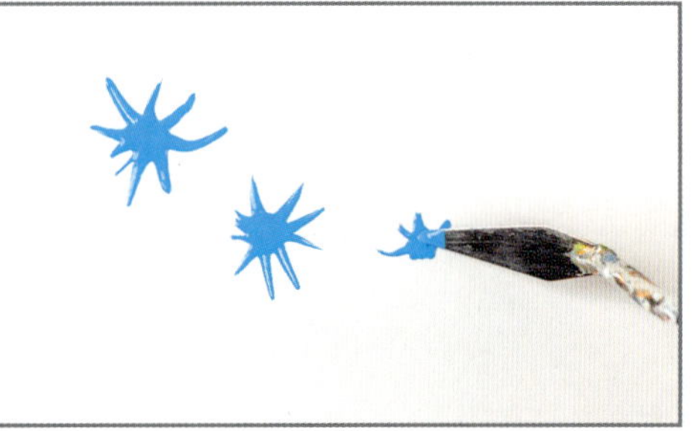

24. Dragging star shapes

The small tip of this knife can be used to create some interesting patterns such as star shapes or other extended marks. Using diluted paint in a disposable cup, collect a small blob of paint on the tip of the knife, or spatter some spots onto the painting surface with the King. Using the tip of a clean RGM 41, drag the edges of the blob outwards to create a star shape.

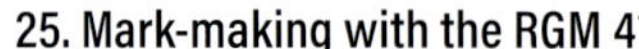

25. Mark-making with the RGM 41

This knife is not designed for applying large areas of paint but smaller versions of the marks already demonstrated in techniques 1 to 21.

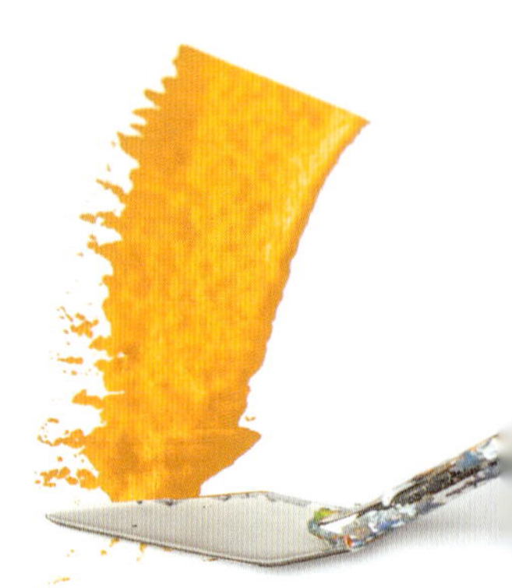

USING THE LARGE ROUND KNIFE

The large round knife is one I developed by adapting the shape of an RGM 6 blade. The slight egg shape of the blade will create interesting oval or half-moon shapes, which helps to represent foliage when denoting summer trees.

26. Semi-circular marks for foliage

To create foliage patterns the paint is first spread on the palette and then the tip of the knife is dragged through. The paint can be picked up at any point around the edge of the knife which helps to create slightly different marks. Once loaded, the knife is placed on the painting surface at an angle and can then be pulled in any direction to create the shapes required.

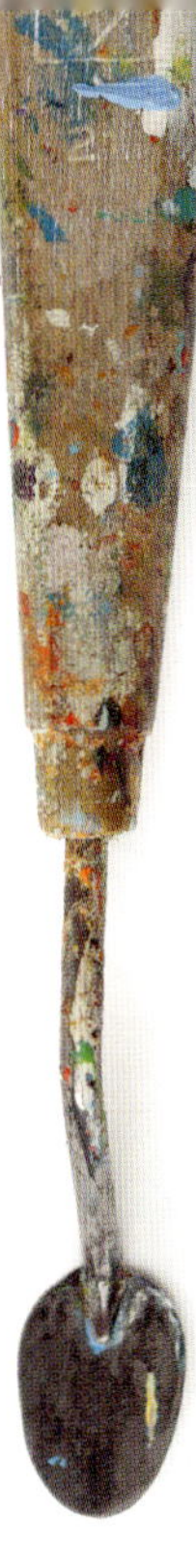

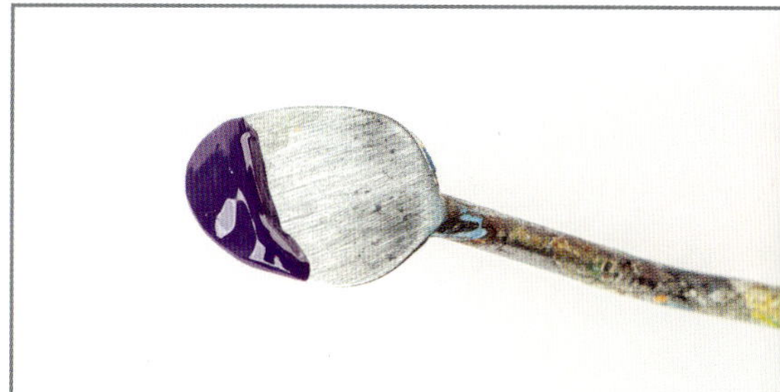

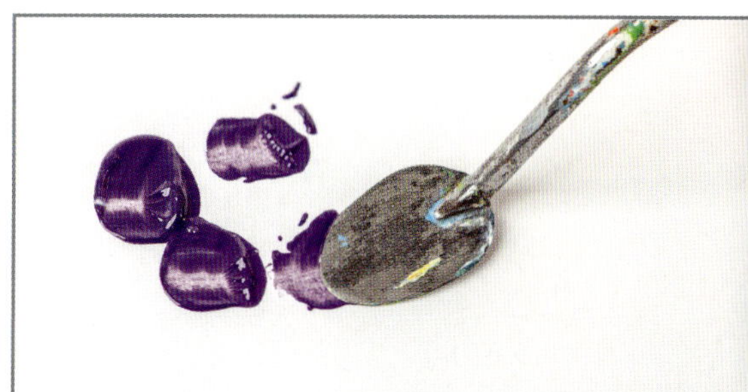

USING THE SMALL ROUND KNIFE

The smaller round knife is another cut-down RGM 6. I use this as an alternative shape to create finer foliage. The shape allows for a different variety of marks to be produced.

27. Mark-making with the small round

The mark-making process is the same as described above (26), though, being smaller, the shapes are more varied, especially if the knife is allowed to run out of paint during use.

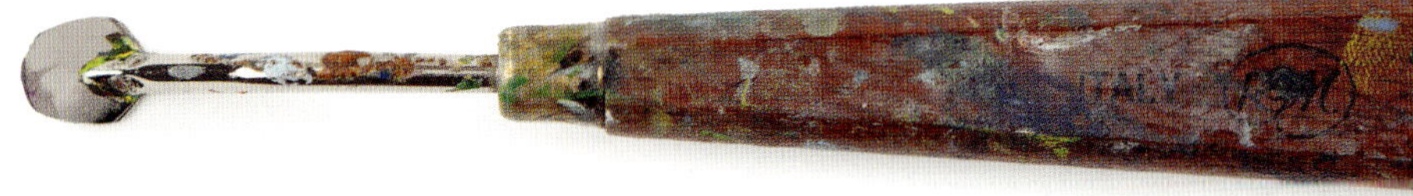

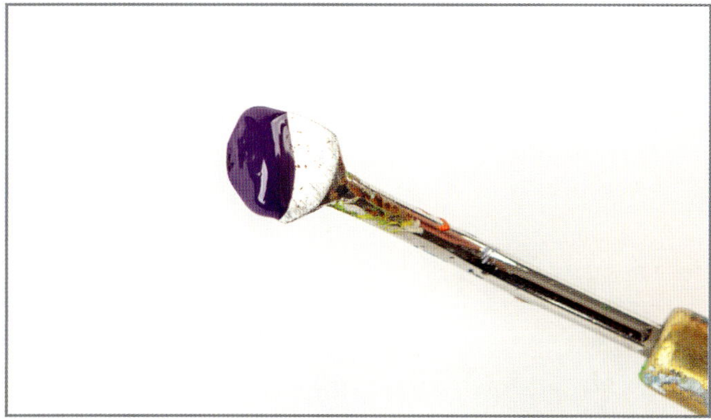

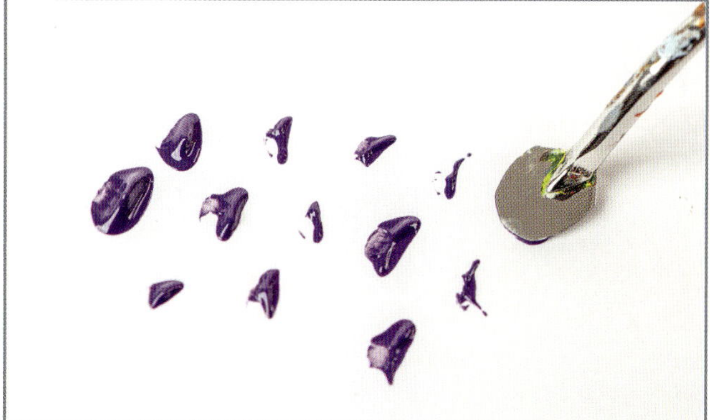

28. Painting over marble dust

For really fine textures, I have developed a method of combining acrylic with marble dust. This material is a by-product of processing white marble and is available in art stores and online (the marble dust I use comes from L. Cornelissen & Son, London). I store it in an old honey jar.

After picking up paint on the tip of the knife, the knife then touches the surface of the marble dust, picking up a small quantity. As the paint is applied to the painting surface, the dust acts as a resist which allows interesting foliage effects to be produced.

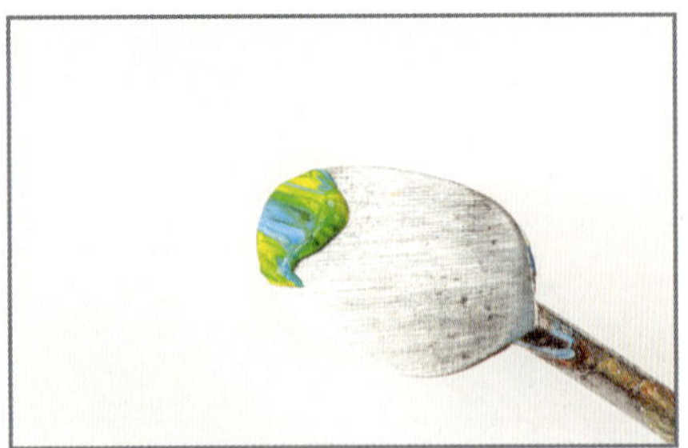
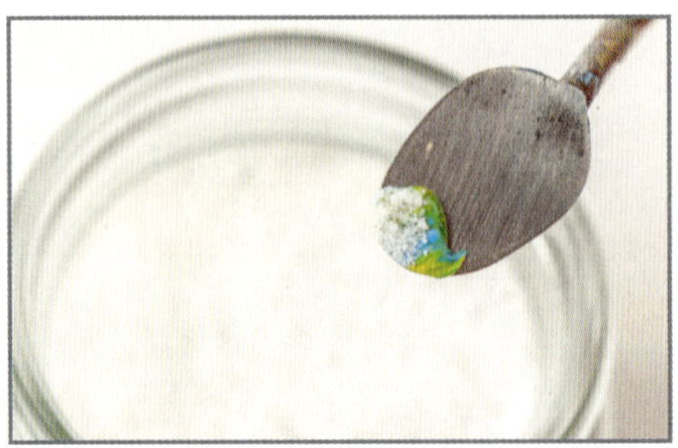
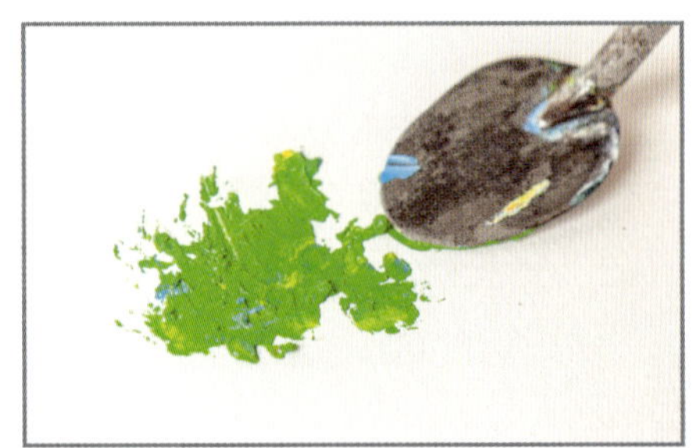

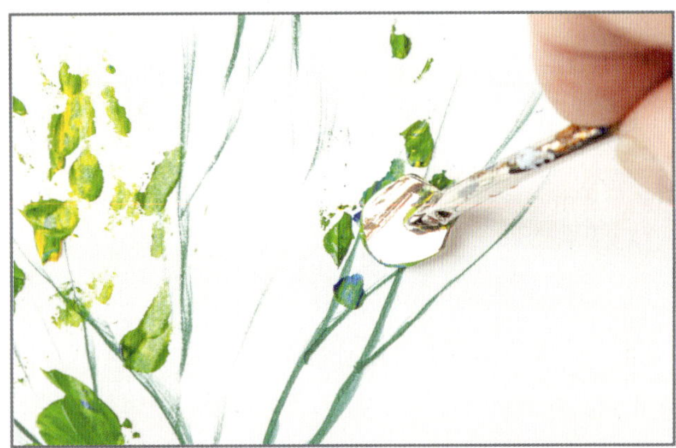

29. Tree textures (leaves)

A variety of leaf shapes can be produced using the same technique as described in 26 and 27 (see page 33), by choosing a different-sized knife. For added interest, I sometimes stack a blue and yellow together, which will then mix as the leaf marks are applied.

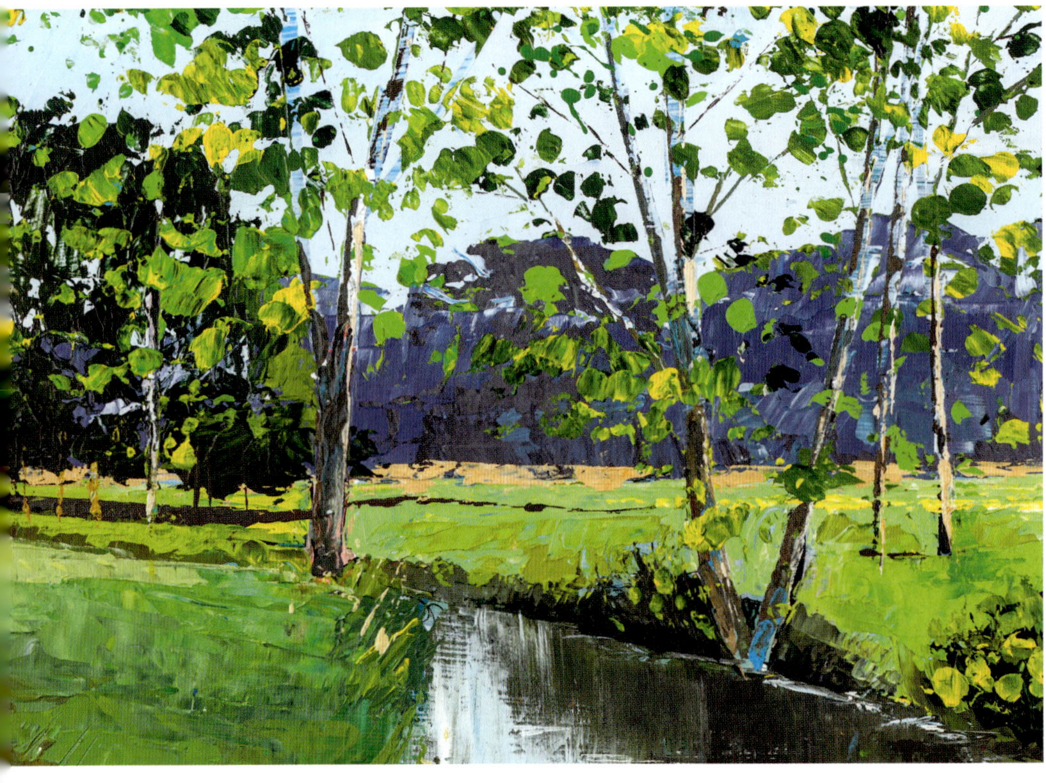

Springtime on Somerton Stream

38 × 30.5cm (15 × 12in)

I was inspired by the early spring greens of the foreground trees in this riverside scene. After completing the background and indicating some of the bare branches using fine strokes with the RGM 6, I proceeded to add the leaves using both the small and large round knives.

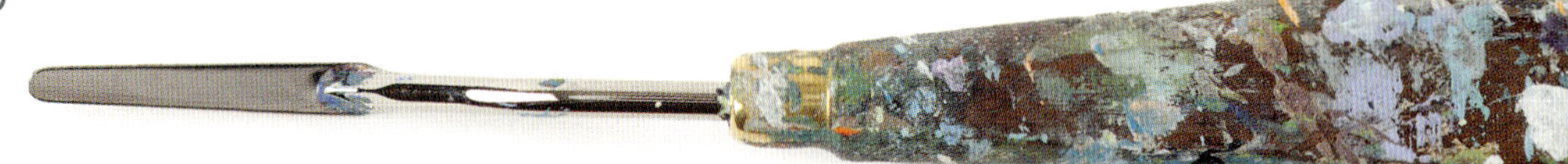

USING THE RGM PASTRELLO

This knife comes from a set of six fine blades that were developed when RGM collaborated with the artist Franco Pastrello. If you decide to specialize in really fine detail work using knives, then the rest of the set is worth investigating. Having used them all, this one has become one of my favourites, having a narrow flexible blade which is ideal for producing curved and straight fine lines.

30. Fine line with slow-drying extender

One of the most challenging aspects of painting with knives is being able to produce a long, straight, fine line. This can be done with some of the other knives described, but is much easier with the RGM Pastrello. When creating fine lines, I usually start by diluting the paint with pouring medium, mixing it 50:50 with the paint. When the two parts are combined, the paint initially takes on a porridgy consistency, but with continued mixing a creamy consistency is achieved.

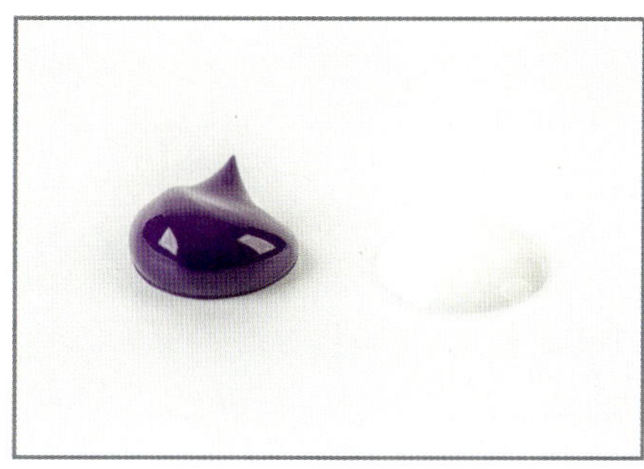

1 Squeeze out roughly equal proportions of paint and pouring medium.

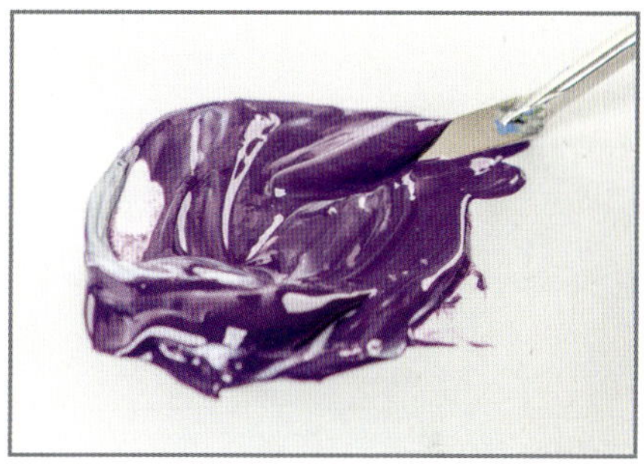

2 Mix the two halves together. The paint initially has a porridge-like consistency.

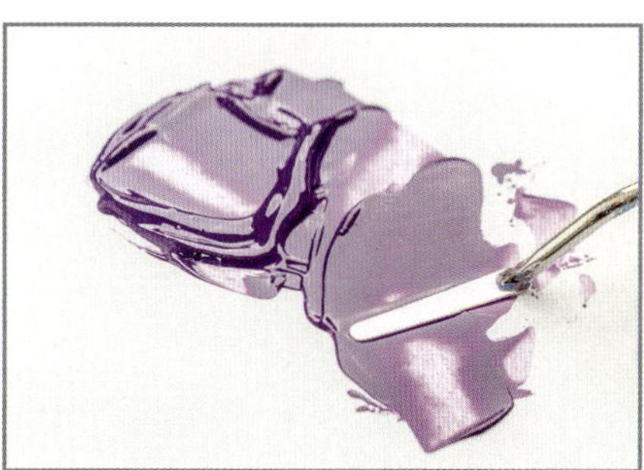

3 Continue mixing until the paint becomes slick and smooth. Spread the paint flat.

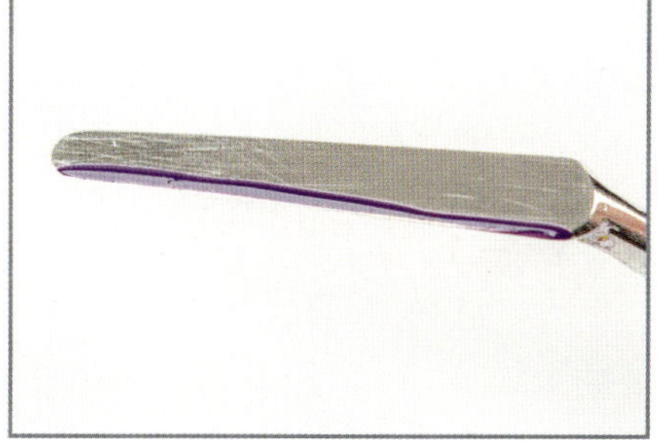

4 Pick up a sliver of paint along the edge of the knife.

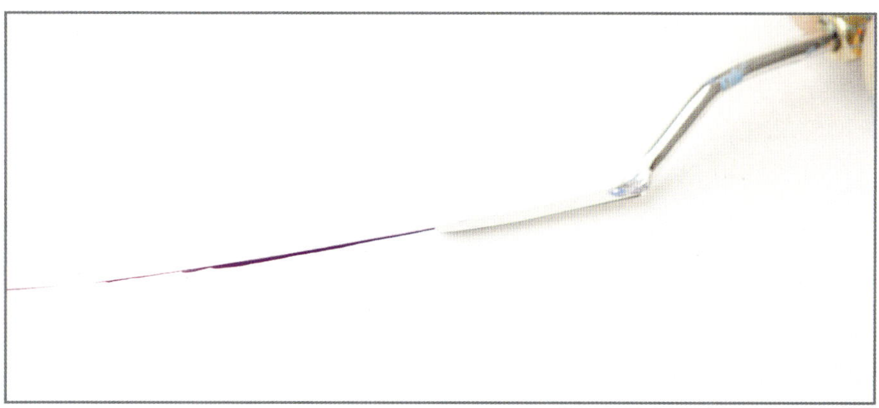

5 Draw the knife over the surface, turning the blade towards the canvas as you proceed.

31. Double-loading the RGM Pastrello

The narrow blade of the knife can be double-loaded when the paint is applied to both sides of the blade. If the knife is then placed level on the surface at a slight angle, a wider straight line can be produced as the heel of the knife is lowered onto the painting surface whilst keeping the tip in contact.

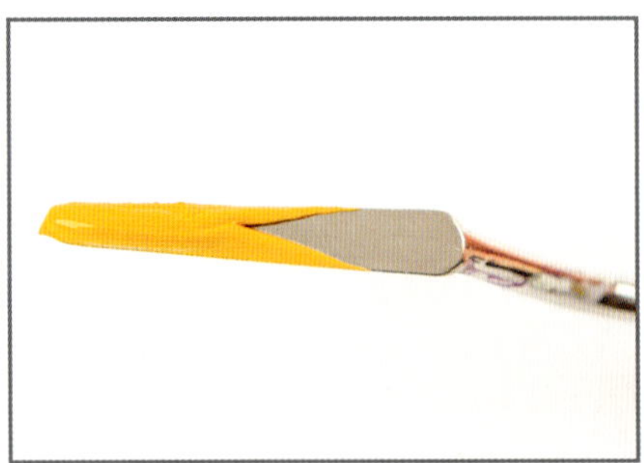
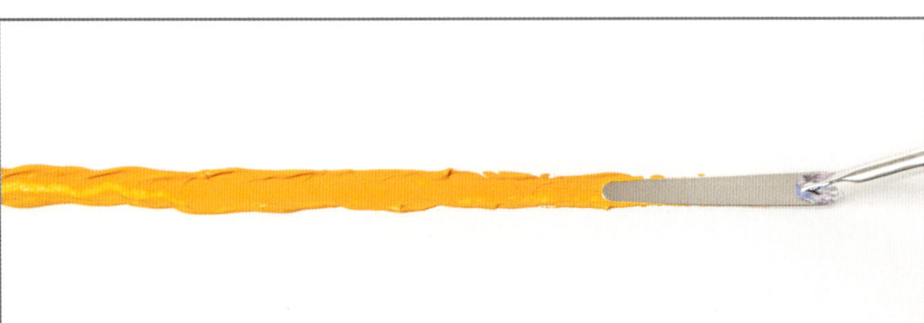

Loaded on both sides.

32. Plain/curved stroke

This is a fine delicate mark that is best achieved using the RGM Pastrello 38. A fine sliver of paint is applied to the edge of the knife and then, using the single-colour fine stroke (4, see page 25), pull the knife in a gentle curve across the painting surface. It may be necessary to dilute the paint with a little pouring medium to improve the flow.

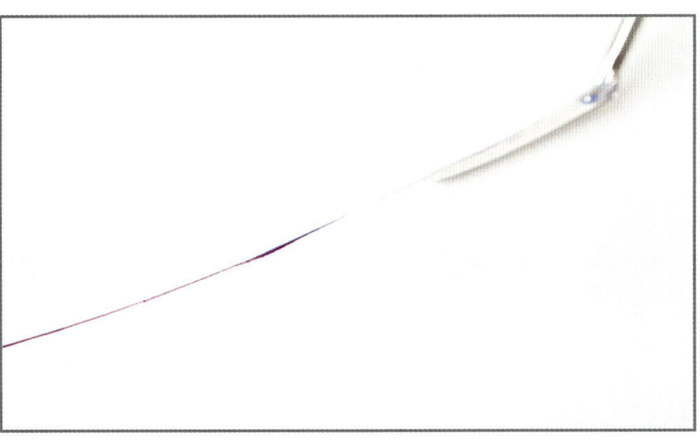

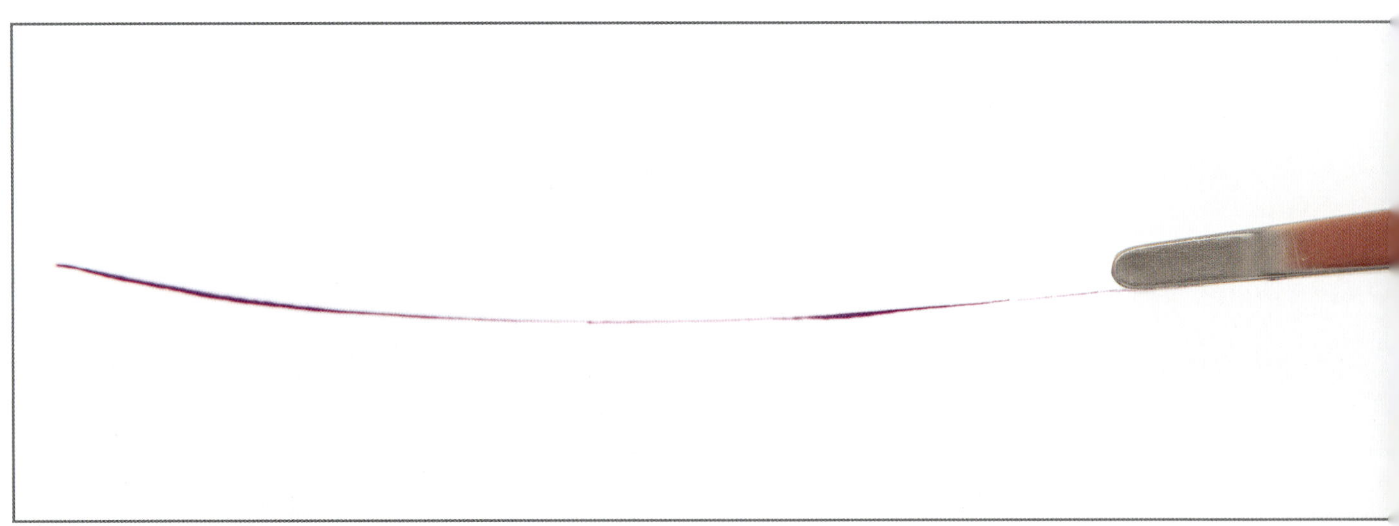

USING THE BULL NOSE

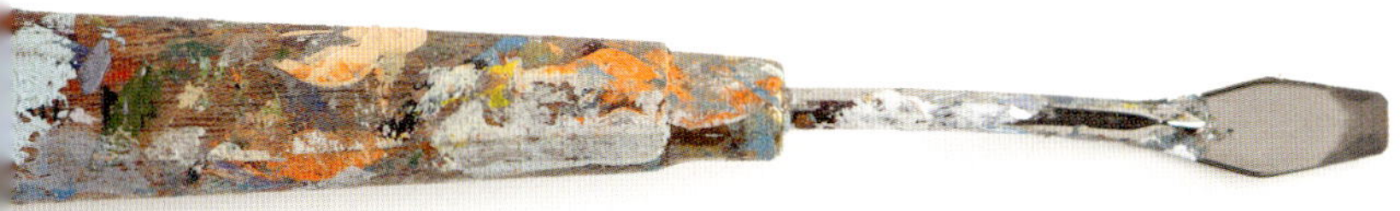

The bull nose is another knife I've created by snipping off the end of an RGM 41 and sanding it smooth. It became a requirement when painting *Stranded Boats, Morston Quay* (page 55). The intricate shapes of the stranded boats called for a knife with a squarer edge. Most commercially available knives today have slightly rounded edges, which do not allow such intricate work to be carried out.

33. Little squares

The straight edge of the knife allows a series of rectangular marks to be made by loading the tip of the knife. The shorter edges on the sides of the knife also allow more detailed work to be carried out when doing a sweep.

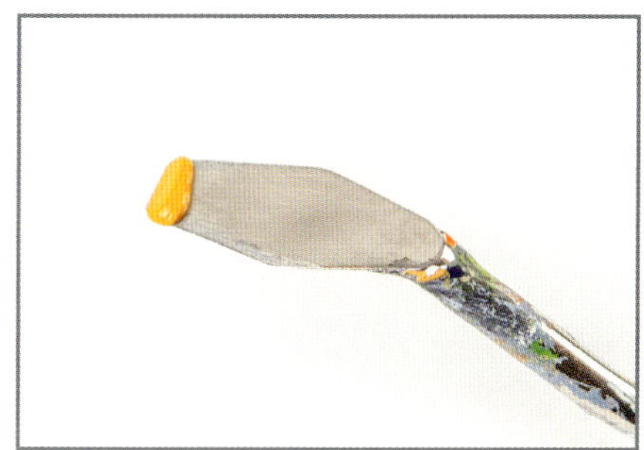

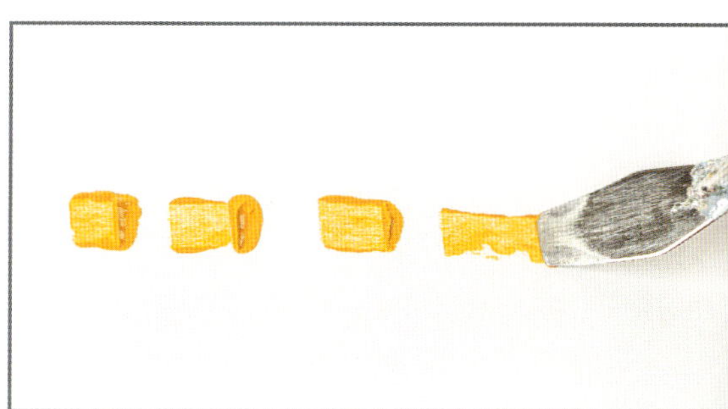

The Laurel Inn, Robin Hood's Bay

29.5 × 35.5cm (11⅝ × 14in)

The Laurel Inn, Robin Hood's Bay was painted entirely using knives. It demonstrates a wide variety of knife techniques; the tree in the background was painted with the large round using paint combined with marble dust. The balloons on the left were added using the small round. Nearly all the windows are painted using the bull nose. The figures were entirely painted using the RGM 41. The remainder of the painting was completed with the RGM 6 including a little *sgraffito* to denote the mortar gaps on the right-hand wall.

CARING FOR YOUR KNIVES

Take good care of your knives and they will give a lifetime of service. Clean regularly while the paint is wet and try to avoid pigment drying on the knife.

WIPE THE PAINT OFF THE KNIFE

While working, wipe the paint off the knife when changing colours.

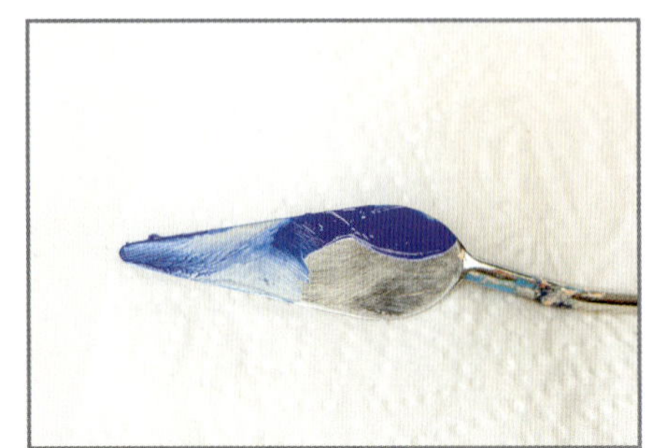
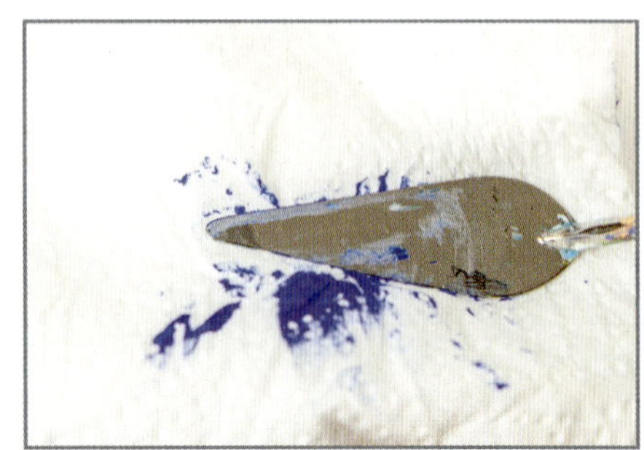

DON'T PRESS DOWN TOO HARD

When working, don't press down too hard, as this can bend the blade. During cleaning, it's worth checking against a straight edge that the blade has not become bent during use. If this happens and is not too serious, the bend can be rectified by gently bending back in the opposite direction.

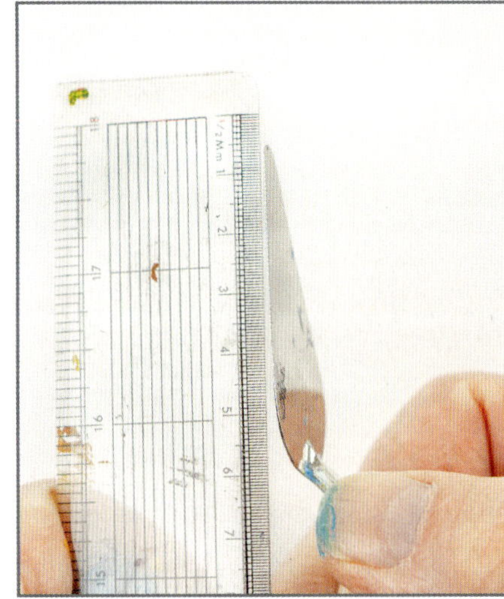

KEEP THE SOLE CLEAN

The base of the knife is called the sole and the point at which the back joins the handle is the heel. The most important area to keep clean is the sole of the knife, as this is where all the work goes on. Whilst the paint is wet, it can be gently wiped away with damp kitchen roll. If allowed to dry, a nail polish remover containing acetone must be used as well. Work in a ventilated area when doing this.

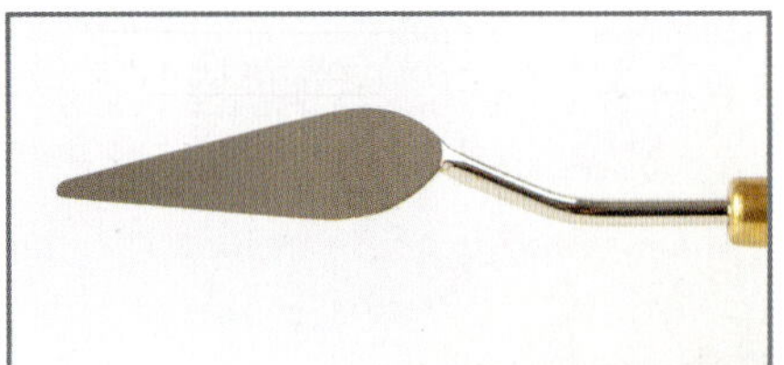
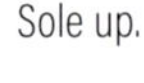

Sole up.

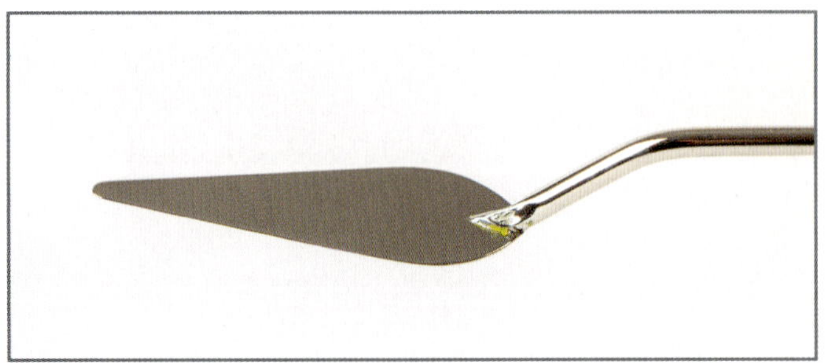

Sole down.

WAYS OF MIXING

There are two main ways of mixing acrylics when using knives. Put more time and effort in and the paint will gradually become more mixed. Work quickly for a short period of time and the paint becomes marbled and will separate out when applied.

HOMOGENOUS MIXING

This is a mixing technique whereby the colour components are thoroughly combined with each other until it is not possible to distinguish the individual colours in the resultant mix.

Tranquil Evening, Nether Meadow
23.2 × 9.5cm (9⅛ × 3¾in)

This little landscape (below) is a good example of where a homogenous mix is required. The uniform blue at the top is made from azure blue and white and spread using the 109. Naples yellow mixed with white is added into the lower half of the sky. Horizontal strokes with a clean knife blend these two areas together. As this is an evening scene, the remaining colour mixes are much more muted. The painting is further developed by adding one colour over another onto the wet paint.

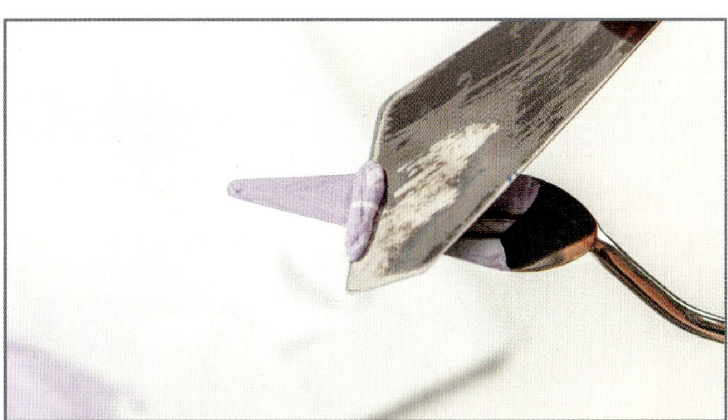

1 I have used the RGM 6 to create a mix of purple and white. Some of the unmixed paint will migrate to the base of the knife. This can be scraped off with another knife and added back to the palette.

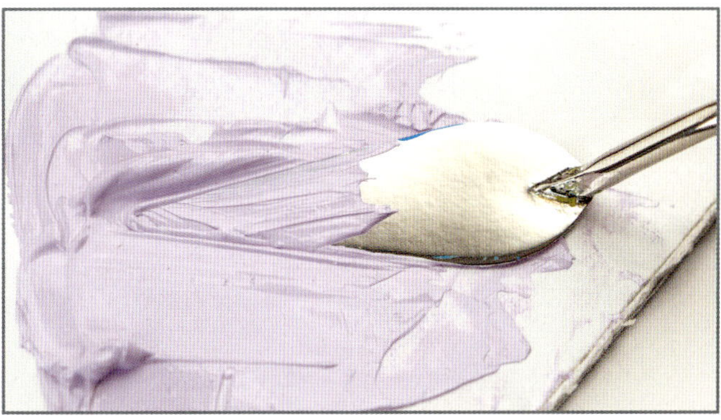

2 Continue manipulating the paint by sliding the knife from left to right until it has a uniform appearance – then it can be applied.

SEMI-MIXING FOR A STRIATED EFFECT

Palette knives really come into their own when you need to partially mix the paint. A palette knife allows you to work quickly without any risk of the acrylic paint drying. Striations usually come from two-colour mixing. Add a third colour and the mix can take on an unpleasant greyish tinge. Use acrylic directly from the pouch without any added water and fold the colours over one another. Keep doing this until the right effect is achieved.

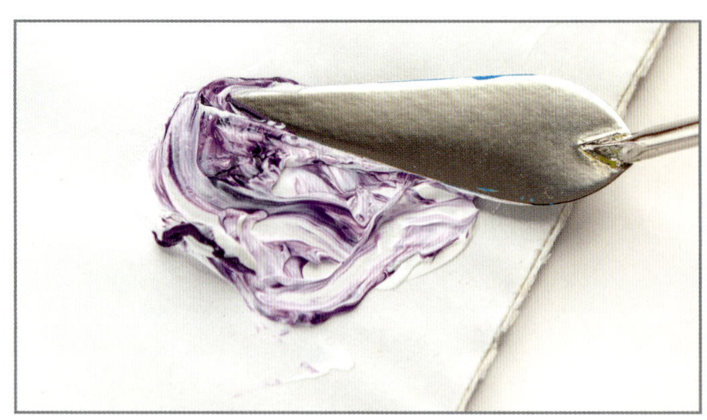

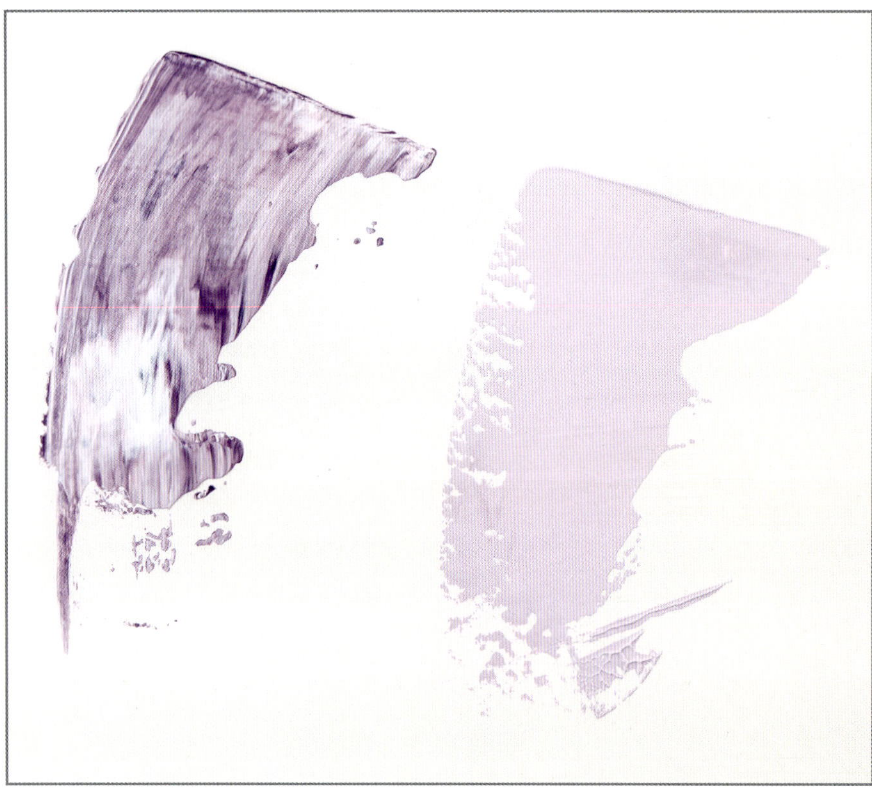

A striated mix (far left) can be seen where the two colours have been combined very quickly and the individual colours can be distinguished when applied by the knife. A uniform, or homogenous, mix (left) is the result of more time spent on the mixing process before applying the paint.

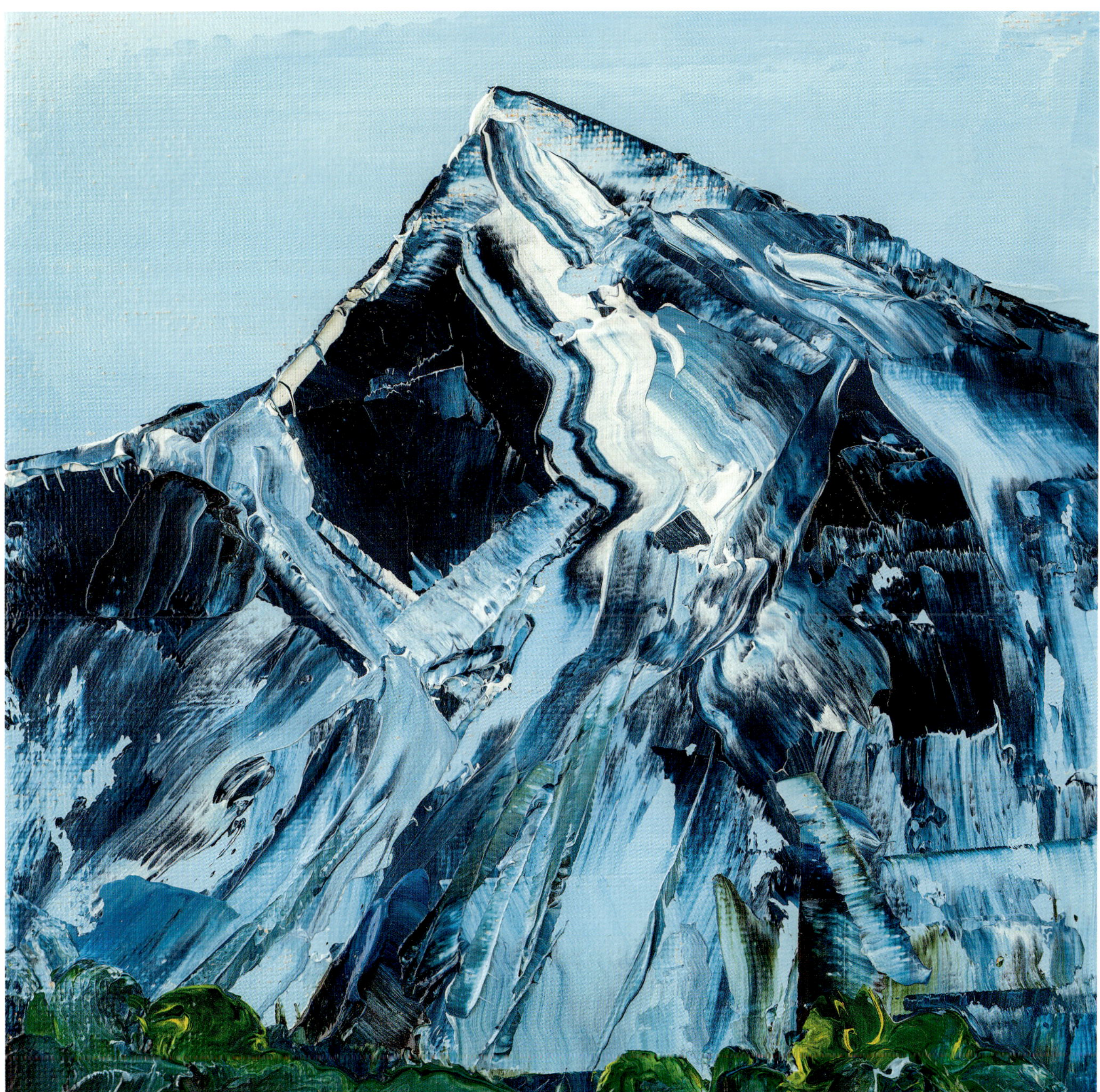

The Highest Peak

17.5 × 17.5cm (6⅞ × 6⅞in)

This painting of a mountain side shows the striated effect where a series of
partially mixed greys are applied to create interesting rock textures and marks.
This is particularly effective when placed against a homogenous sky.

The importance of sketching

I find that it's not always possible to find the perfect subject in the landscape. Some experimentation and manipulation is often necessary to create an image that will eventually become a finished painting.

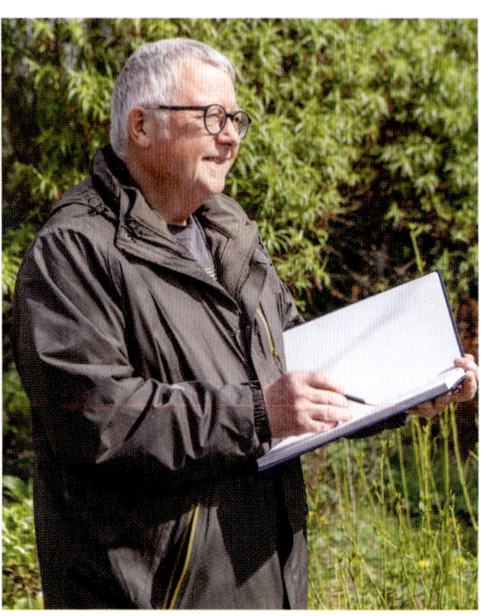

Sketching is an enjoyable process that enables me to work through a number of design ideas. The most important component of drawing is the composition: the large forms, and the position of those shapes in proportion and relation to one another.

I usually start the process by working through a series of thumbnails onto which tone is added. The size of the sketch (usually no bigger than 5 × 7.5cm, or 2 × 3in) allows me to work quickly and see the whole concept quite readily. If the idea doesn't work, I can quickly move on to the next one. This method helps to refine my vision of the subject, until I have something that can be developed into a final painting.

I also like to explore negative shapes within a sketch. This often helps with sorting out the pespective within a subject such as that involved in developing the beach huts scene.

This is a powerful process, as it helps provide new ideas and solutions to your design issues very quickly.

As John Singer Sargent once said,

You can't do sketches enough. Sketch everything and keep your curiosity fresh.

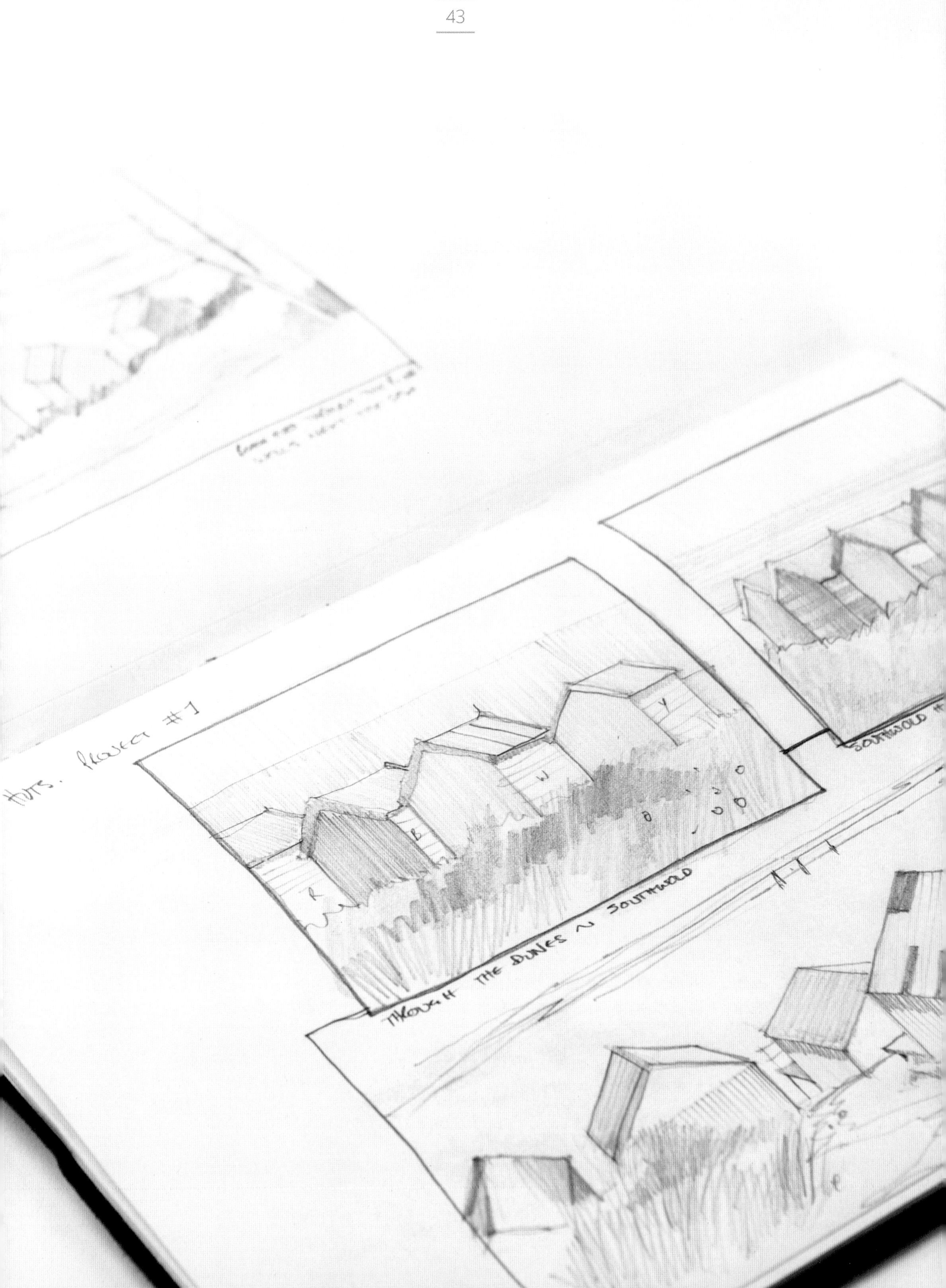
HUTS. PROJECT #1
SOUTHWOLD #
THROUGH THE DUNES ~ SOUTHWOLD

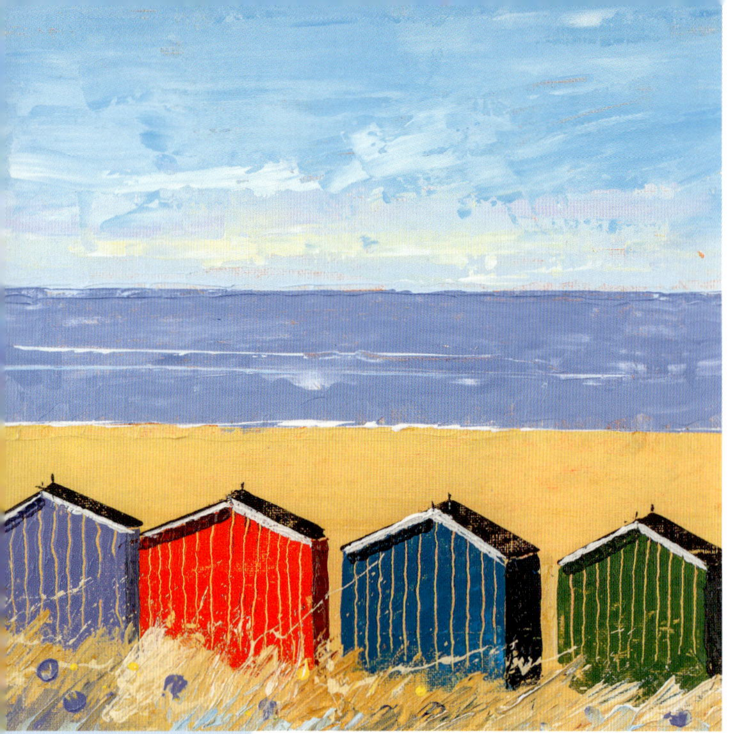

{ Beach Huts | page 46 }

The time has come for action! There is now no better opportunity than to pick up one of these fascinating tools, squeeze out some paint on your palette and learn the essence of palette knife painting.

The PROJECTS

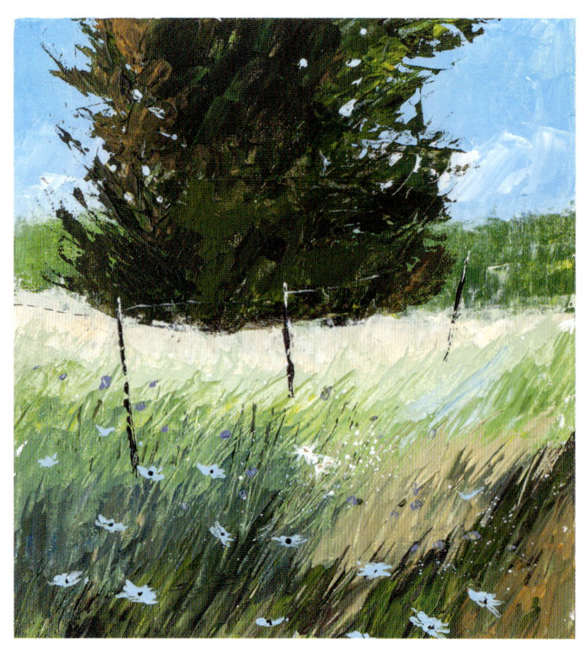

{ Summer Meadow | page 56 }

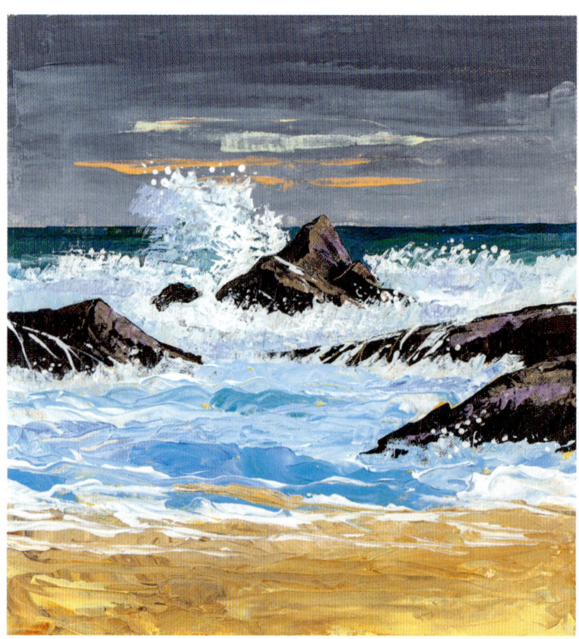

{ Big Rock Splash | page 66 }

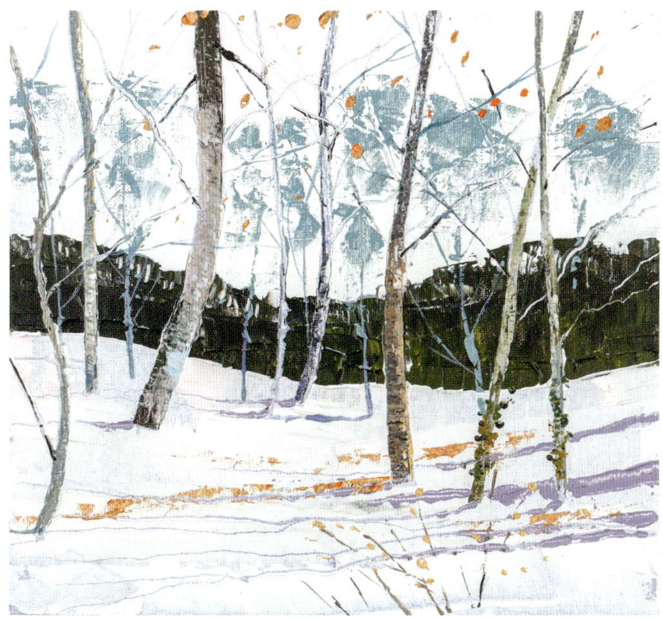

{ Winter Woodland | page 74 }

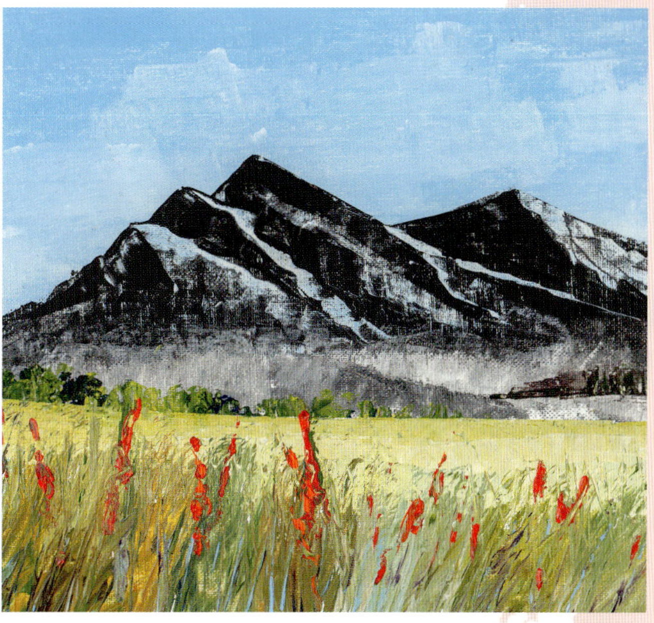

{ Alpine Pinkweeds | page 106 }

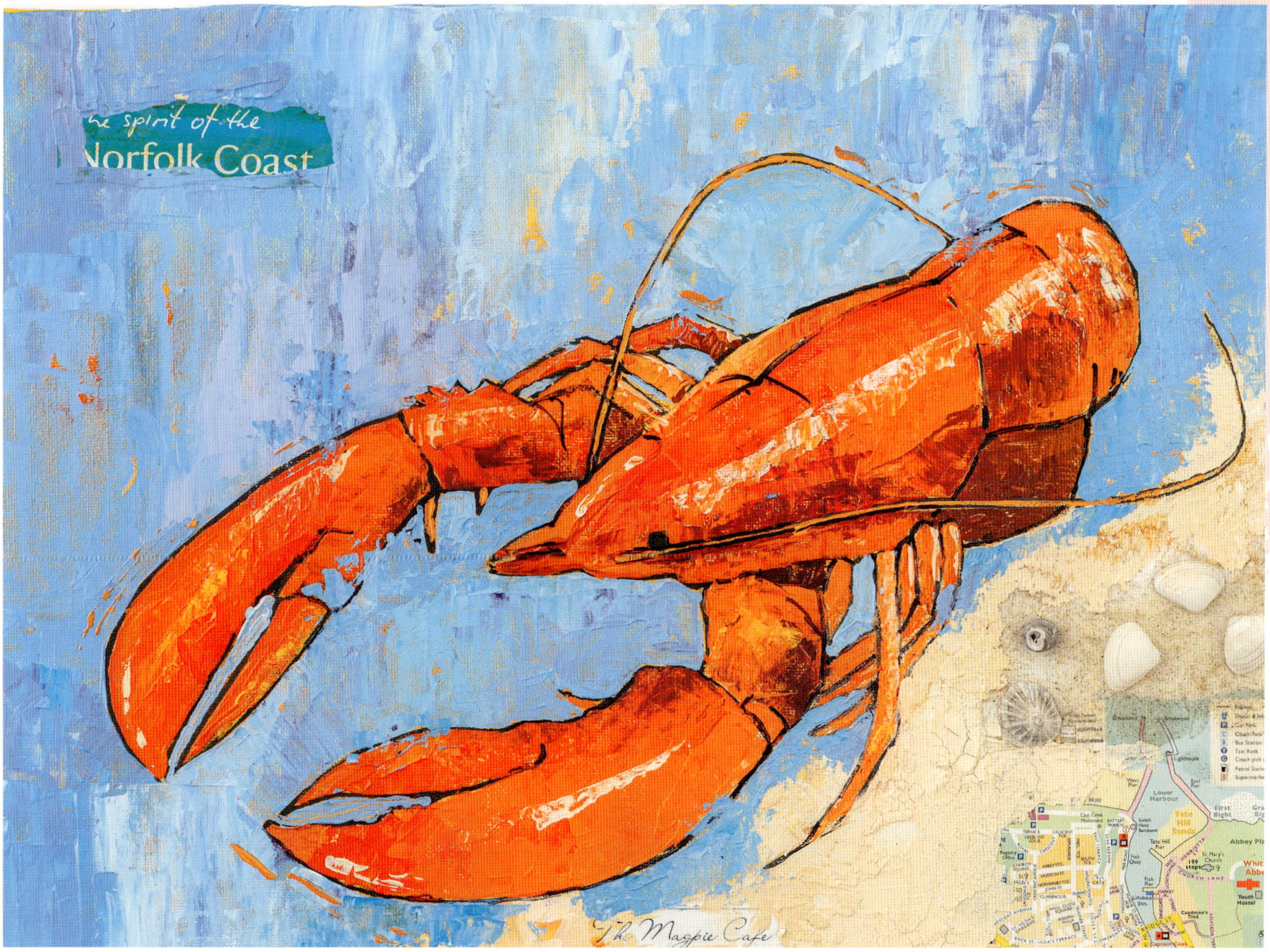

{ Salty Seaside Lobster | page 84 }

BEACH HUTS

This is a simple project to help build your painting skills. It is designed to very quickly get you accustomed to applying single colours and shapes and also creating a simple striated mix. We will be using the basic palette knife shapes and introducing some new ones for additional effects.

To begin you will need to pre-tint the canvas board with a diluted wash of primary yellow and cadmium red light hue using a 2.5cm (1in) flat brush, then allow to dry.

► ## You will need

SURFACE:

Plain white primed canvas board tinted with primary yellow and cadmium red light hue, 30.5 × 30.5cm (12 × 12in).

KNIVES:

RGM 109, 6, Pastrello 38, small round and flat-bladed (for mixing only).

PAINTS:

Titanium white, azure blue, Naples yellow, purple, ultramarine blue, yellow ochre, Mars black, cadmium red light hue, primary yellow, sap green, Chinese blue and light violet.

OTHER TOOLS AND MATERIALS:

2.5cm (1in) flat brush, Neocolor water-soluble oil pastel (black), ruler, kitchen paper and pouring medium.

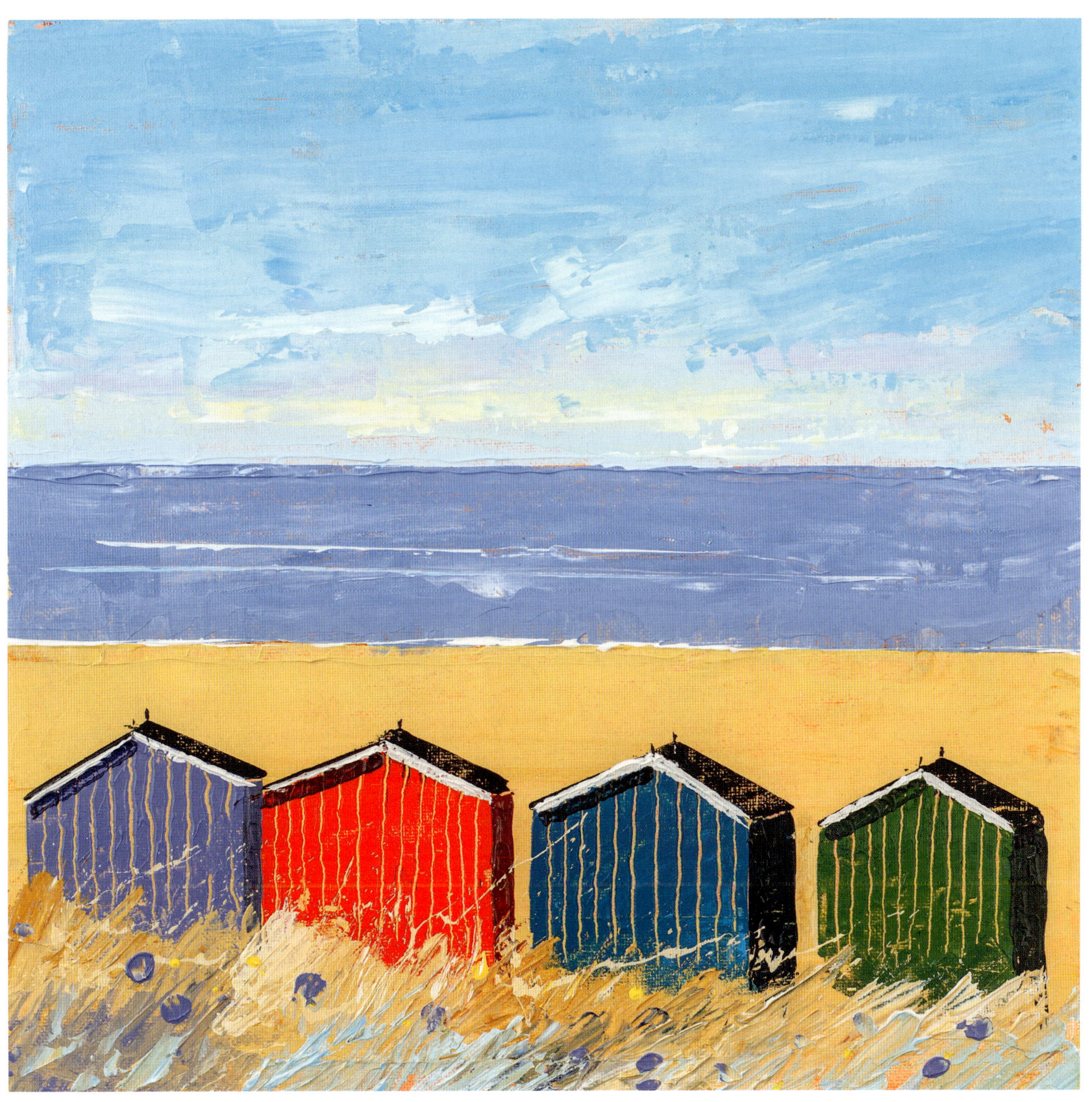

Beach Huts
30.5 × 30.5cm (12 × 12in)

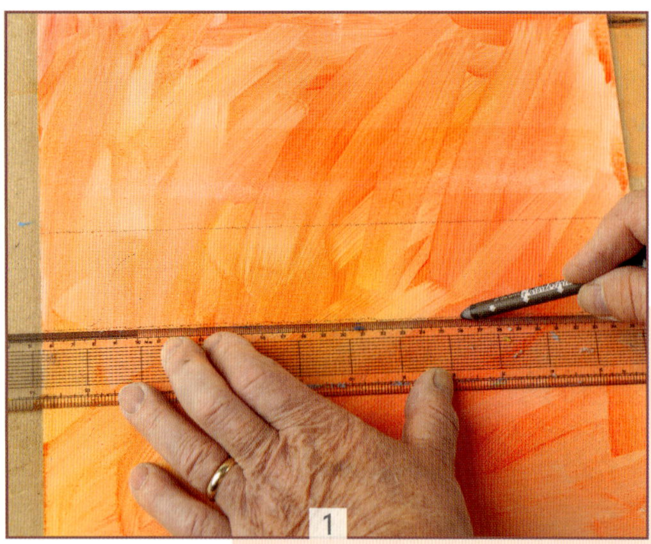

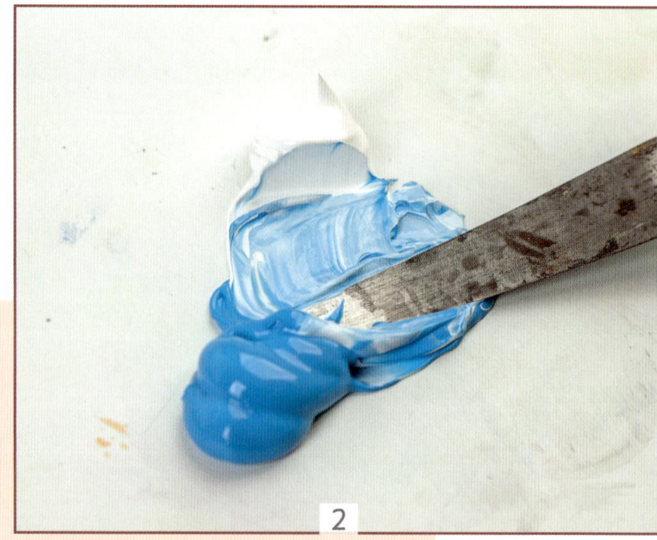

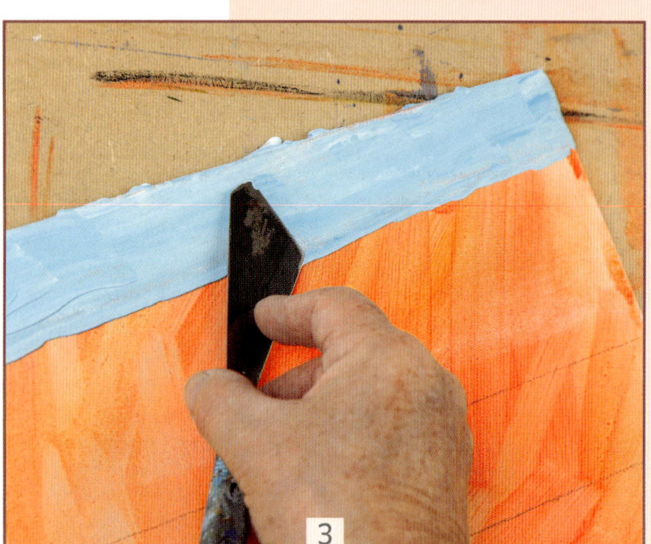

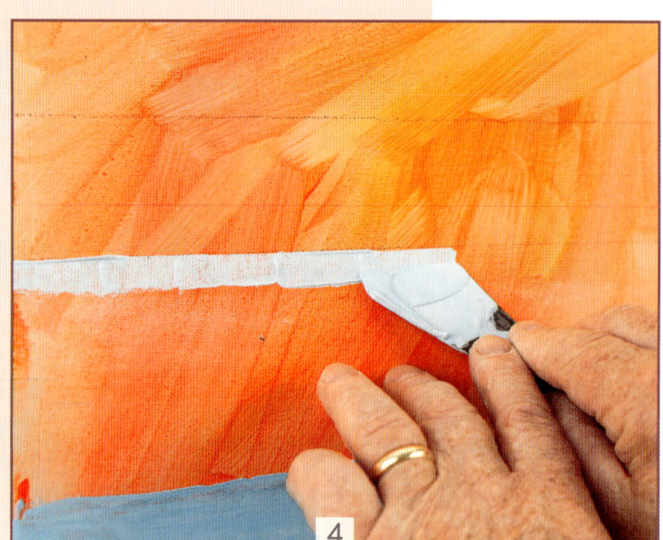

1   Mark the horizon line with a Neocolor II water-soluble wax pastel. This offers a useful edge to guide the palette knife later. Add a second line where the shoreline breaks onto the beach.

2   For the sky, mix a combination of azure blue and titanium white using a flat-bladed palette knife. Keep going until it's possible to just distinguish the white from the blue, creating a gently striated mix.

3   Flatten the mix and pick up a large roll of paint onto the broad edge of the RGM 109. Apply the paint in horizontal strokes applying pressure so that an even coating is achieved. As the paint is pulled over the surface, individual colours should be visible suggesting blue sky and clouds. Be careful not to lift the knife halfway across; keep contact with the surface.

4   Squeeze out more white and a little purple for the sky near the horizon, which is generally paler than the rest. It is not necessary to clean the knife when mixing this new colour. Turn the board upside down and, using a smaller roll of paint, work along the drawn horizon line, touching the line with the blade and then pulling down.

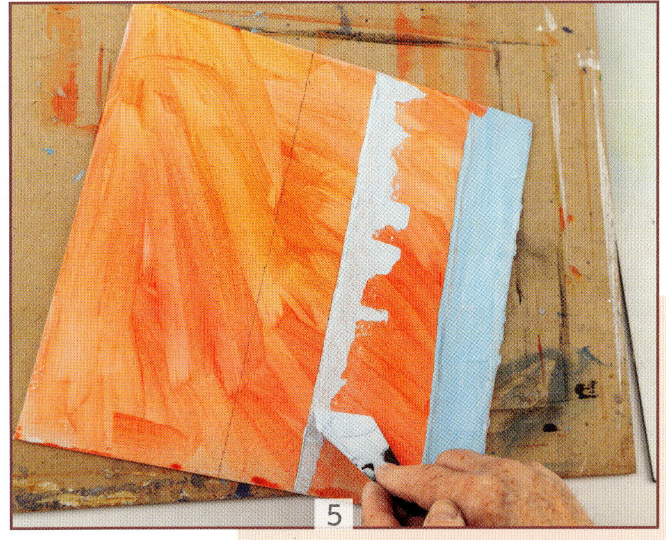

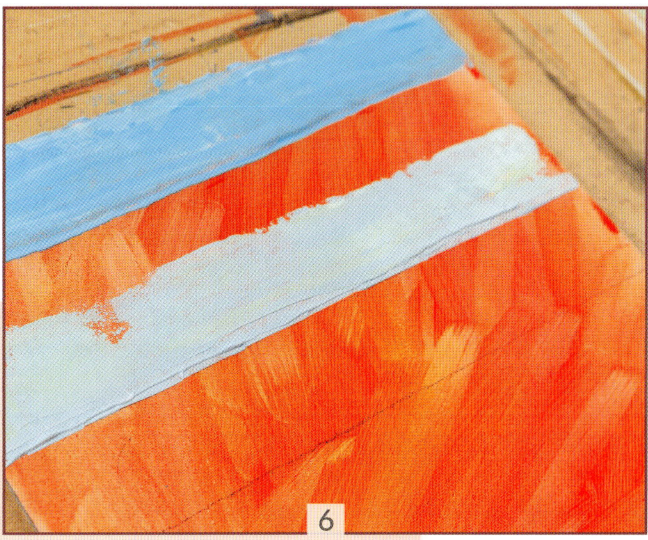

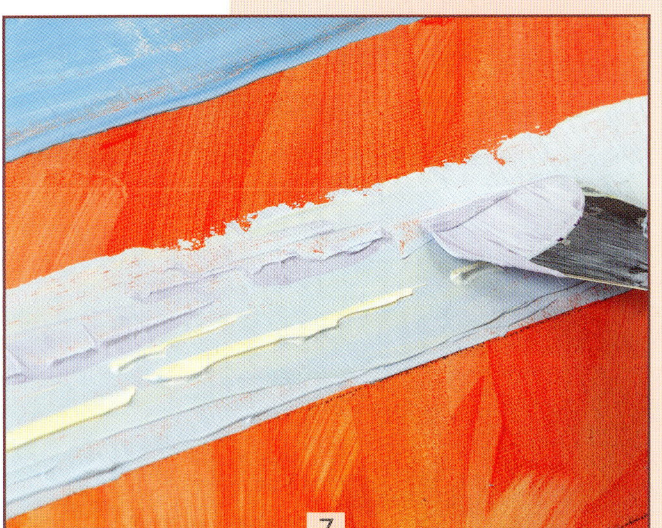

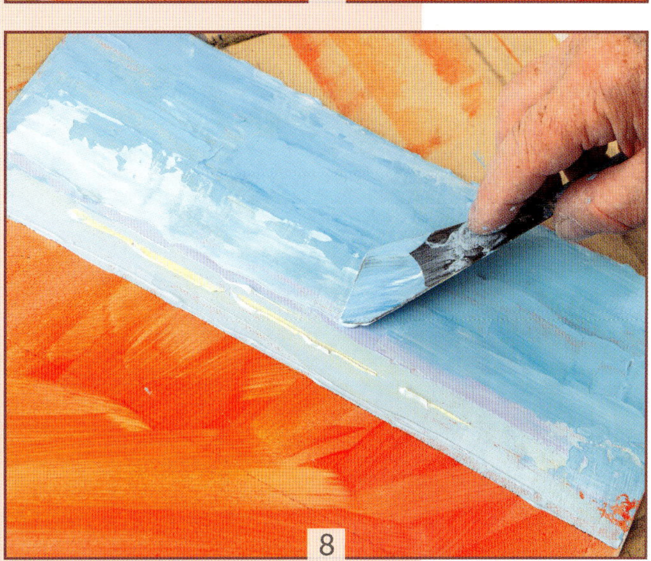

5   Cut across the marks just made with more paint to create the lower band of sky.

6   Stack a pale blue mix and Naples yellow onto a clean knife. Drag horizontally over the lower sky and the yellow should separate out.

7   Add a fine roll of Naples yellow to the knife. Touch horizontal lines of yellow onto the lower sky, then add similar marks using a mix of purple and white. Fill in the mid-sky area with the sky mix from steps 2 and 3.

8   For the final stage of blending the sky, add white from the broad edge of the knife, gently pulling over the wet paint already applied.

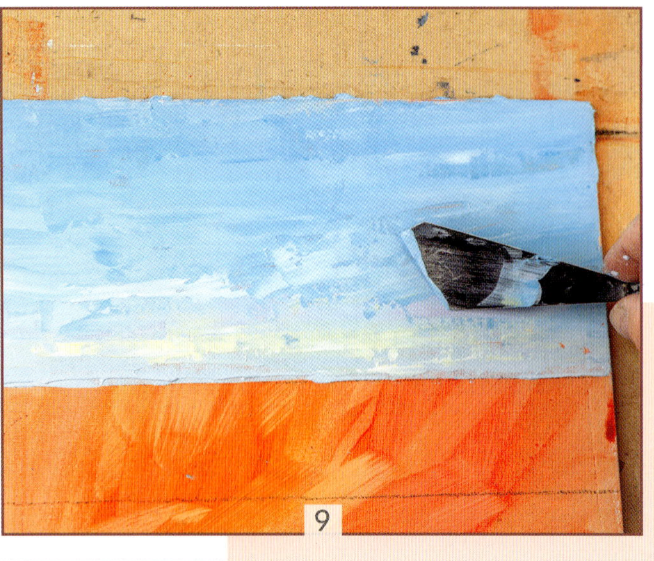

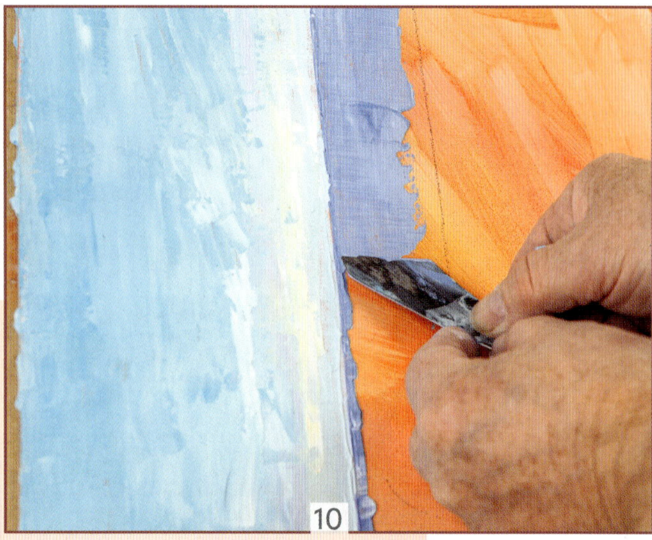

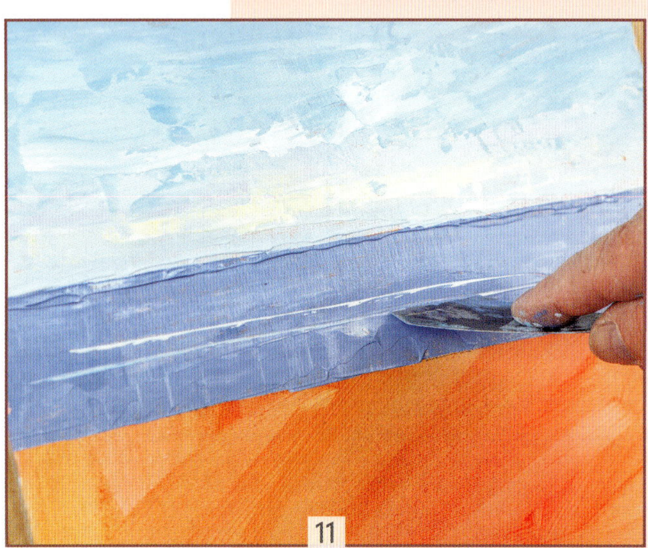

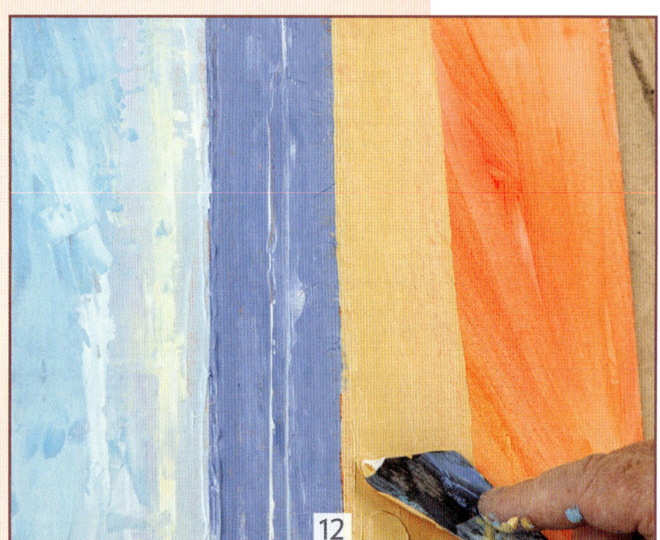

9   Manipulate the added white paint until a satisfactory sky is created. Work quickly as the acrylics have a fast drying time.

10   The band of sea is painted with the same knife but with a mix of ultramarine blue and a touch of purple. Add a little of the previously mixed sky colour and loosely mix in. Pull the paint down from the marked horizon, then pull horizontally across these marks. The mix should separate out to suggest distant waves.

11   Add a fine roll of white to the knife and drag this horizontally through the wet paint to suggest breaking waves.

12   The edge of the beach is created by mixing a sandy colour, using yellow ochre, Naples yellow and titanium white. The paint is applied the same way as previously to achieve a straight edge on the shoreline. The paint application at this stage needs to be quite smooth to allow the beach huts to be painted on top. This can be done by applying pressure to the knife strokes. Paint all the way to the bottom of the board.

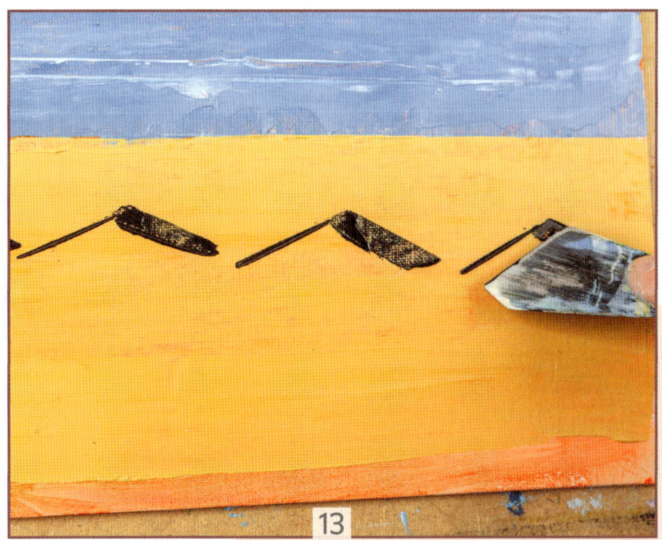

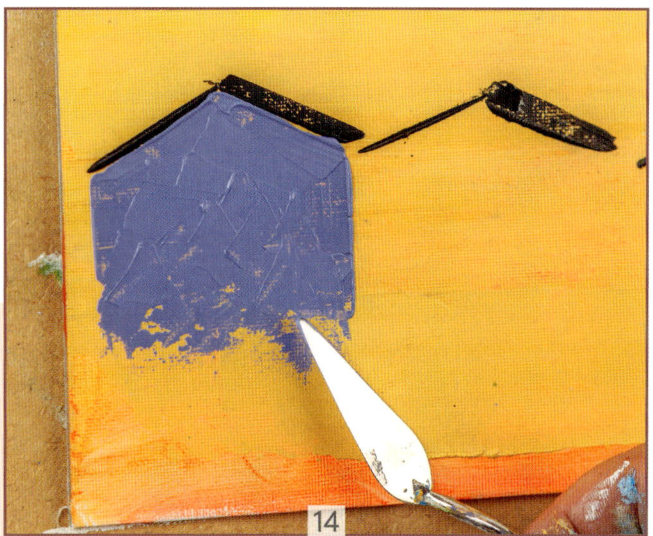

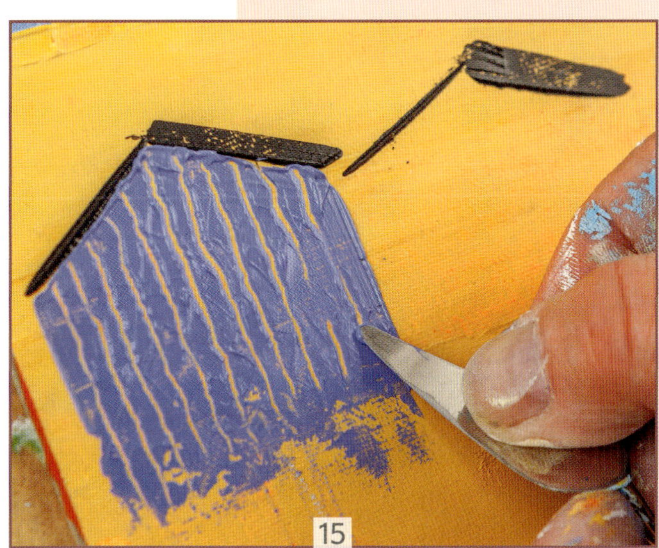

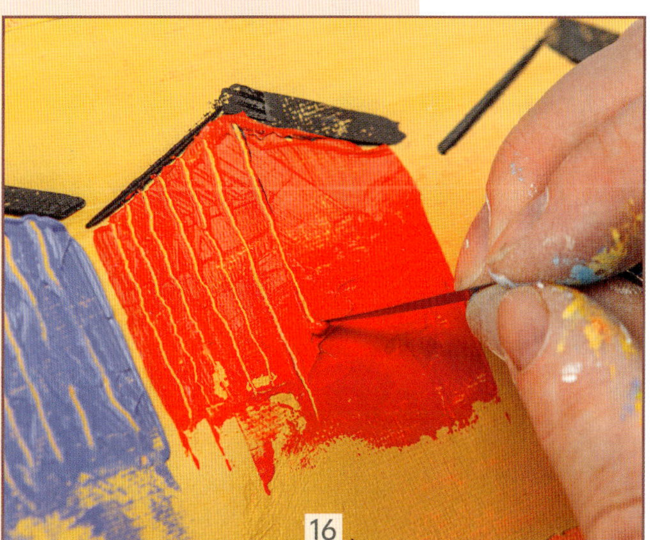

13 Once the paint has dried, the beach hut roofs can be added. Using Mars black and a thin roll of paint on the same palette knife, add the broad strip on the right of each roof. Then go back and touch in the narrower, left strip until the row of roofs is complete.

14 Paint the first hut using unmixed light violet, with the RGM 6 knife. Deciding beforehand on which side to load the blade makes working easier. Also, partially loading the blade along the edge helps with any awkward spots. Scumble the paint at the base of the huts so that the edge can be easily concealed later behind the sand dune.

15 While the paint is still wet, use a method called *sgraffito* to scratch vertical marks that represent the hut boards, still using the RGM 6 knife. The coloured background should be revealed as you do this.

16 Next, move on to the next beach hut and, using cadmium red light hue, repeat the procedure.

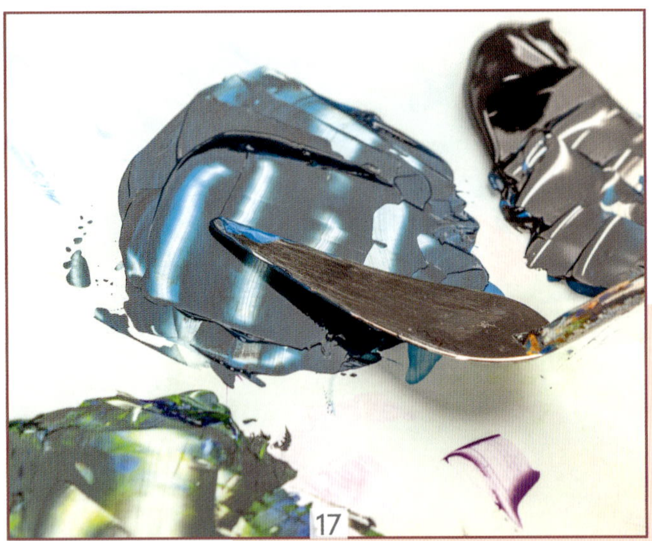

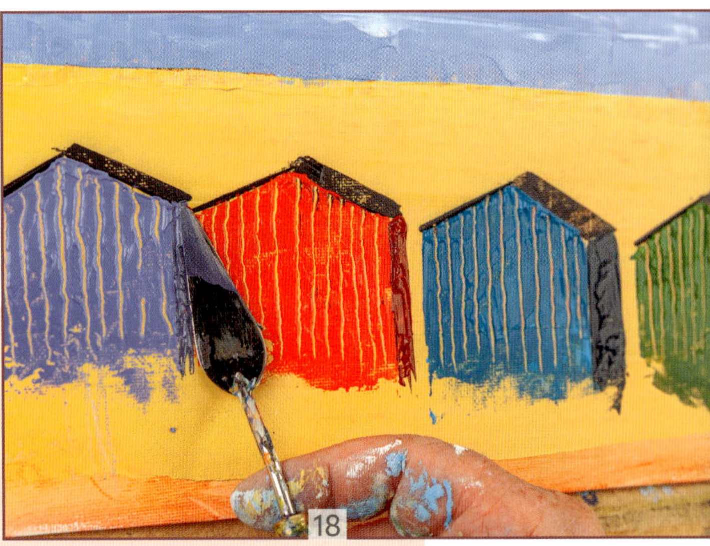

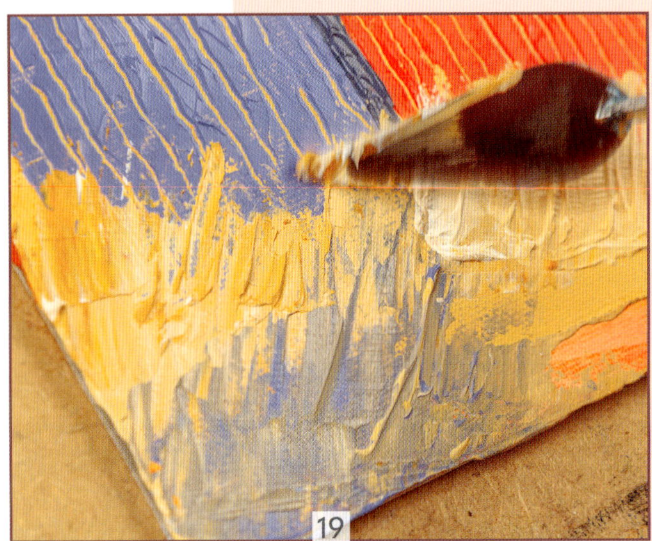

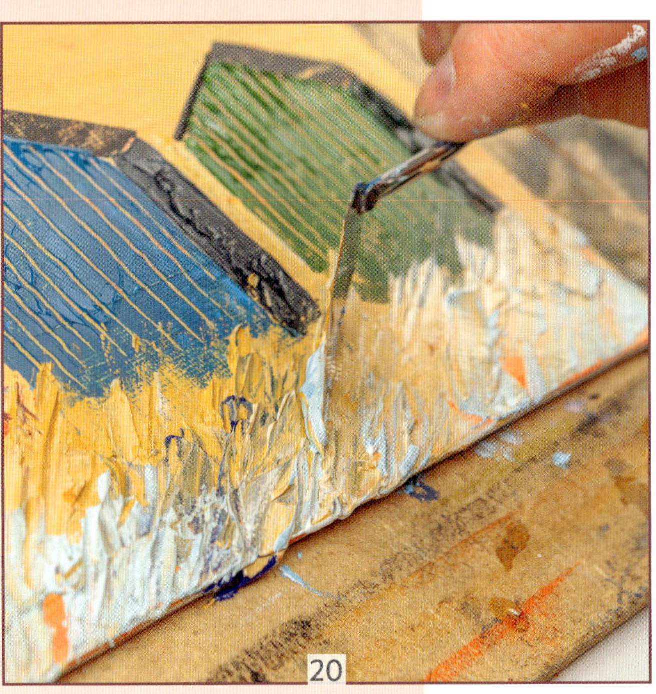

17   Use Chinese blue for the third hut, still using the RGM 6 knife; complete using sap green. Mix in a little black and apply this to the shadow side of the last hut.

18   Work back along the shadow sides of each hut, mixing in a little black to the base colour used to paint each hut.

19   The foreground sandbank uses quite thick layers of yellow ochre to ensure any previous marks are covered up. If there are any colours left over in the palette, these can be stacked onto the wet paint when creating the sandbank. Use side strokes with the knife to form the shapes of grasses. Add some light violet into the base of the sandbank to suggest shadow areas. Scratch through the wet paint with the blade edge to create finer grasses.

20   Using the same knife, add a little ultramarine blue to echo similar colours throughout the painting, thus creating harmony.

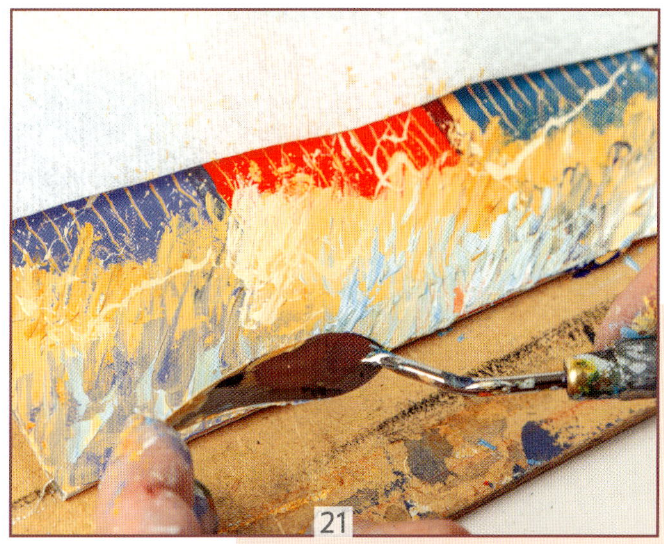

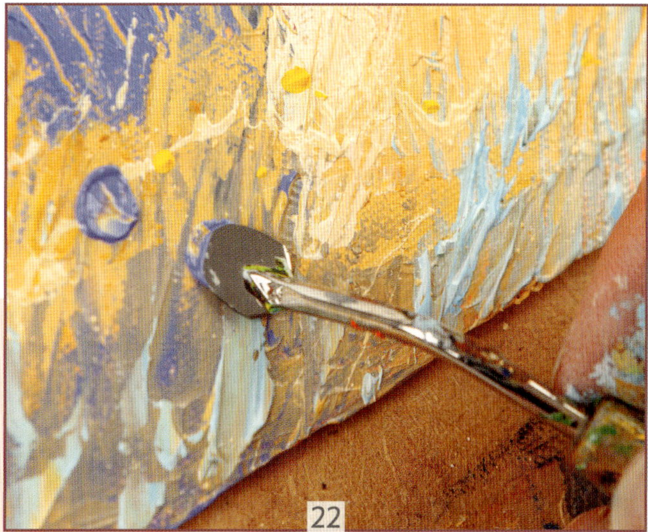

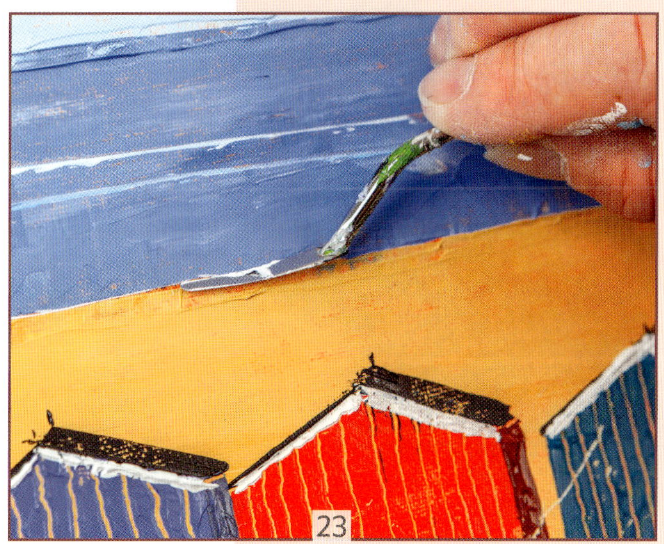

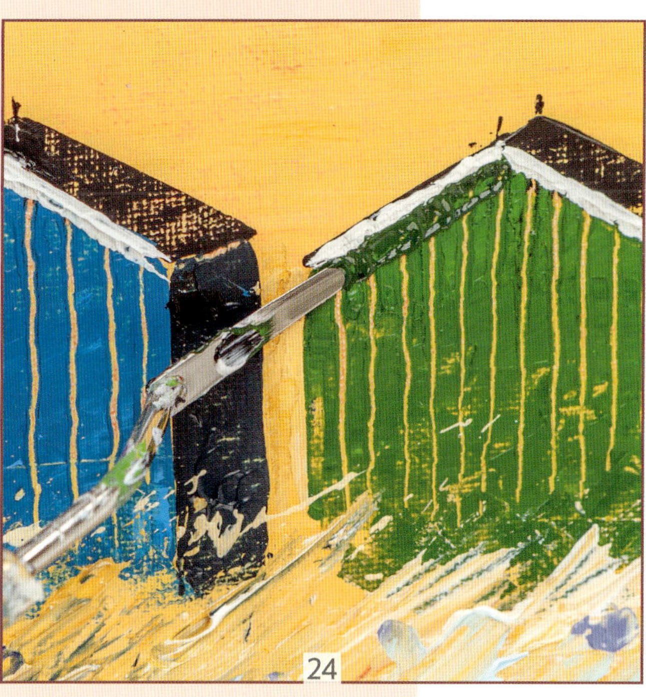

21 Mask carefully just above the dune with kitchen roll and then flick paint off the tip of the RGM 6 knife. Add a little pouring medium to make the paint more fluid if need be.

22 Add a few dots of blue using the tip of the knife to create some buttons (see page 25). For larger marks, switch to the small round (modified) knife, shown on page 33.

23 Using the RGM Pastrello 38 with titanium white added to the side of the blade, create breaking waves along the shoreline.

24 The same knife is used to add white soffits to all the huts. Finally, shadows are placed under the eaves using each individual hut colour with a bit of added black.

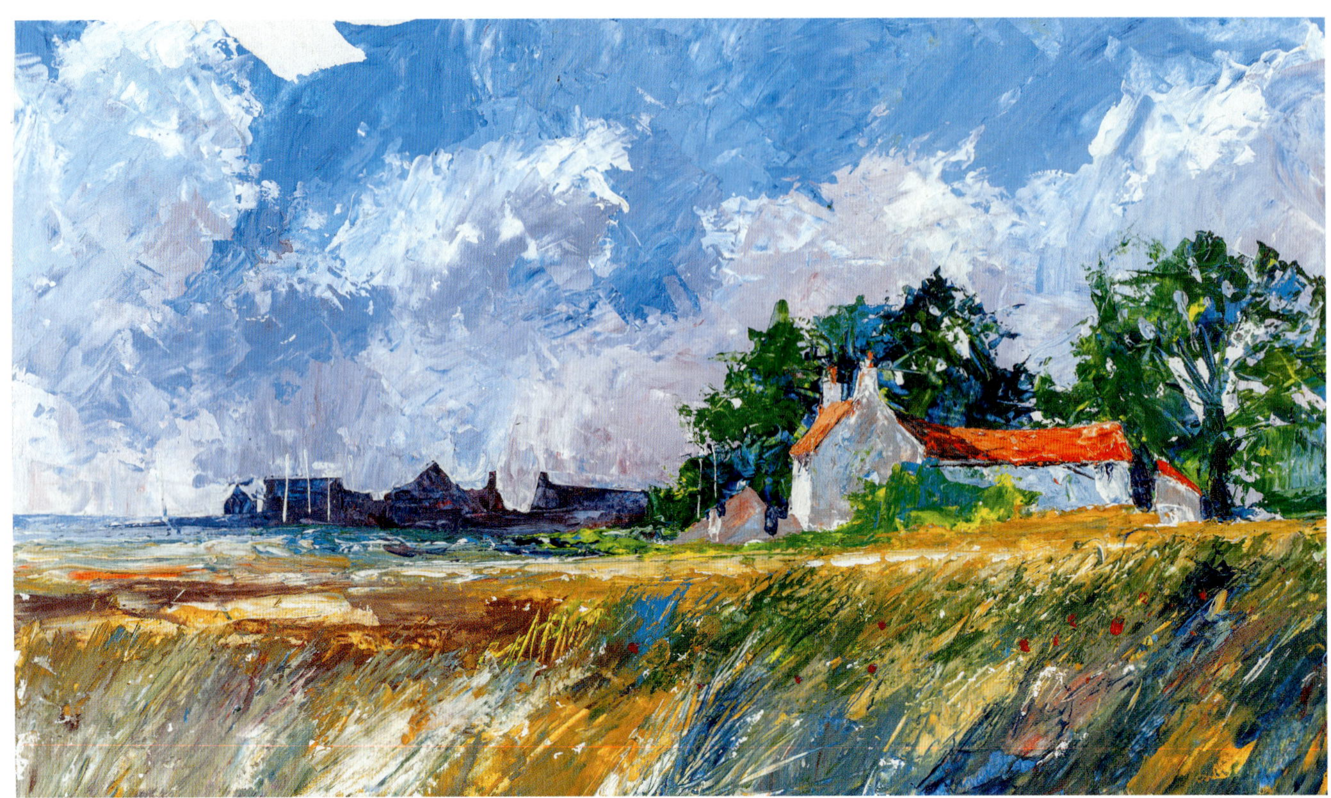

Brancaster Staithe, Norfolk, UK

43.2 × 23cm (17 × 9in)

This subject embraces the principles demonstrated in the previous exercise, in a much more loosely treated manner. The cottage in the distance is quite small and a looser approach allows it to be painted more simply.

I have also had great fun with the foreground using heavy acrylic textures, paint flicking and *sgraffito* with the palette knife.

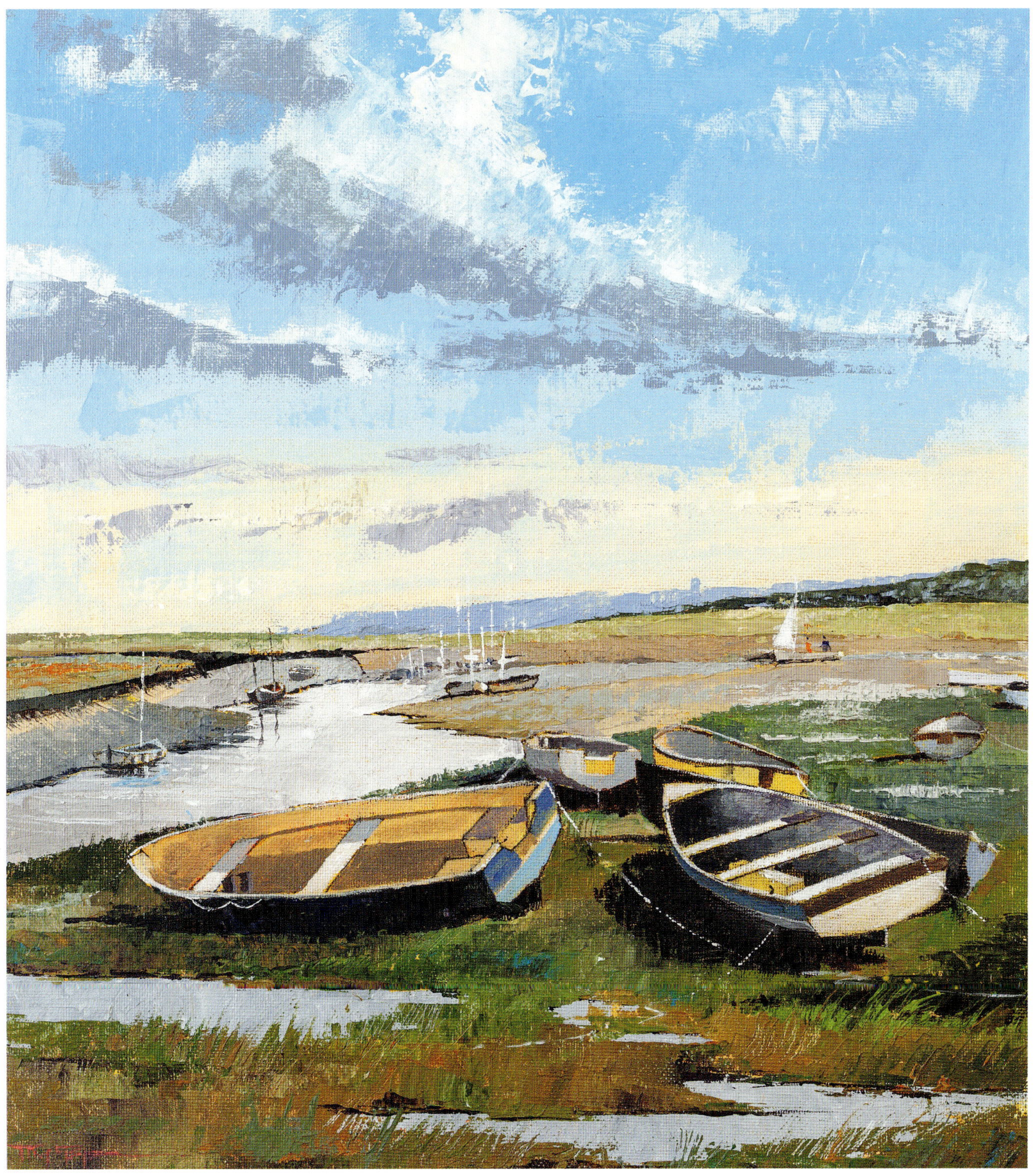

Stranded Boats, Morston Quay, Norfolk, UK

35.5 × 40.5cm (14 × 16in)

With practice, it's possible to create really sophisticated shapes with the knife. The boats in this larger painting were created entirely using the much finer RGM Pastrello 38. This was ideal for detail and for adding the fine mooring lines to the boats. The foreground grasses are added using the same technique as the sandbank on page 52.

SUMMER MEADOW

This project is designed to take you further along the path of palette knife painting. The project involves applying a number of specific marks such as fine lines, spatter and flower shapes to represent a summer meadow in full foliage. Some of the broader marks express a freedom and freshness of working that are well away from the restraints that a heavily outlined drawing would give. I recommend that you work on a plain white canvas in this instance, which will encourage you to go all-out for coverage and achieve a heavier impasto effect.

▶ ## You will need

SURFACE:

Plain white primed canvas board, 30.5 × 35.5cm (12 × 14in).

KNIVES:

Small round, RGM 109, 6, 38, 41 and King.

PAINTS:

Burnt umber, titanium white, azure blue, cadmium red light hue, purple, ultramarine blue, yellow ochre, Mars black, sap green, primary yellow and light violet.

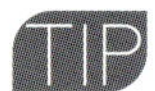

When starting to paint, we naturally pick up a brush to make marks. It is not until we switch to working with a knife that the wonderful textural marks and effects that can be made in a landscape painting can be truly appreciated. Each method of painting has its own benefits, though there is a particular beauty in a landscape produced using knives.

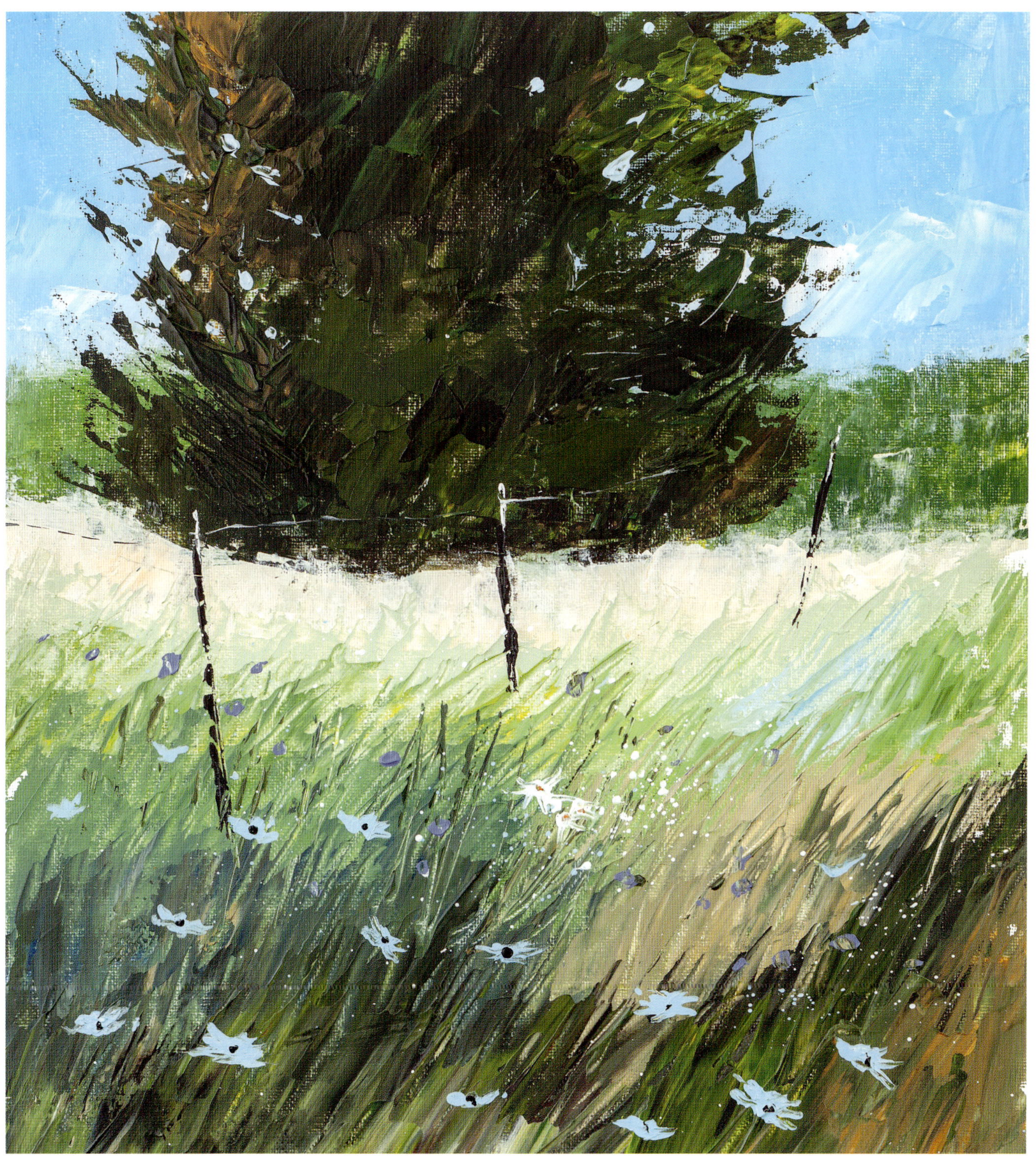

Summer Meadow
30.5 × 35.5cm (12 × 14in)

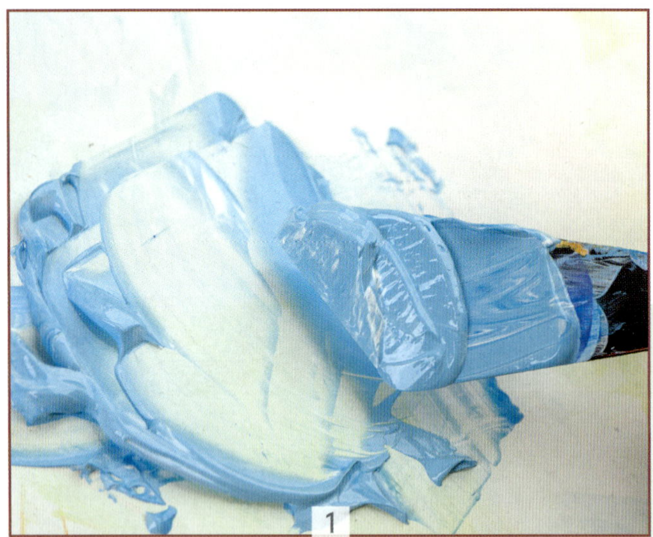

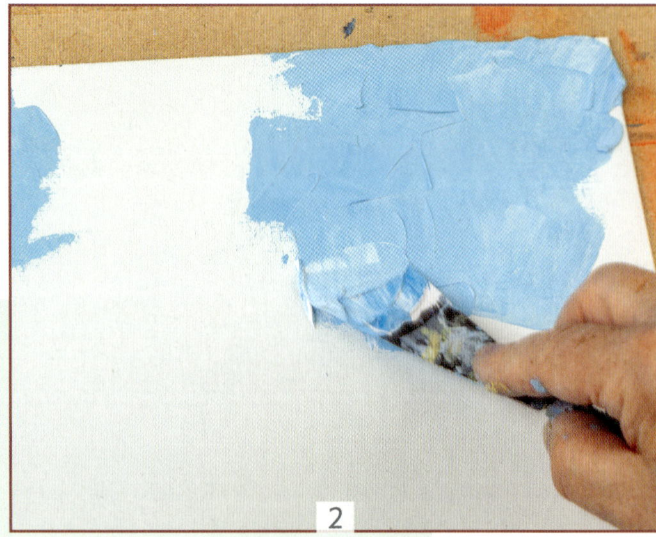

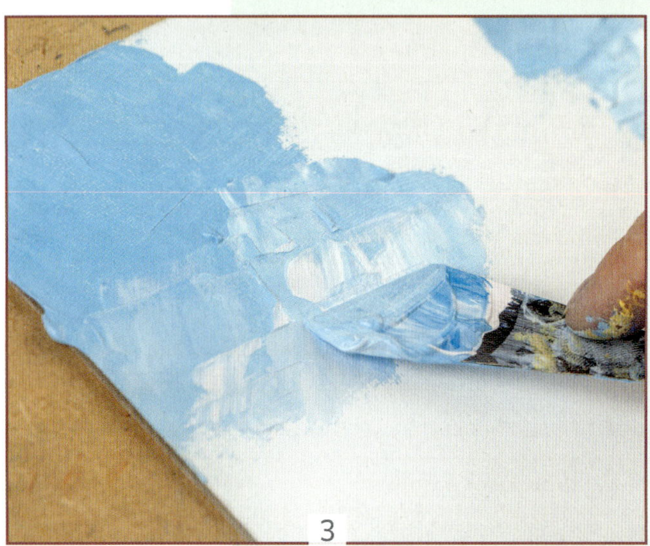

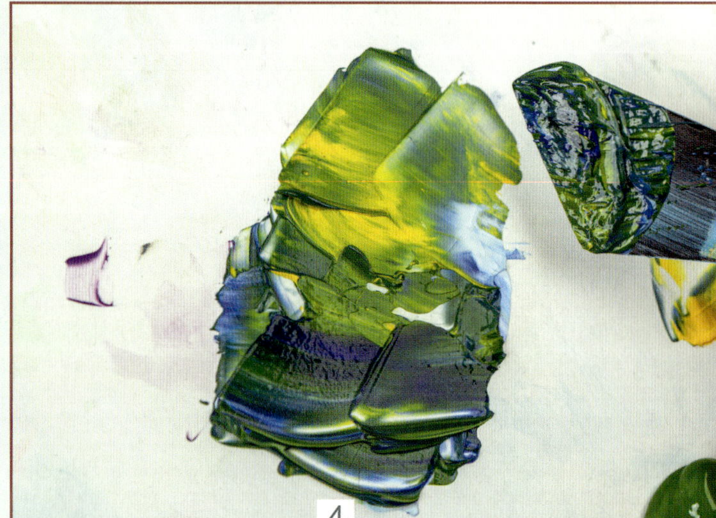

1 Lightly mix azure blue, titanium white and a tiny amount of cadmium red light together until the different colours can just be distinguished as a slightly striated mix.

2 Paint the sky into the spaces surrounding the tree using the RGM 109, leaving a blank silhouette or negative shape to roughly describe the form of the tree. Allow some of the unmixed white paint on the knife to go onto the surface to suggest clouds.

3 To create the lighter lower part of the sky, add some premixed pink made from white and red into the sky colour already in use. Drag this very subtle colour down your canvas.

4 Prepare the mix for the background hedge. To reflect how it will appear on the painting, start from one side of the palette, add ultramarine blue, then sap green followed by primary yellow, all placed in a line. These colours should only be loosely mixed so that the individual colours can be easily distinguished. The mix should appear dark green on one side and pale green on the other.

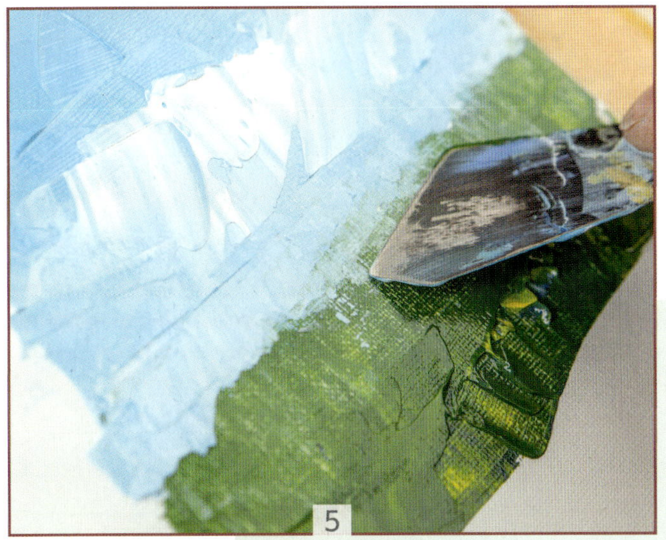

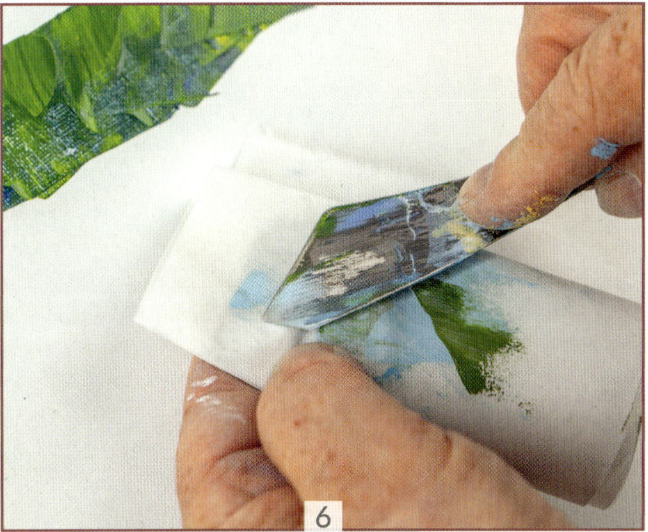

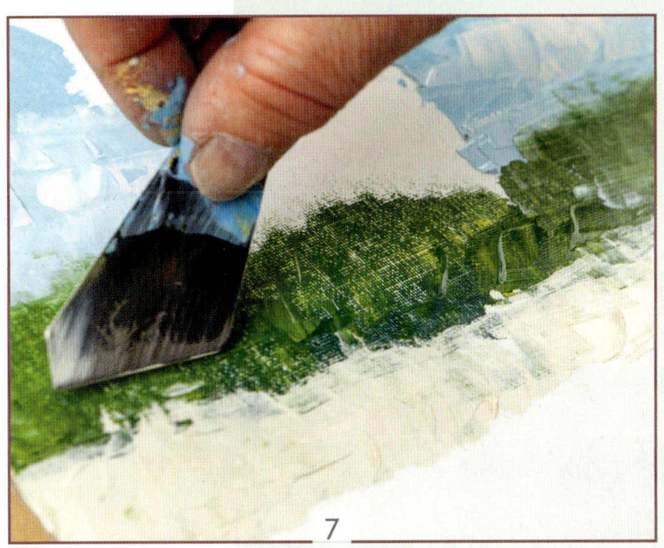

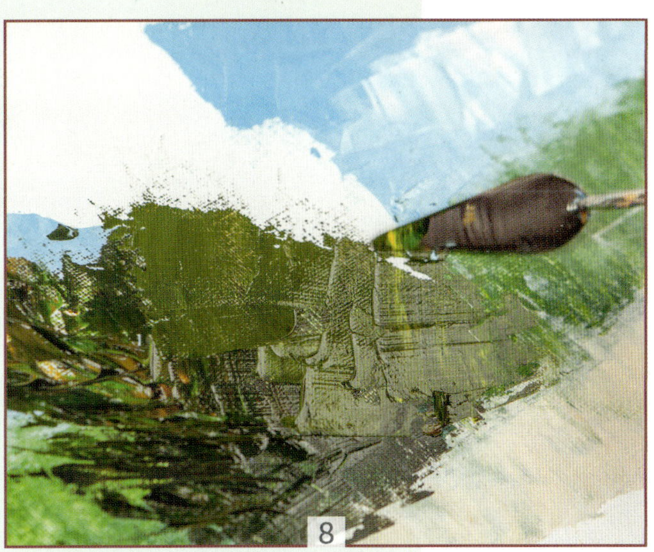

5 Apply a roll of paint with the RGM 109. Allow the knife to run out of paint to create a soft edge scumble where the edge of the foliage meets the sky. The different colours should separate out as the paint is applied. Add thicker paint over these marks and loosely blend together. Continue to scumble the blade upwards.

6 Wipe the blade edge on tissue to keep the colours clean and prevent the green from being dragged into the sky.

7 Add a band of yellow ochre mixed with white below the background hedge. Scumble the paint into the base of the hedge to create a soft edge.

8 Start constructing the tree by mixing sap green, Mars black and yellow ochre together as a striated mix and then adding it to the base of the tree near the centre of the painting using the RGM 6 knife. Working upwards, primary yellow is then applied to the outer leaves, which will turn green when it touches the other colours just added.

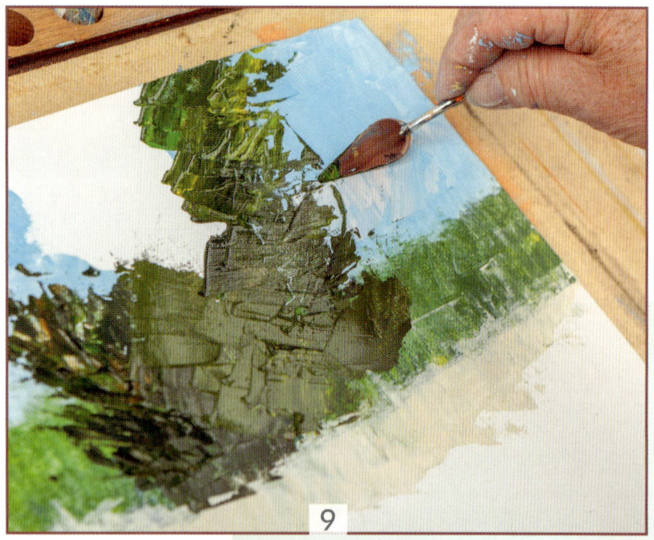

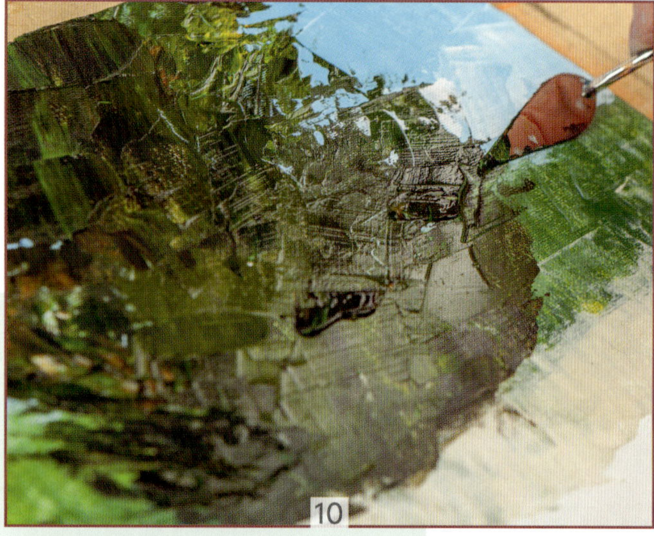

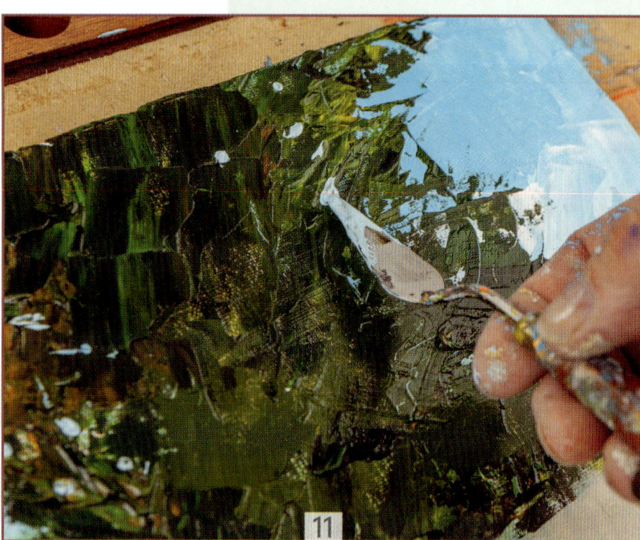

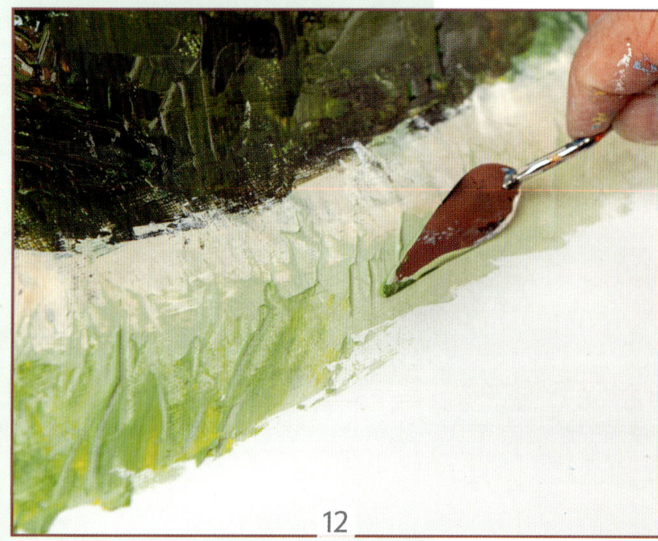

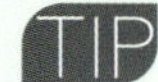

TIP

Mix a slightly lighter colour for the sky holes, which will then stand out more when applied.

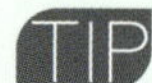

TIP

It may be necessary to add some gloss glazing medium after this point to keep the paint mobile, wet and workable for longer.

9 Vary the proportions of sap green, yellow ochre and black as the tree is painted from the ground upwards. Rotate the wrist so the position of the knife edge changes. These actions help to create the impression of dense, random foliage.

10 When approaching the edges of the tree, load the knife edge less so that it runs out of paint and scumbles over the now slightly uneven painted surface, creating a ragged edge.

11 Clean the knife and mix white with azure blue. Work along the outside of the tree to create a feathered edge, then add buttons where the sky holes in the foliage should be.

12 Add a pale mix of yellow ochre and titanium white where the meadow meets the base of the tree. Over this apply sap green mixed with white. Using the edge of the knife and keeping the handle parallel to the horizon, stroke upwards towards the tree until the colours overlap slightly. Put additional strokes into the wet paint with a slight curving motion of the tip.

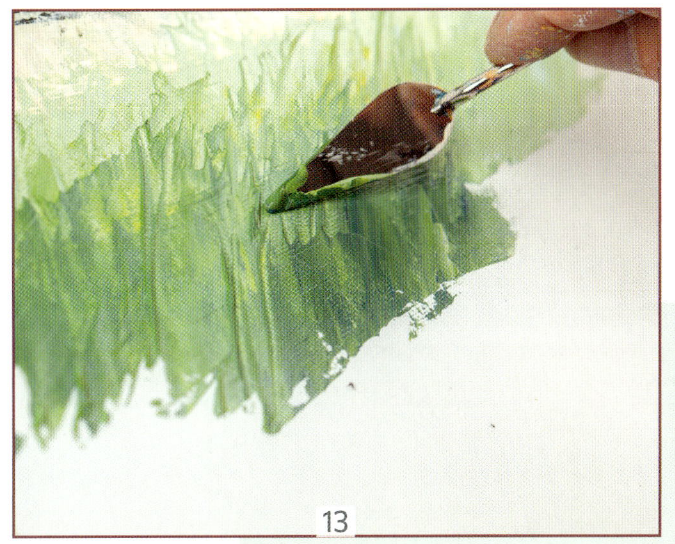

13

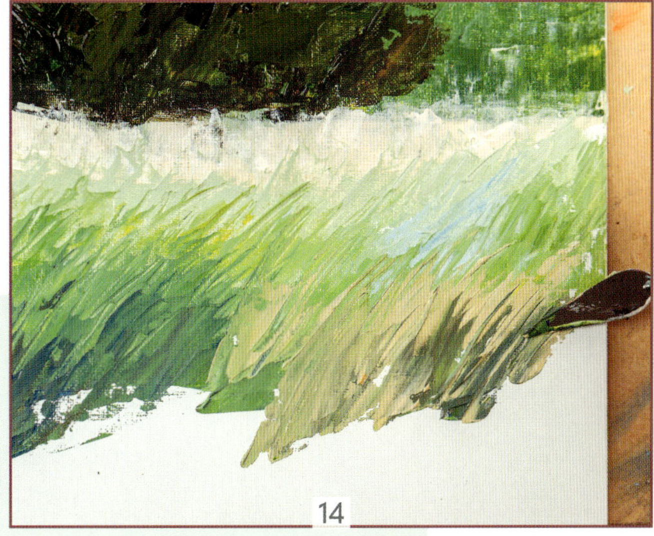

14

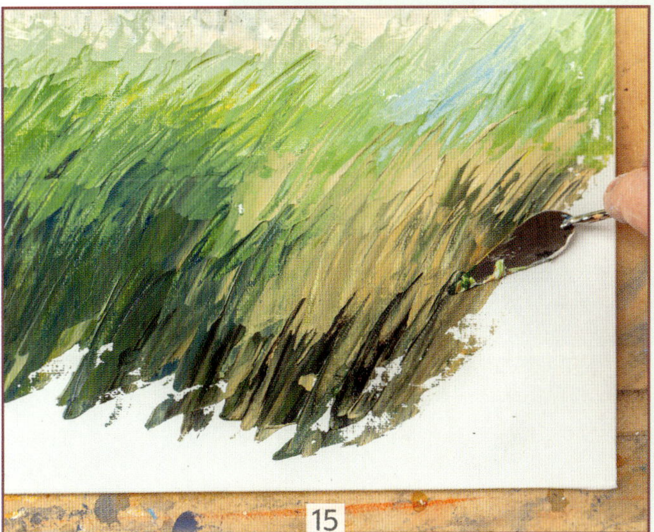

15

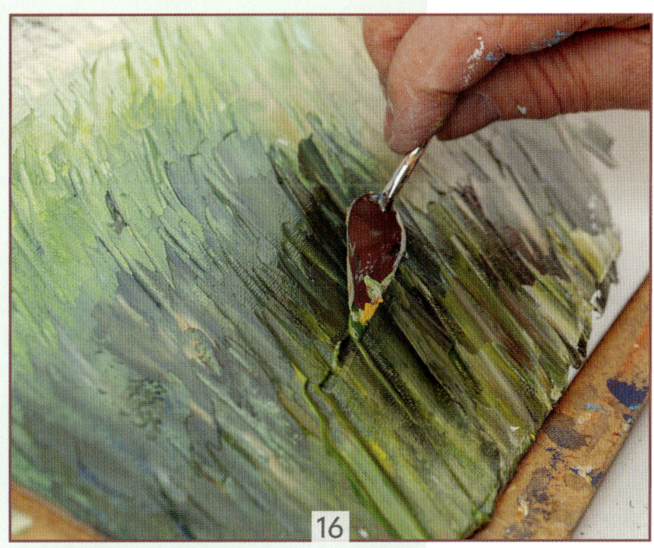

16

> The thing I love about the palette knife is that there are no hard and fast rules for using one.

13 Working towards the base of the painting, make the greens gradually darker by mixing a little burnt umber with sap green. Continue using the same stroke as in step 12. Try to place the darks against the lighter colours already applied.

14 Add a few touches of left-over sky colour into the marks as the foreground progresses, followed by a few strokes of yellow ochre on the right side.

15 Darken the greens even further towards the base using Mars black with just a hint of primary yellow. Using the tip of the knife, scrape into the wet paint to suggest grass stalks.

16 Mix primary yellow, Mars black and a touch of cadmium red light hue to complete the grasses at the base of the painting.

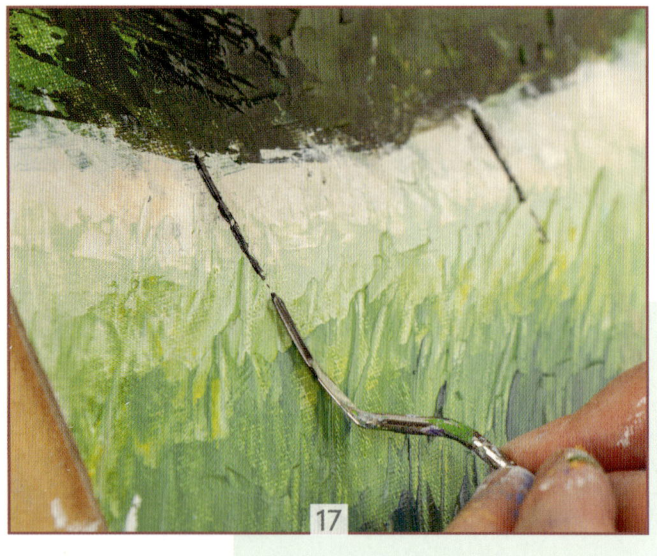

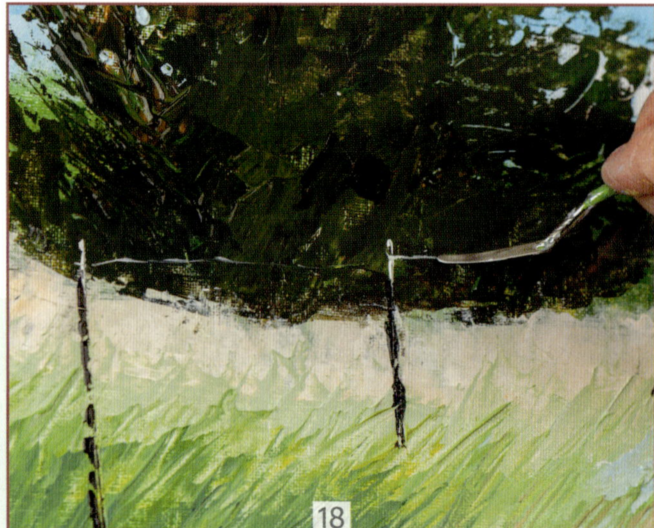

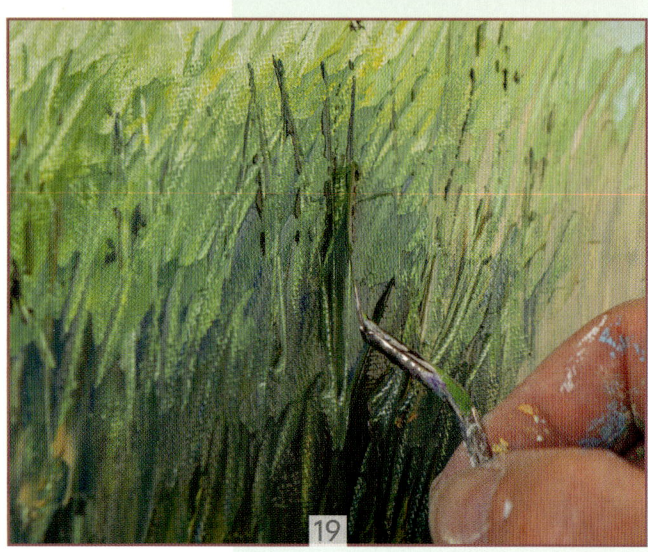

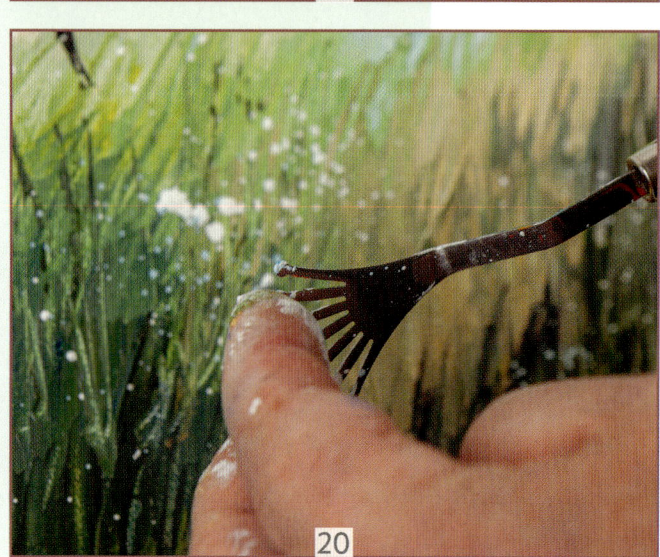

17 Add a line of fenceposts using the RGM Pastrello 38 and Mars black before the grass area dries. Double-load the knife for the nearest post, then use the side of the knife for the remaining posts.

18 Mix some white with pouring medium and add a fine sliver of paint to suggest highlights on the posts. Make a curved line between the posts for the connecting wires.

19 Clean the RGM Pastrello and work the edge through the wet paint at the base to create a few grassy stalks.

20 Using the paint already prepared for the fence wire, add a little water with a syringe and, with the King, flick paint into the lower half of the painting.

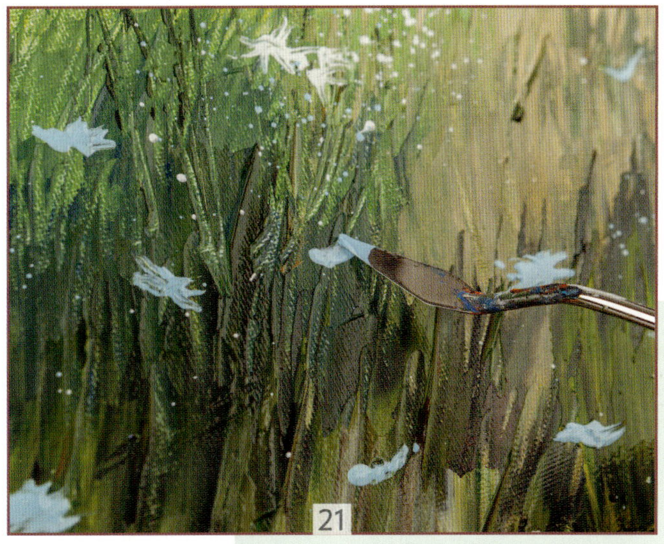

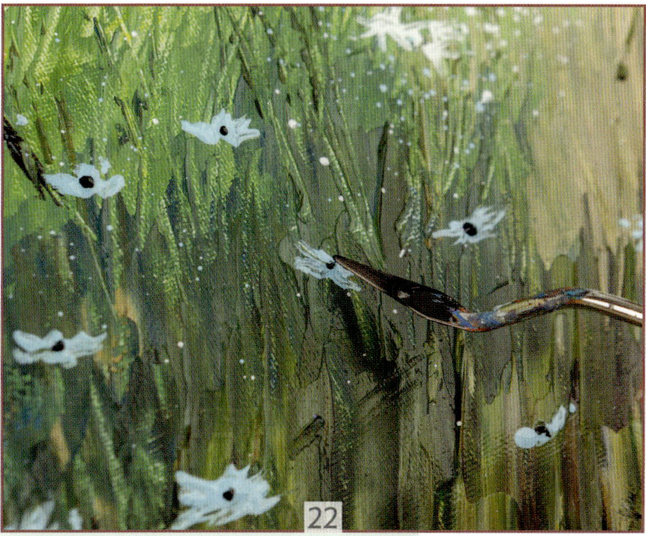

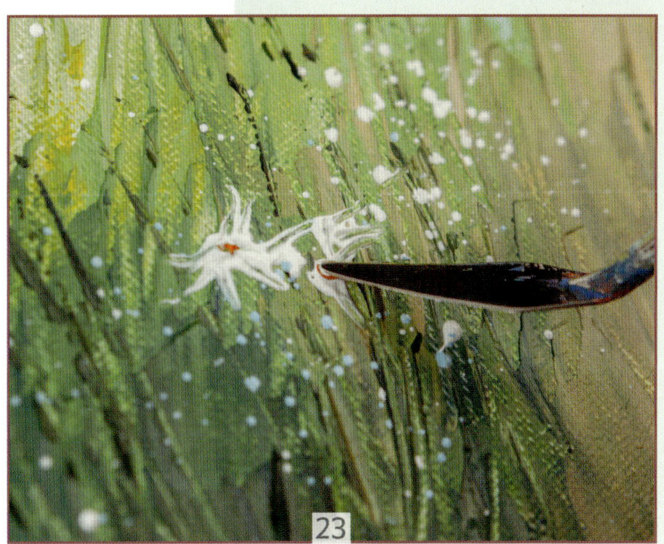

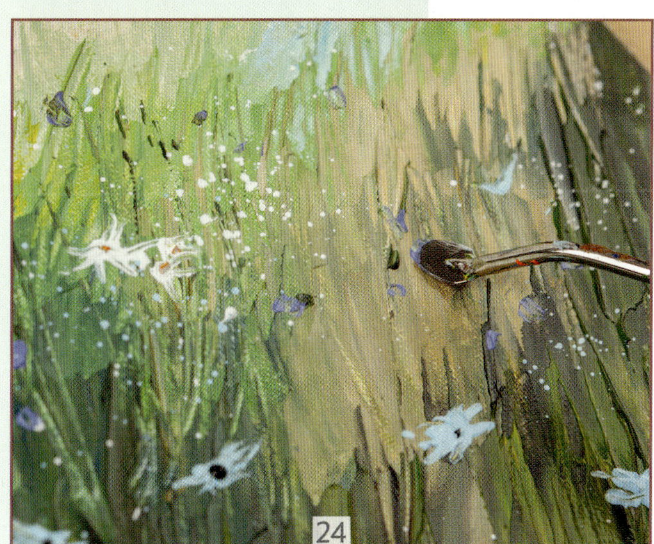

21 Add azure blue into the mix and flick more colour onto the surface. Add a blob of paint to the canvas with the RGM 41 and then drag out the edges to create a petal (see page 32).

22 Add dark centres to the flowers using Mars black. If the blue is still wet, the black needs to be even wetter to make it stick.

23 Add a few paler flowerheads and add orange button centres from primary yellow mixed with red.

24 Complete the scene by adding some small round flowerheads using the small round and light violot.

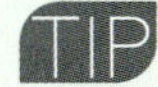

Flowers tend to grow randomly in a meadow. To find their positions, scatter a few grains of rice onto the dried surface and paint the petals where the grains land.

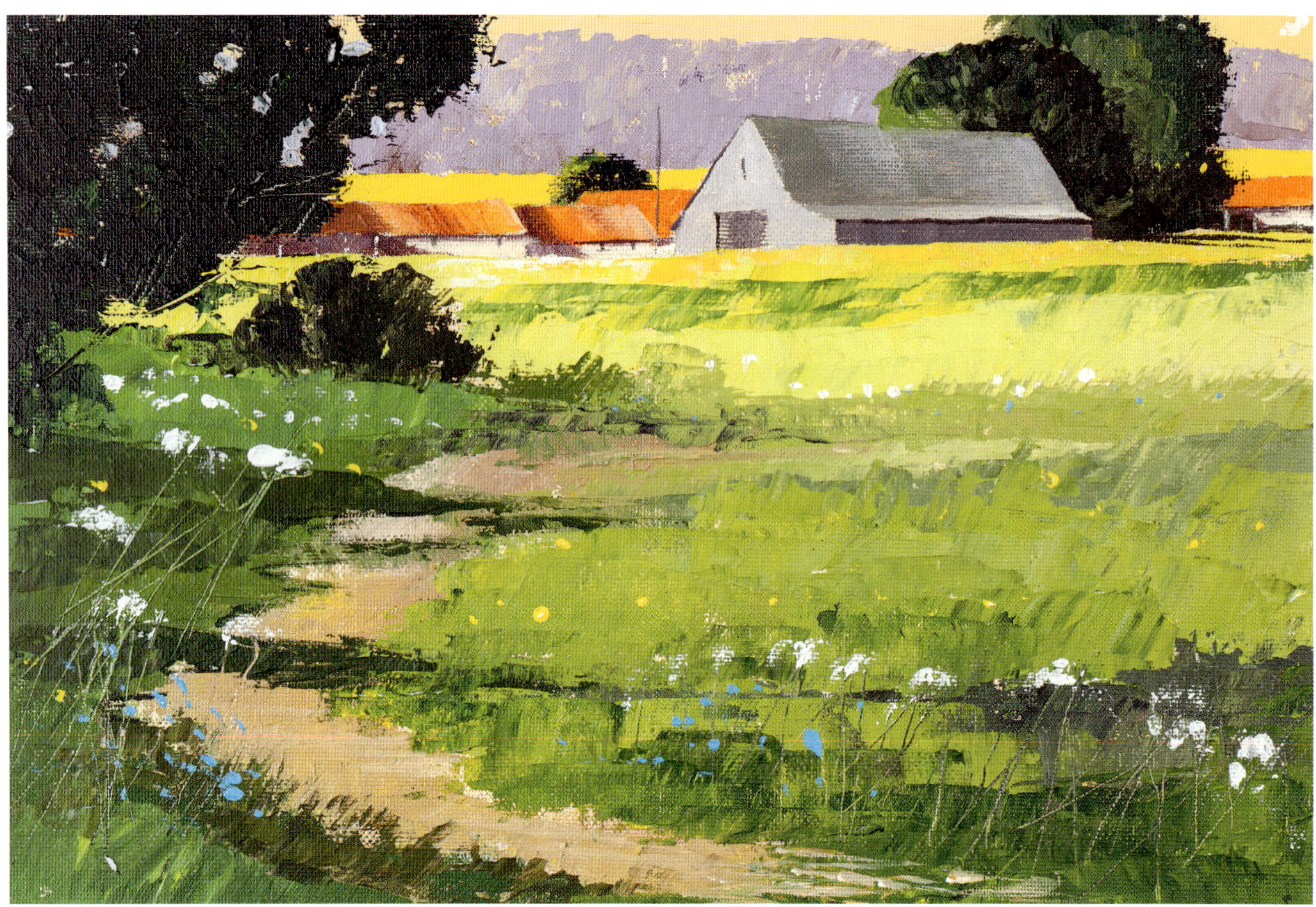

Kentish Farmstead, UK

35.5 × 25.5cm (14 × 10in)

This painting employs a number of techniques demonstrated in the previous
exercise for the handling of the tree on the left and the foreground grass textures.
Sgraffito has been used to define the foreground stalks amongst the cow parsley.
Buttons made with the small round knife have been used to define some of the
cow parsley flowerheads in the foreground.

Blackshore Cottages, Walberswick, UK

40 × 27.5cm (15⅝ × 10¾in)

Here, I've painted a heavily textured foreground using a variety of colours, the most dominant being Mars black and yellow ochre; I've overlapped these pure colours in the foreground. A similar line of fenceposts and wire has been placed on the right of the painting. Azure buttons suggest cornflowers in the foreground.

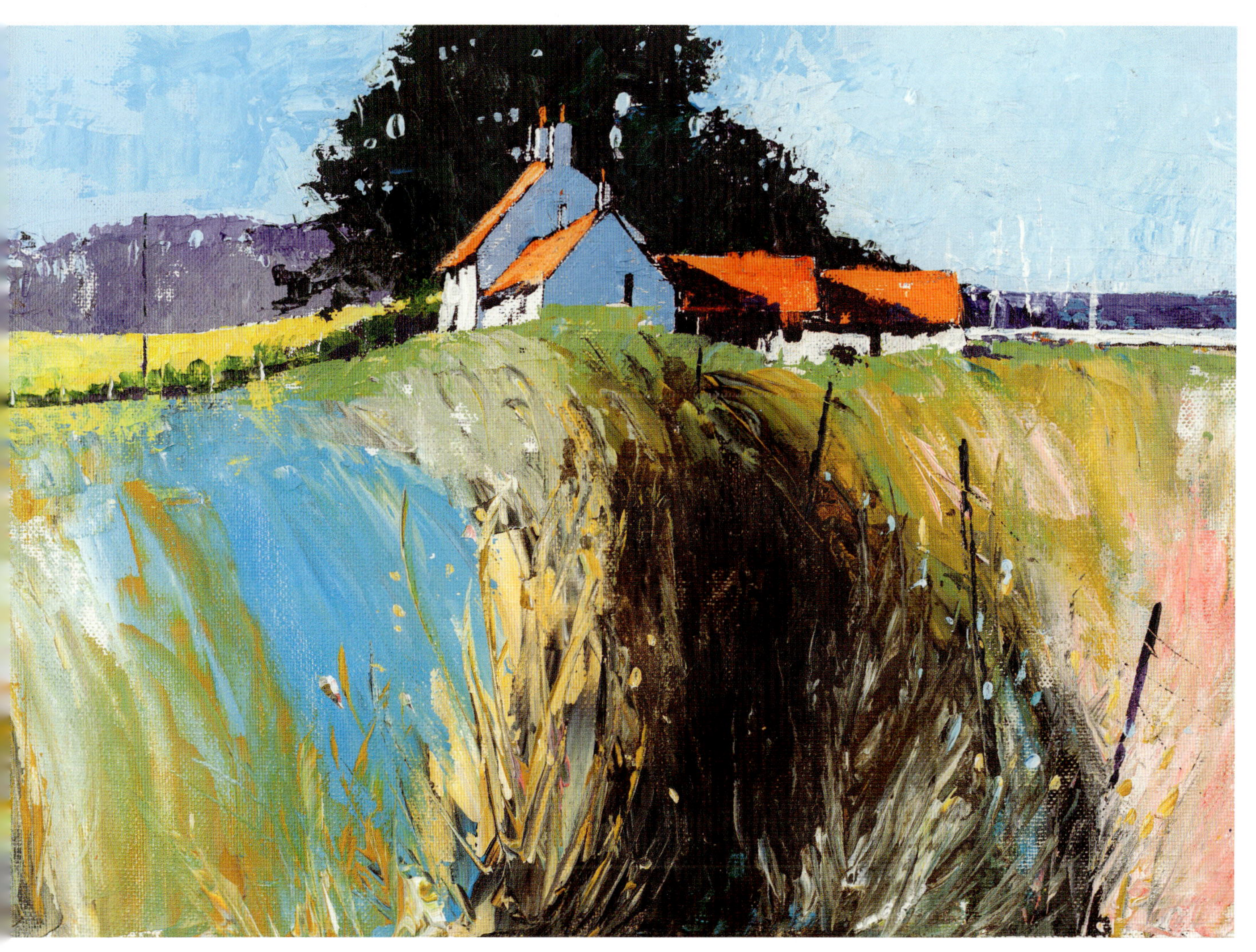

BIG ROCK SPLASH

I'm inspired to paint seascapes with knives, as I love the deep textures that can be achieved. The paint becomes almost like the sea itself, as it swirls and ripples through the foreshore. All of this is offset by the dark rocks and brooding skies that make this type of subject the perfect thing to paint.

This project will help you to capture the gesture and movement of a seascape. The approach takes advantage of the unique harmony between the different knifes and paint to allow the colours to flow through each other. We get to see how particular knife shapes are ideal for defining different parts of the painting. Capturing the perfect moment when a wave breaks against a rock can be difficult to freeze with a camera. But by observing with small thumbnail sketches (see below), an idea of composition and form can be quickly understood. I usually produce a series of thumbnail sketches until I'm happy with a particular composition.

▶ You will need

SURFACE:
Plain white primed canvas board tinted with cadmium red light hue and yellow ochre, 30.5 × 33cm (12 × 13in).

KNIVES:
RGM 109, 6, King, RGM Pastrello 38 and 41.

PAINTS:
Titanium white, azure blue, Naples yellow, cadmium red light hue, purple, ultramarine blue, yellow ochre, cadmium orange, cobalt teal, burnt umber, Mars black, Chinese blue, sap green and light violet.

OTHER TOOLS AND MATERIALS:
2.5cm (1in) flat brush, pouring medium, Neocolor II raw umber water-soluble pastel and ruler.

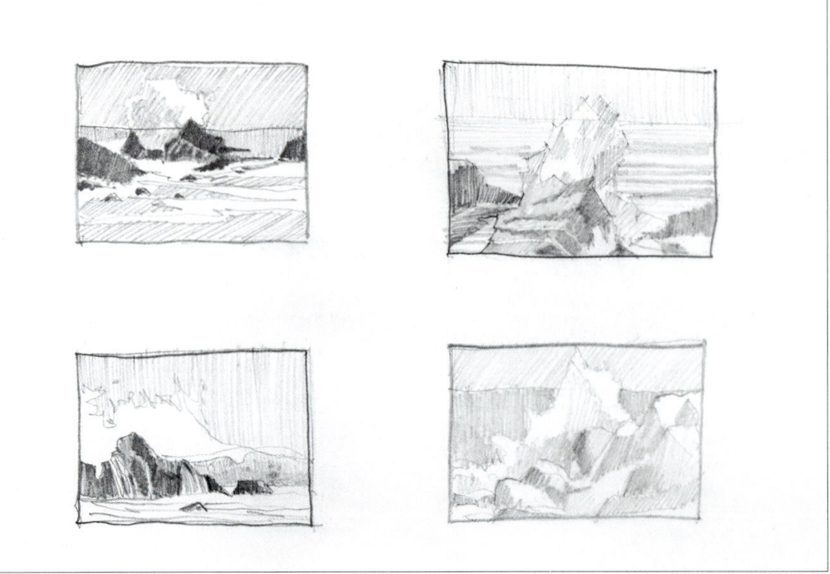

Compositional sketches.

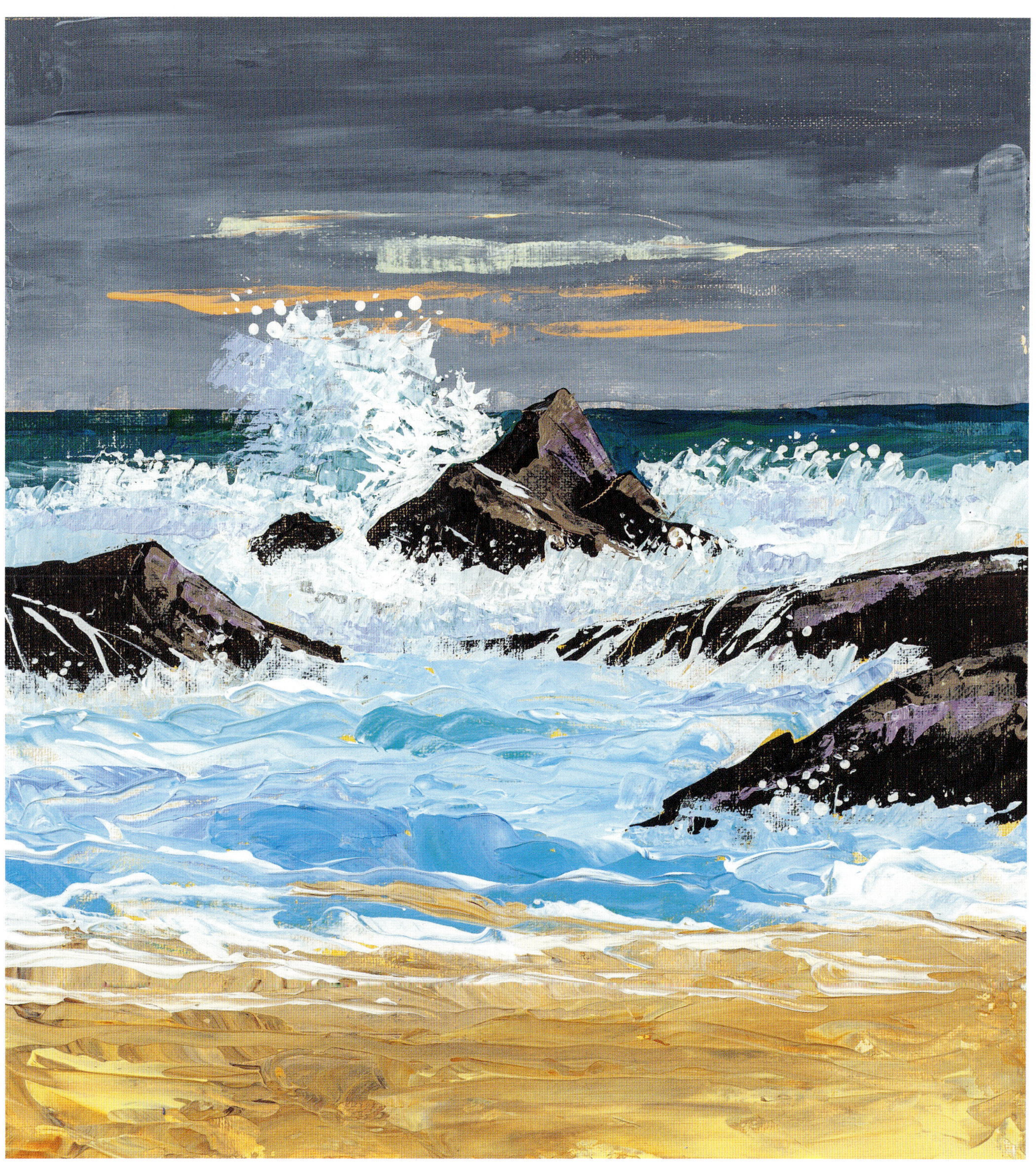

Big Rock Splash

30.5 × 33cm (12 × 13in)

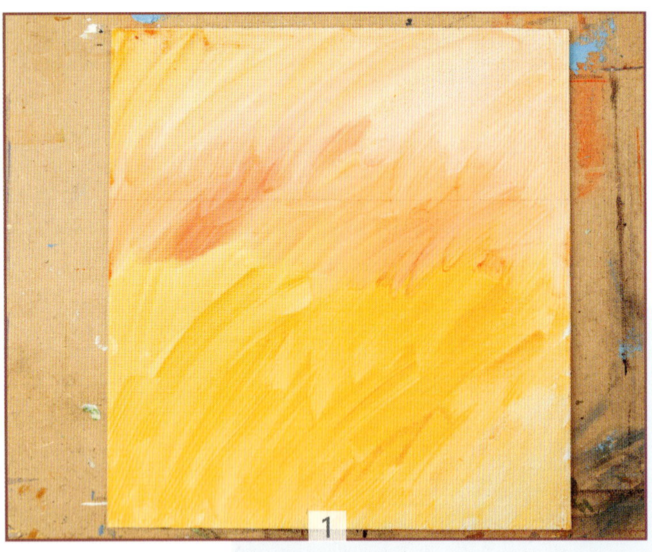

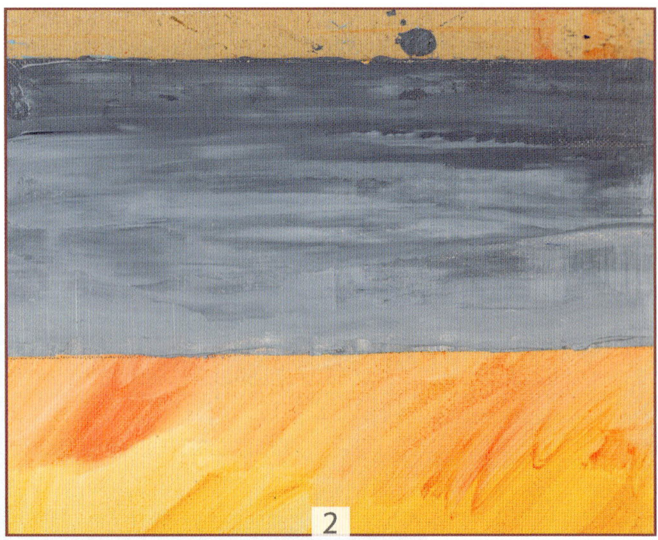

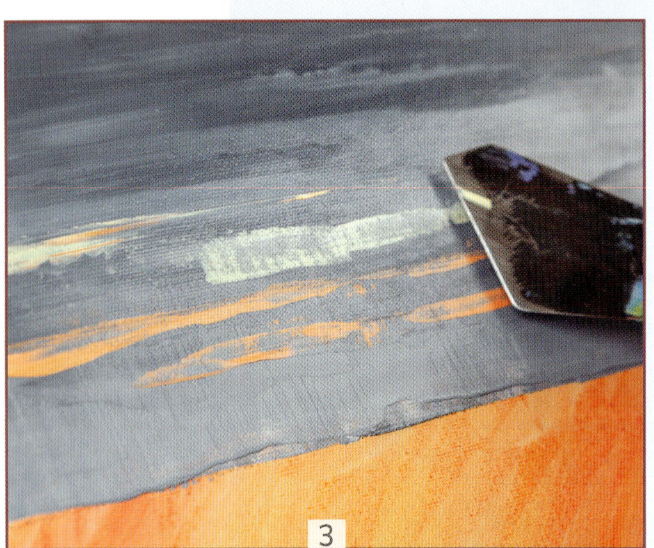

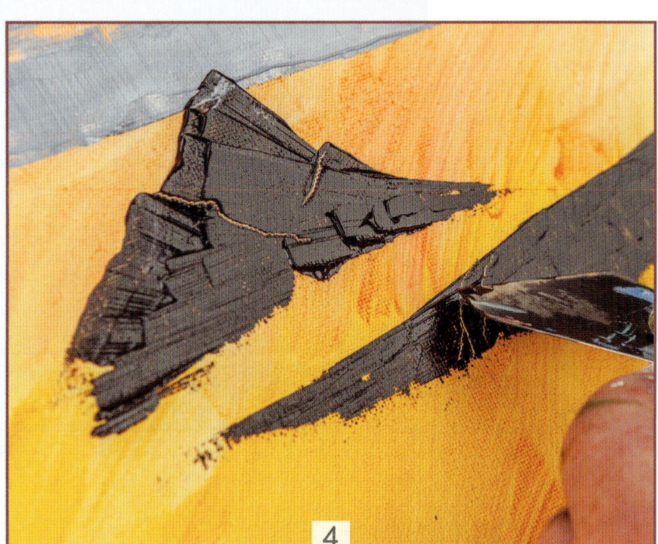

1 Tint the canvas board with a diluted wash of cadmium red light hue and yellow ochre using a 2.5cm- (1in-) wide flat brush. Leave to dry, then mark a horizon line across the upper third using a ruler and a Neocolor II raw umber soluble wax pastel.

2 I usually like to add a dark sky to my seascapes to make the crashing waves and foam really stand out. Mix a grey using ultramarine blue, Mars black and a touch of burnt umber to warm it a little. Lighten the sky by adding a little titanium white as the blade approaches the horizon. Apply the paint into the sky area using the piggyback technique (see page 31).

3 Make two separate mixes of Naples yellow and cadmium orange, each with a little white added. Add each colour in turn to the edge of the RGM 109 and make a horizontal mark on the lower horizon, placing the orange below the yellow. Clean the knife, then gently sweep the knife over the paint to blend it in.

4 Make a striated mix of burnt umber, Mars black and ultramarine blue. Pick a thick roll of paint on the wide tip of the RGM 109 and apply the paint in the shape of the foreshore rocks.

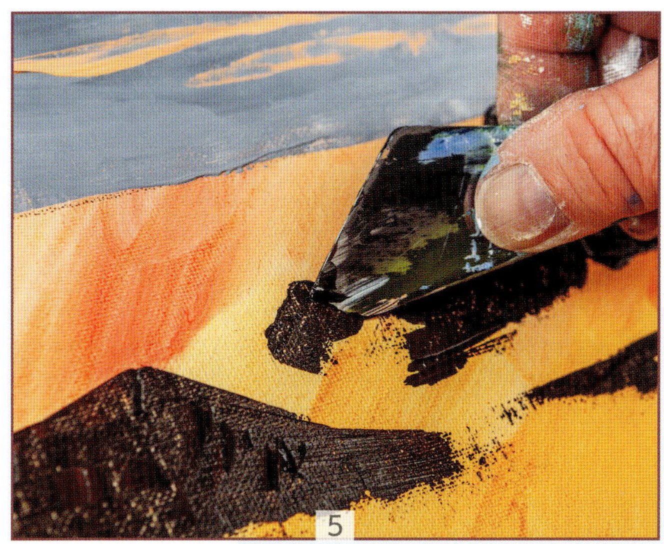

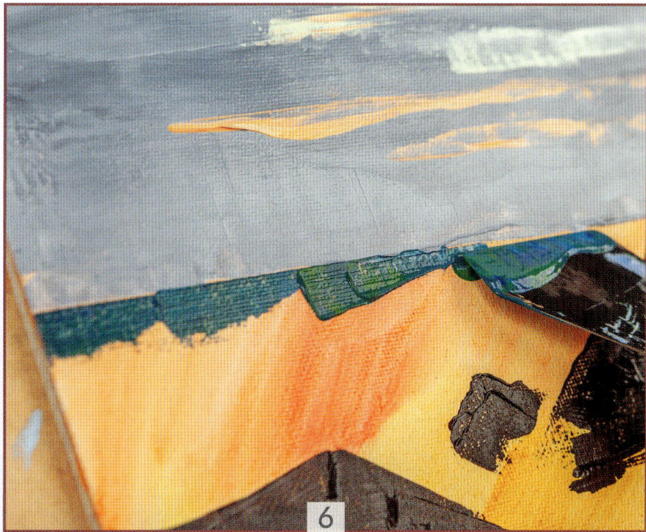

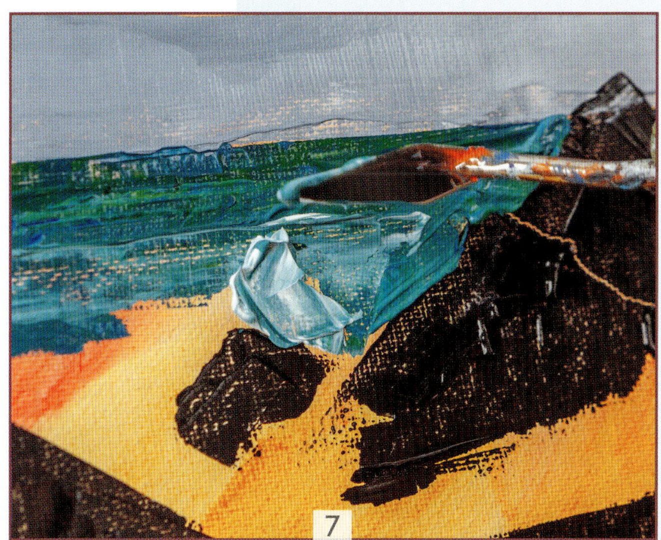

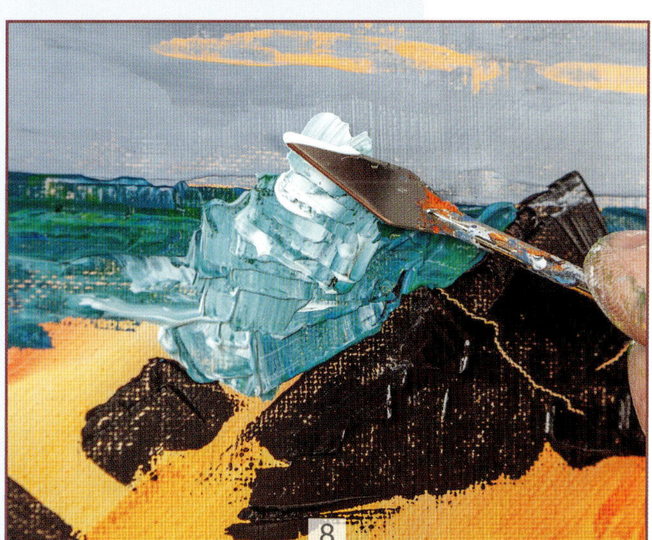

5   For smaller rocks, the front narrow edge of the knife can be used. Use *sgraffito* to scratch out any fissures or light areas in the rocks that may be visible.

6   Create a striated mix of Chinese blue, ultramarine blue and sap green to develop the greeny blue of the distant sea. Add paint following the marked horizon line using the RGM 109.

7   Turn the board through 90 degrees to make access easier. Switch to the RGM 41 knife to work in the more difficult areas between the rocks. Add a little more white for the foam as the sea gets nearer to the rocks.

8   Start to develop the large breaking wave by working white upwards with the knife. Allow the knife to pick up some of the already wet paint to tint the white.

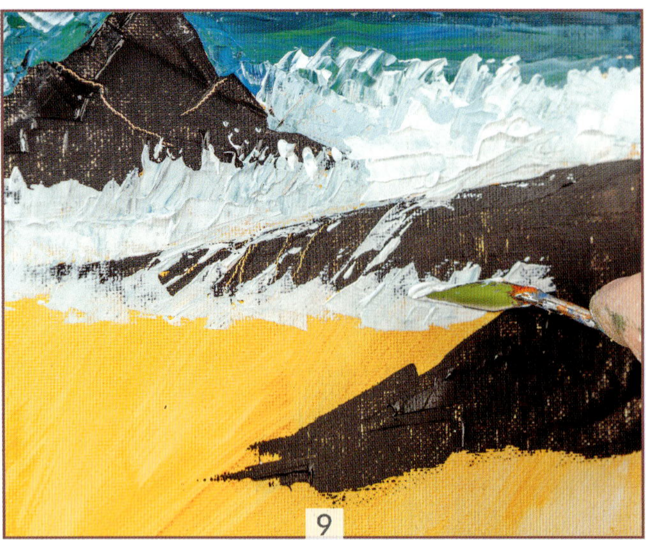

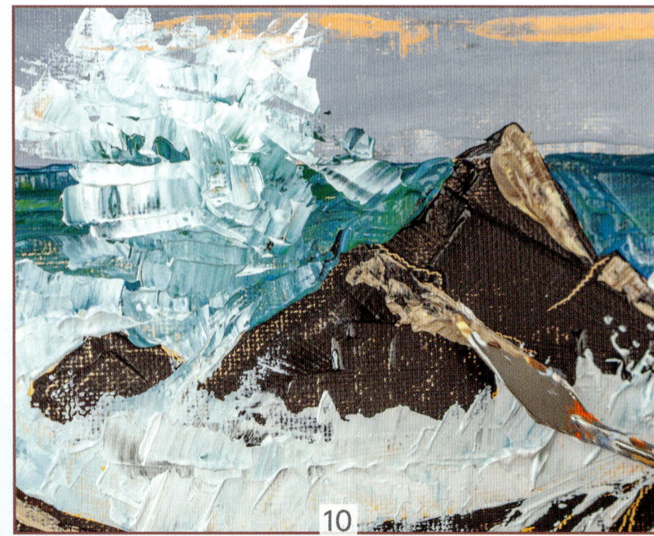

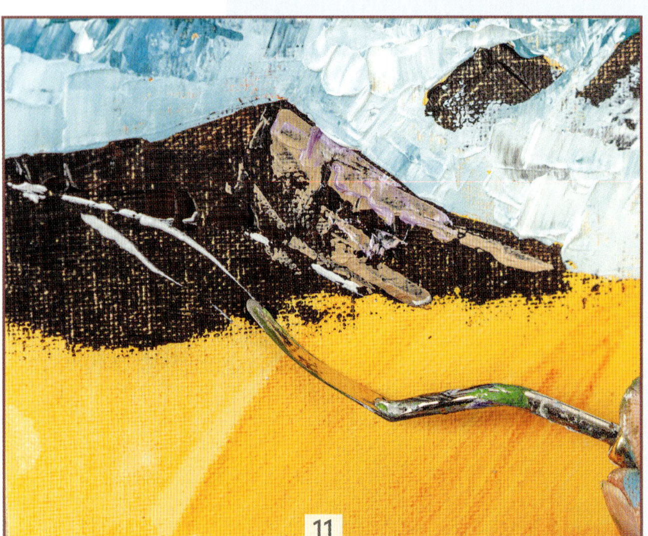

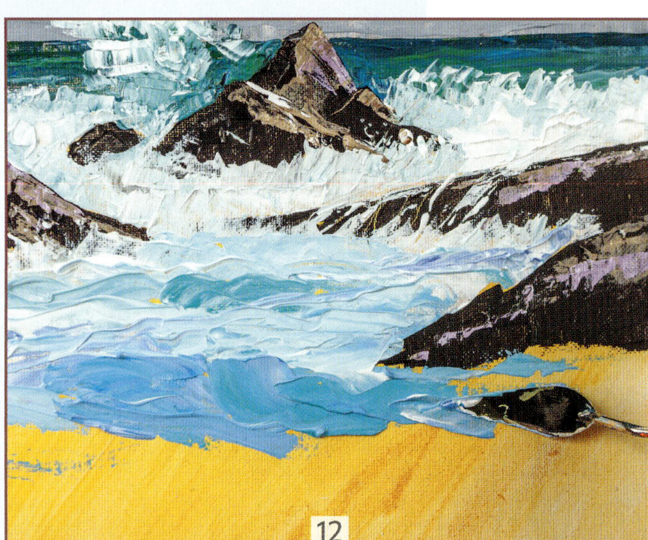

9 Add the foam and spume surrounding the rocks using a pale blue mixed from titanium white and a little ultramarine blue. Using the edge of the RGM 41, drag some fine lines of water spilling over the rocks. Start to develop the breaking waves around the rocks using the same knife and titanium white, using upward strokes with the side of the knife. Allow the knife to run out of paint at the crest of each wave to create a feathered edge.

10 Mix burnt umber with Naples yellow and apply to one side of the rocks to suggest highlights.

11 Add a mix of purple and white over the rocks for added interest. Using the RGM Pastrello for a finer line, dilute the pale blue mix with pouring medium and suggest more water spilling over the rocks using fine curved lines.

12 Switch to the RGM 6 knife and, using a striated mix of azure blue, cobalt teal and white, add heavier layers of paint where the water starts to meet the shoreline. Move the paint in a wave-like motion from left to right to allow the colours to mix and interact with each other. Satisfying wave patterns should appear.

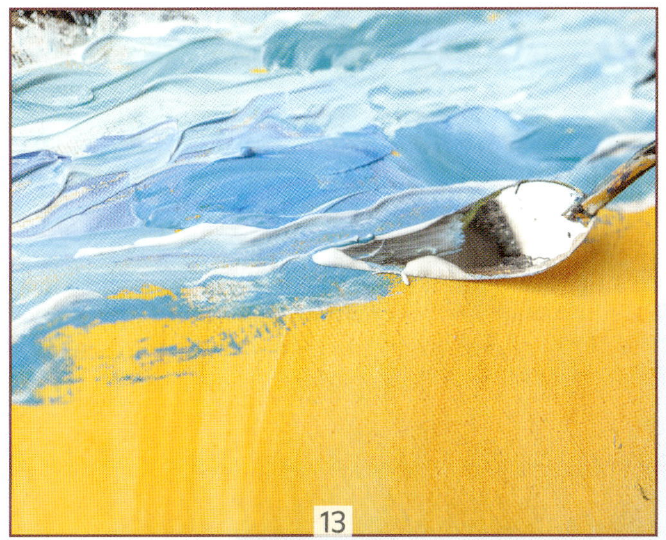

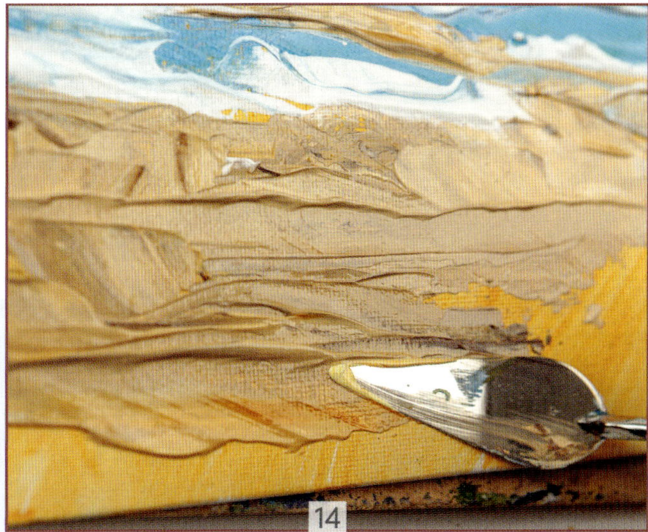

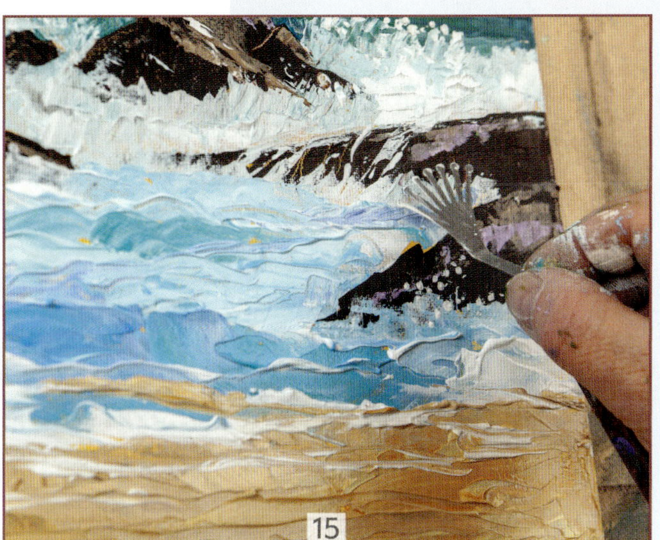

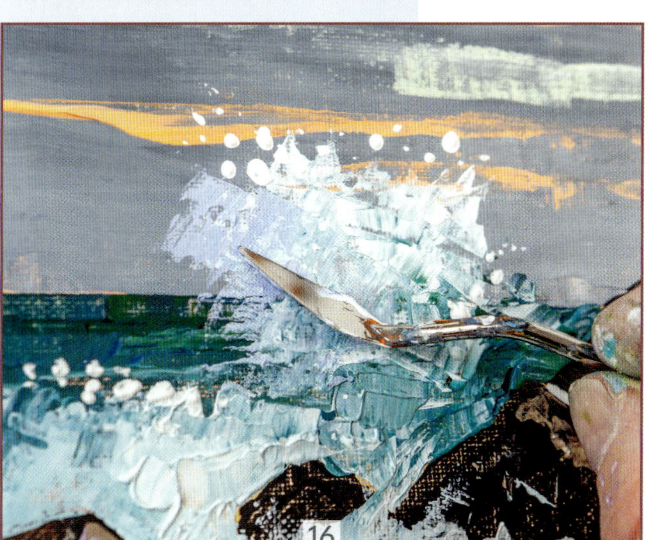

13 As the knife approaches the edge of the shoreline, add ultramarine blue to deepen and vary the colour. Add more pouring medium to alter the way the paint flows at this point and pull the white as fine lines through the darker blue areas.

14 Paint in the sandy foreshore using a striated mix of yellow ochre, burnt umber and titanium white. Using the RGM 6, apply this mix to the base of the painting, adding a little Naples yellow into the wet paint at the base of the painting.

15 Mix titanium white with pouring medium in a disposable cup. Add a little water and mix to a consistency representing single pouring cream. Use the King to add splashes and droplets of water that occur around the breaking waves by touching the prongs onto the surface.

16 To complete the painting, add light violet thoroughly mixed with titanium white into the shadow sides of the big splash and the breaking waves using the RGM 41.

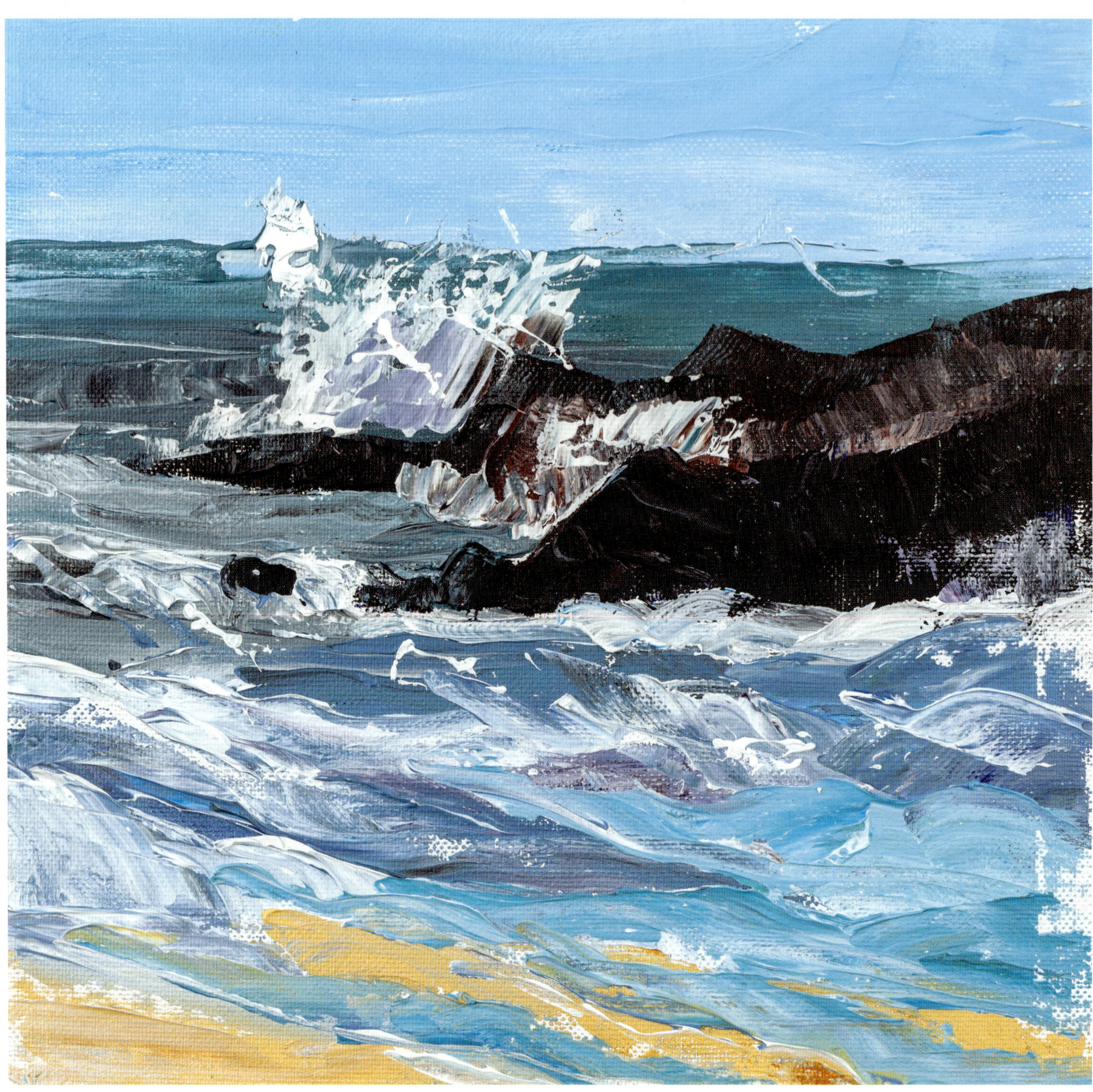

Waves on the Shoreline

25.5 × 25cm (10 × 9¾in)

This is another painting from my many pencil compositions (see page 66).
I particularly like the wave textures that were created on this one.

Crashing Waves

30.5 × 25cm (12 × 9¾in)

I liked the energy that was depicted in this painting. The knife and the strokes give a real sense of movement and dynamism.

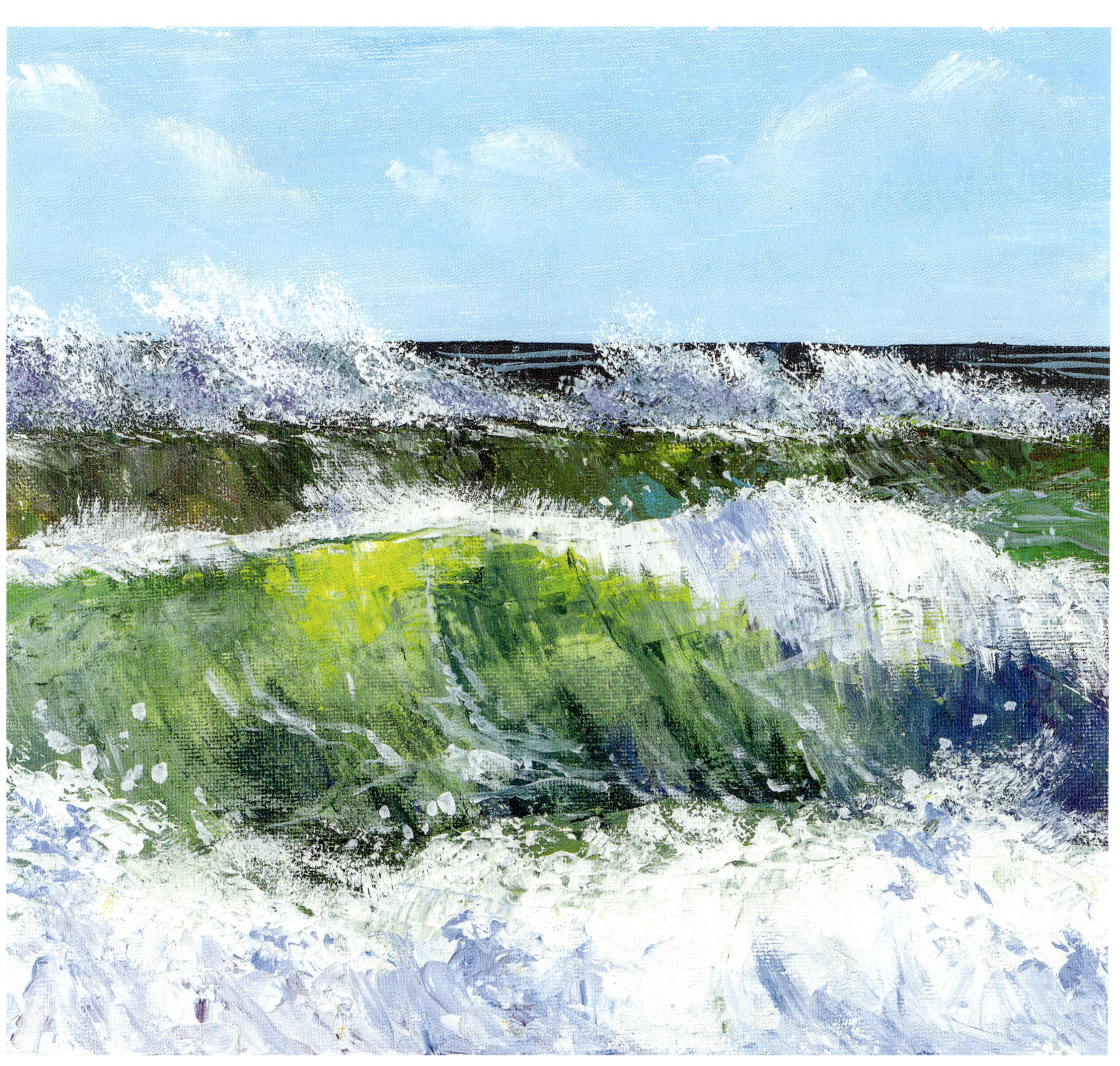

WINTER WOODLAND

To grow your skills even further, this project is designed to contain some slightly more challenging subjects when using knives. With the correct knife shapes and the right approach, painting trees and fine branches is relatively straightforward, as this project explains. In this instance, the canvas is primed with light violet and allowed to dry. For this painting, it's important that we use gloss glazing liquid, which extends the drying time without affecting the quality of the paint finish and keeps the painting surface workable for longer.

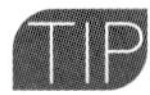

The fact that knives are being used, as opposed to brushes, will help you to develop a much more Impressionistic style when creating trees and foliage. There is no need to dilute paint as you would with a brush, allowing for much more vibrant colours and broken textures to be created.

► ## You will need

SURFACE:

Plain white primed canvas board tinted with light violet, 30.5 × 29cm (12 × 11½in).

KNIVES:

RGM 109, Pastrello 38, 41, bull nose and small round.

PAINTS:

Titanium white, light violet, yellow ochre, burnt umber, Mars black, cadmium red light hue, primary yellow, sap green, ultramarine blue, cadmium orange and azure blue.

OTHER TOOLS AND MATERIALS:

Zhu Ting angled flat brush, size 12, and gloss glazing liquid.

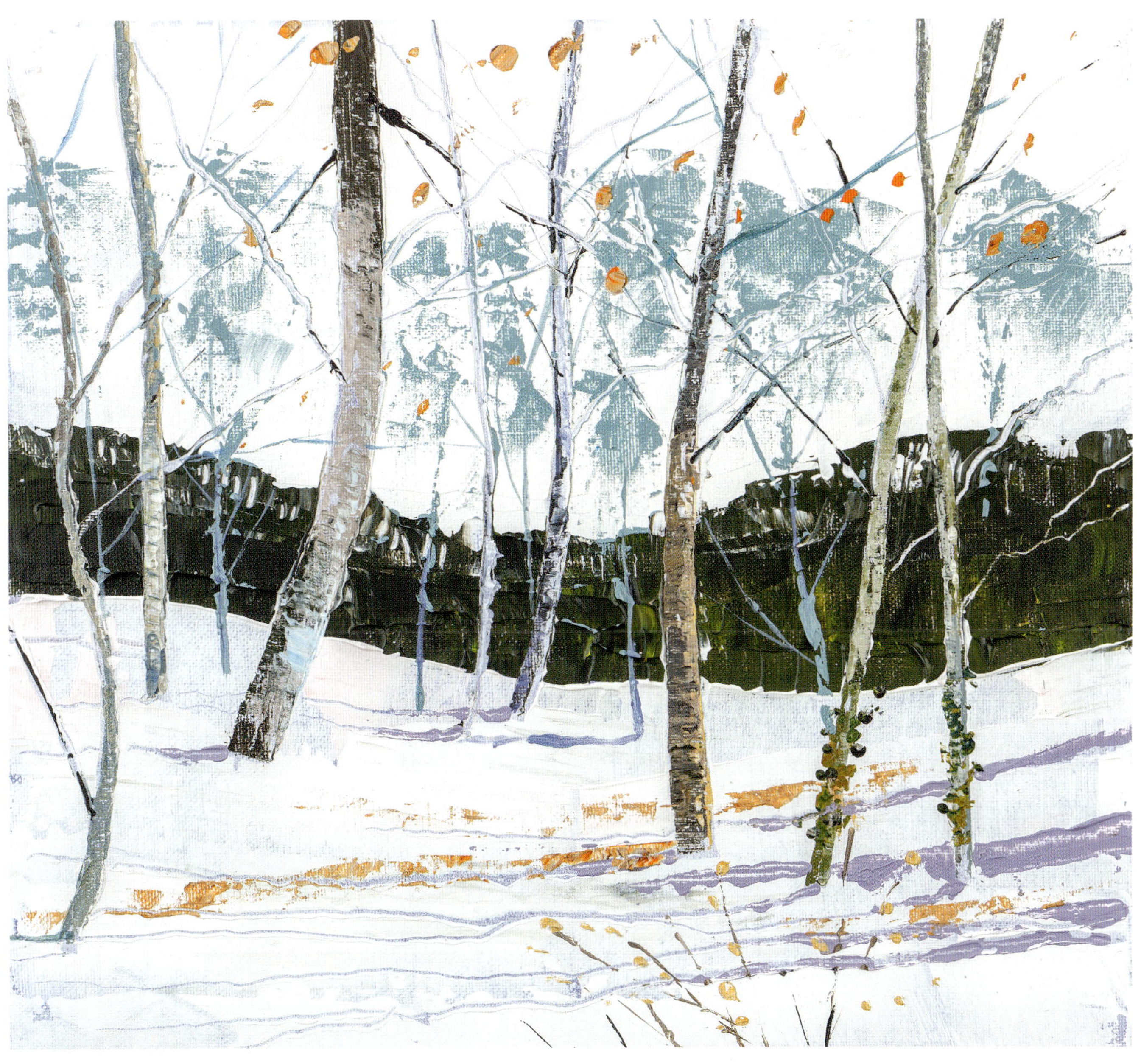

Winter Woodland

30.5 × 29cm (12 × 11½in)

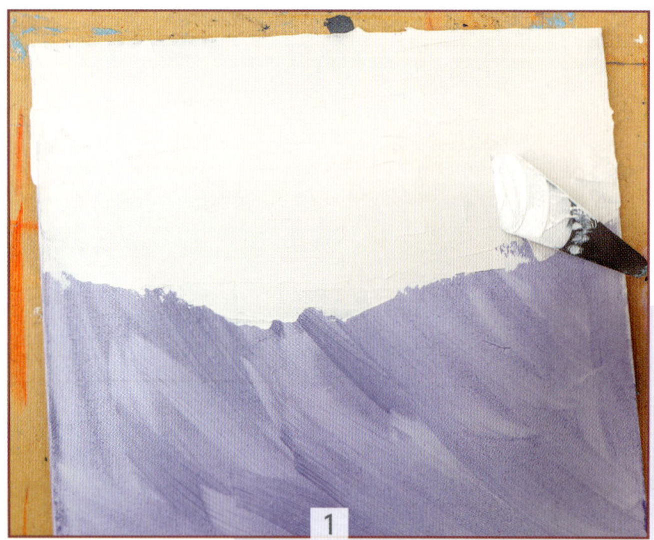

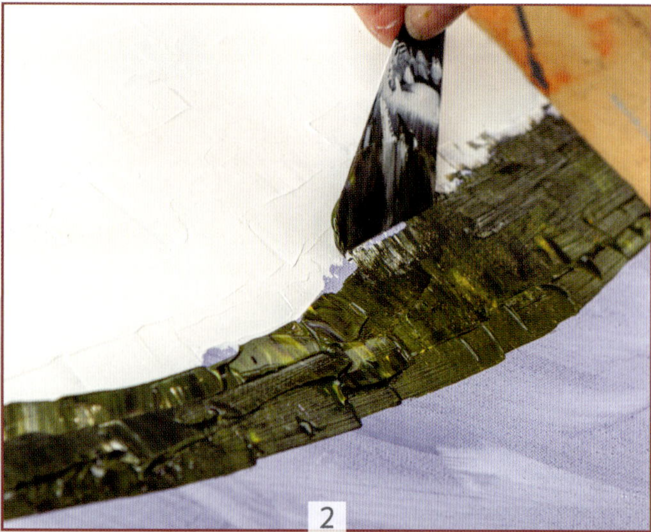

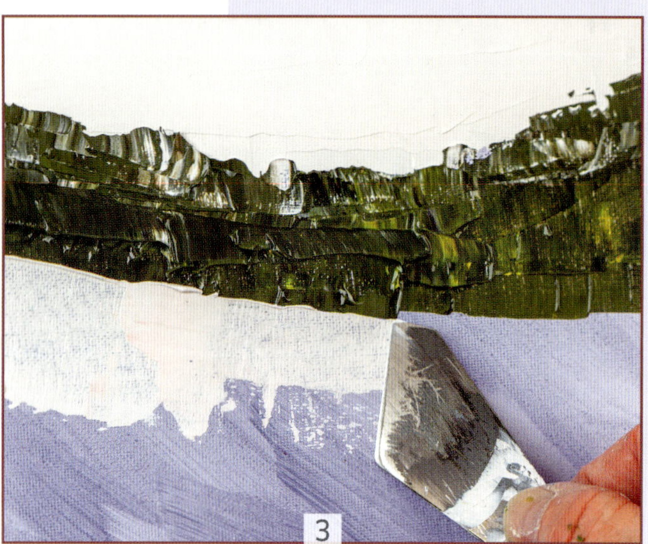

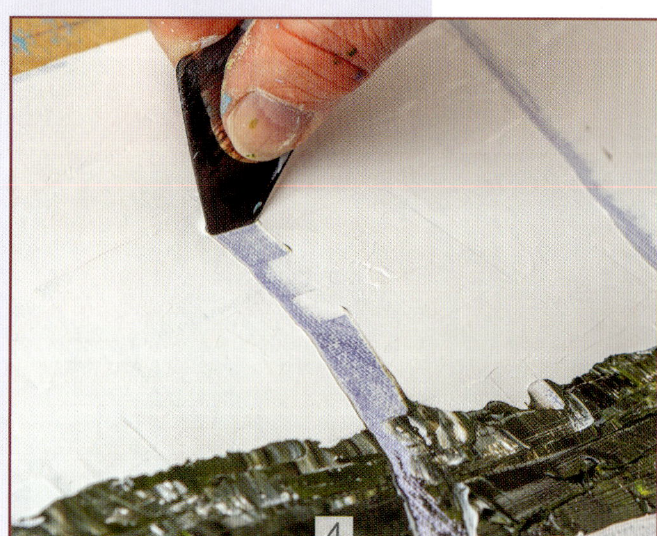

1 Create a quantity of very pale pink by thoroughly mixing white and cadmium red light hue roughly 50:50 with glazing medium using the RGM 109. Ensure there is enough paint to cover the upper part of the sky. Glide the colour over the canvas without applying too much pressure, leaving a thick layer of paint on the surface.

2 Mix Mars black, primary yellow and glazing medium and thickly apply this for the tree line in the middle ground, feathering the edges into the applied sky.

3 Add the fallen snow into the foreground using the same sky mix, with a little more cadmium red light hue added.

4 Use the narrow edge of the RGM 109 blade and working from bottom to top, scrape out the shape of the largest tree trunk, revealing the light violet underpainting below.

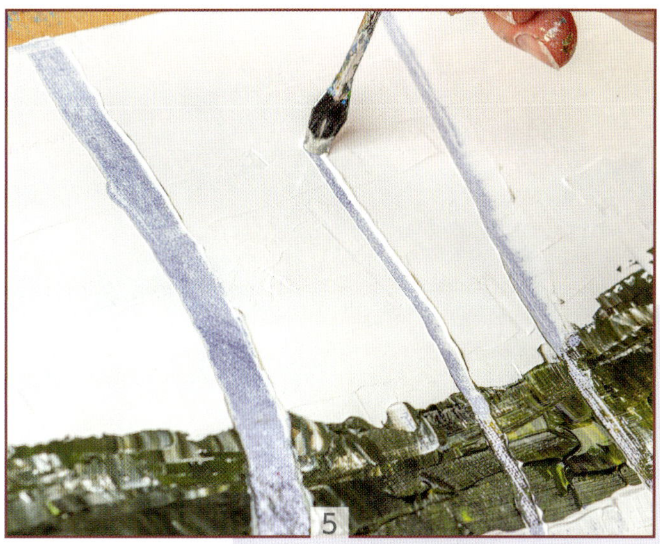

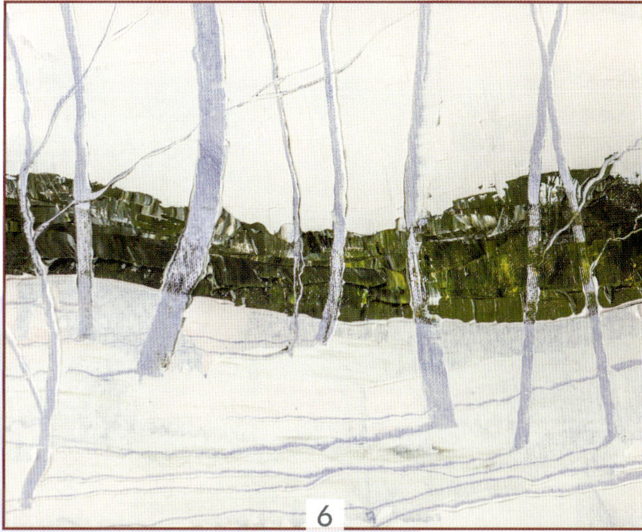

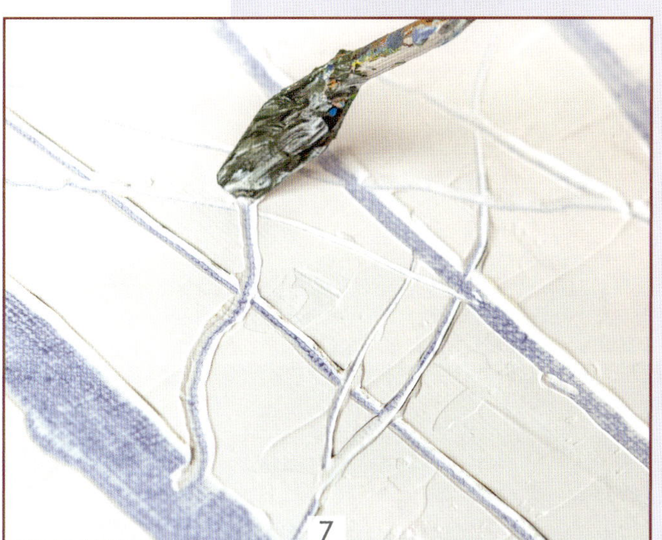

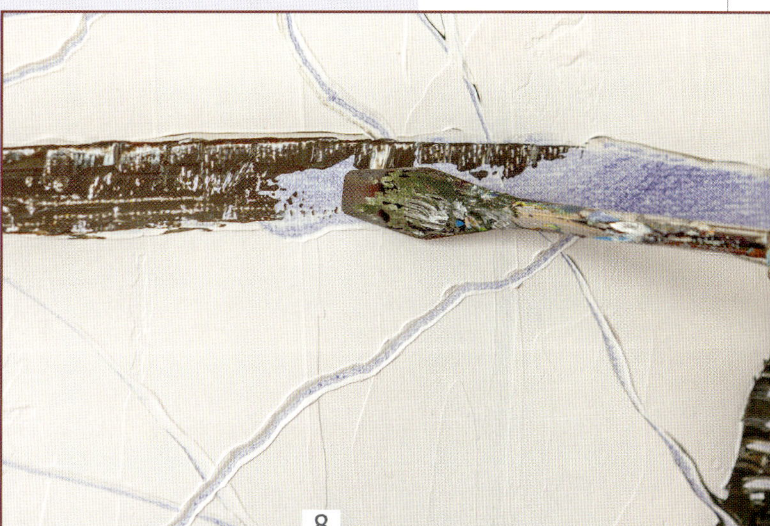

5   With the bull nose, scrape out some narrower trunks in the background. Wipe the knife clean as it passes through the tree-line in the distance to prevent colour being dragged into the sky.

6   After all the trunks of varying widths and some branches have been added, scrape the bull nose sideways from the base of each tree to suggest shadows.

7   Experiment with the angle of the knife when scraping out to vary the width of the lines created for the tree branches.

8   Mix burnt umber into the left-over background tree colour, then turn the board sideways and sweep paint using the short edge of the bull nose over the scraped-back area at the top of the large left-hand trunk to suggest bark textures.

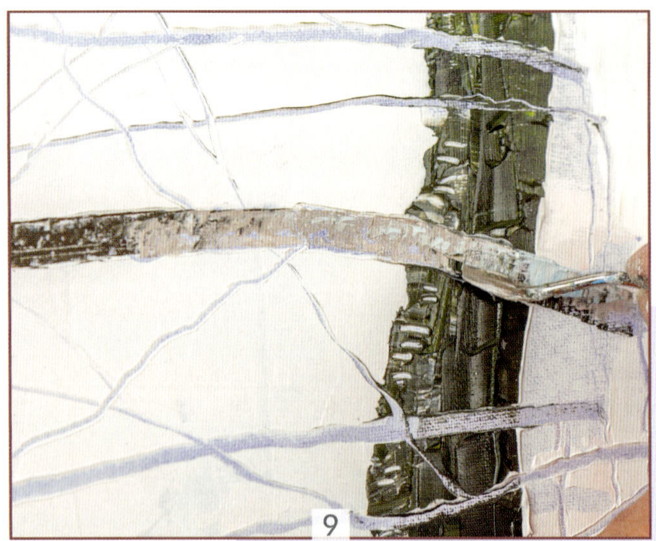

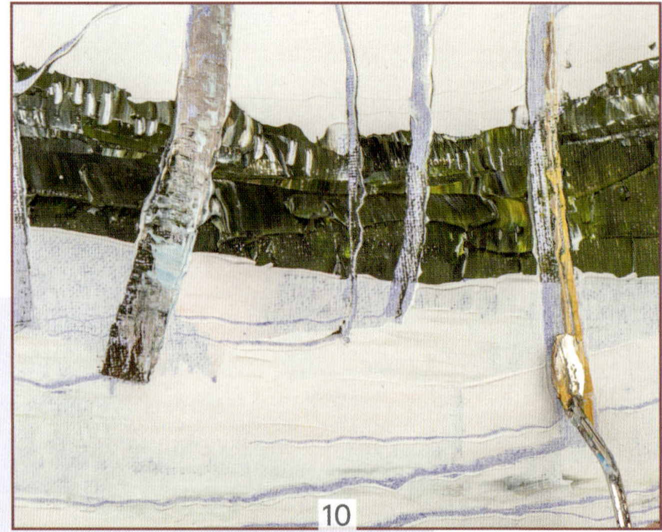

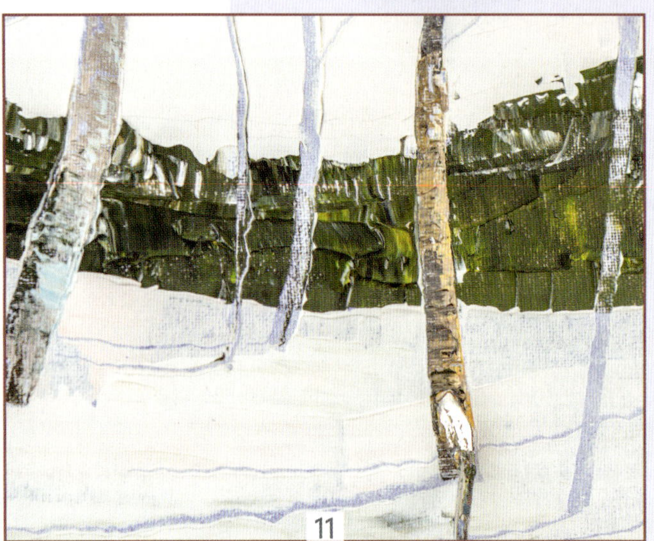

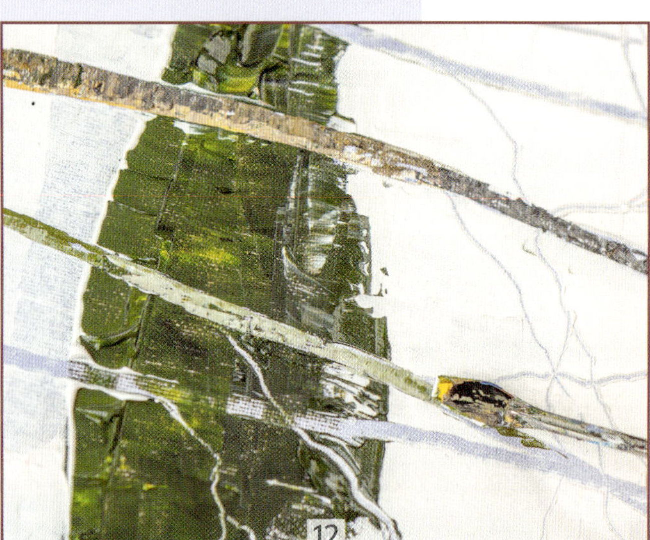

9 Mix titanium white with burnt umber to create a pinky tone and continue down the tree, until all the scraped-out parts on the large trunk are filled in. The patches of pale-blue light on the sides of the trunk can be created from a mix of titanium white and azure blue.

10 Working on the slightly narrower tree on the right with the same knife, add yellow ochre onto the lower part of the tree using side sweeps.

11 Turn the board upside down and start to add darks to the tops of the trunks using purple with a little burnt umber. Turn the painting around the correct way and add side sweeps of violet mixed with white across the trunks to suggest bark texture.

12 We now have some dark trees against a light background. Add a lighter colour of yellow ochre and white where the trunk crosses over the darker distant trees, creating light against dark counterchange.

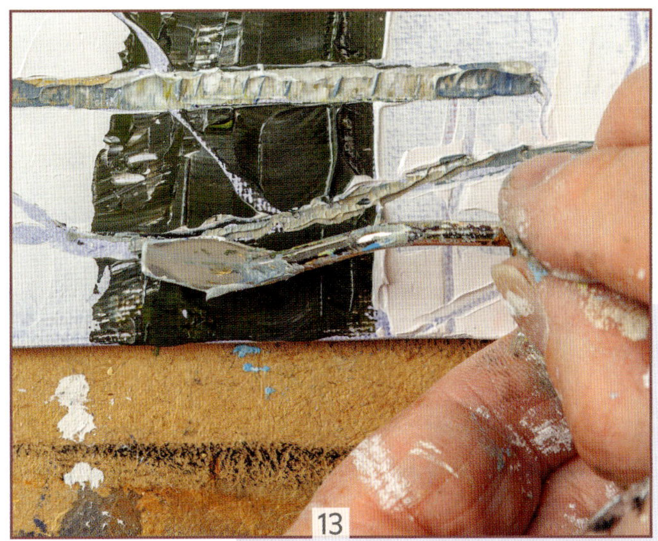

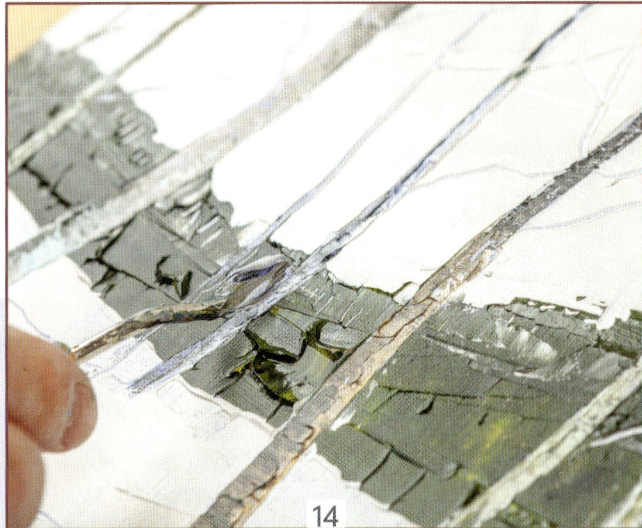

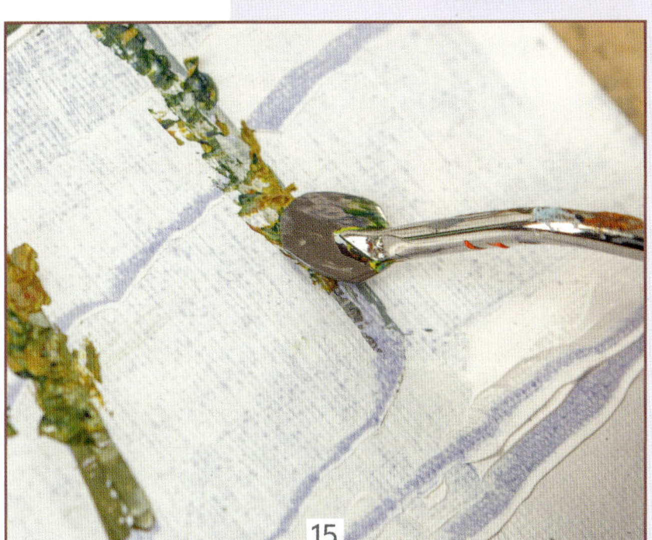

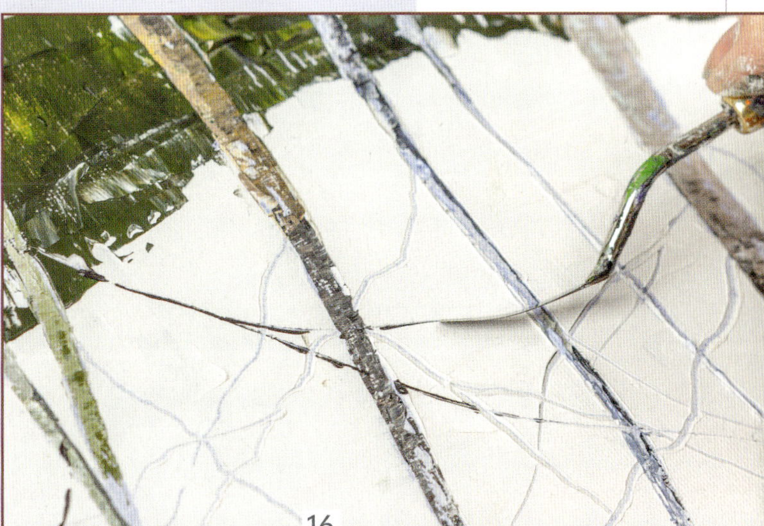

13 Continue to add more texture to the remaining tree trunks using a mix of burnt umber and yellow ochre. Partially mix in sap green and, using the narrow side of the bull nose, sweep these colours across the tree trunks making the marks lighter on the left and darker on the right.

14 Build up the colours on the remaining trunks. Avoid muddy colours by frequently wiping the knife clean.

15 Mix ultramarine blue, primary yellow and a touch of cadmium red light hue and then apply to the lower halves of some of the trunks on the right to suggest ivy.

16 Create a dark mix of Mars black, ultramarine blue and burnt umber, with a little pouring medium. Take a fine sliver of paint onto the edge of the RGM Pastrello 38 and then make a curved stroke through the wet paint applied earlier for the sky. To vary the direction and shape of the twigs being drawn, it sometimes helps to turn the work upside down or sideways.

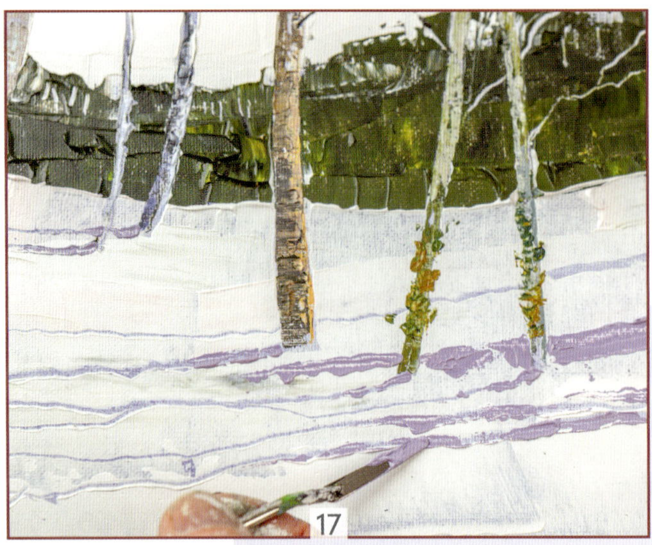

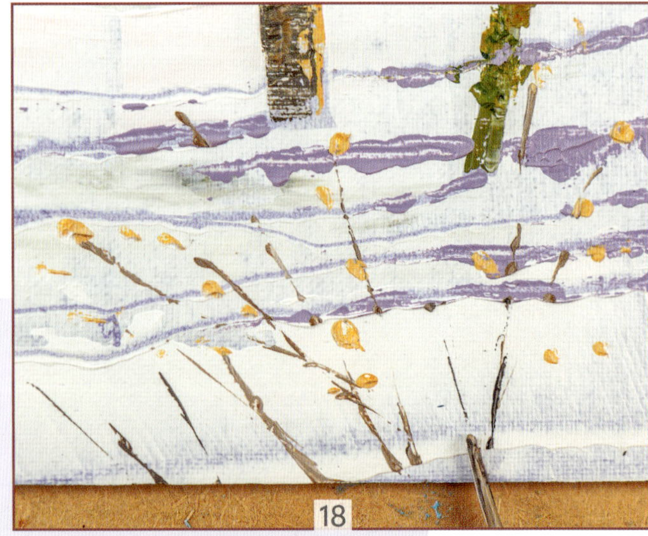

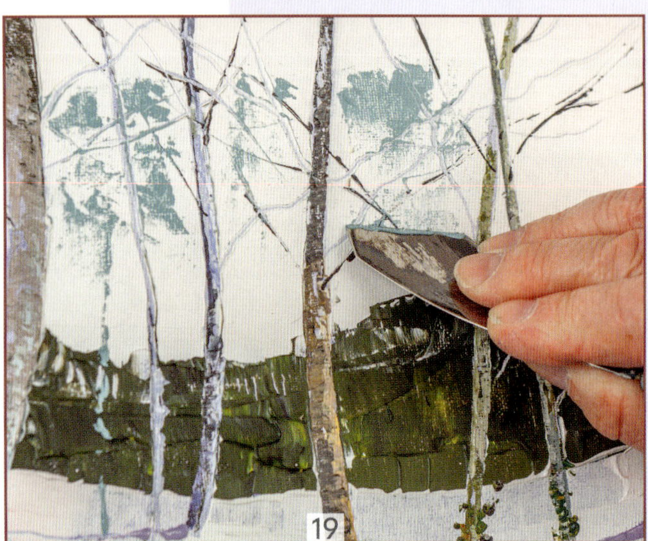

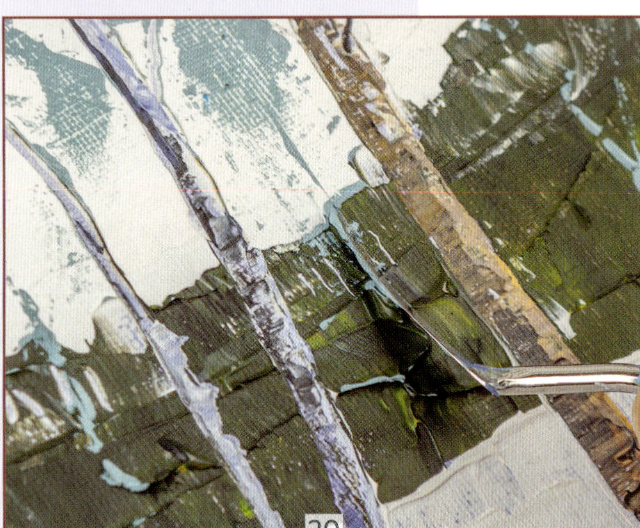

17 Extend the shadows from the ones scraped out earlier by adding purple and white. Vary the white in the mix to get the depth of shadow required. The cast shadows should appear lighter as they get further from the tree and darker near the base of the trunks. Use the RGM Pastrello 38, double-loading the blade to get the marks required.

18 Create twigs and branches projecting into the foreground with the RGM Pastrello 38 using a mix of burnt umber, Mars black and white with some pouring medium added. Use the tip of the knife to add a few yellow ochre buttons.

19 Allow the painting to dry – this may take a little while depending on how much glazing liquid has been added. Use the RGM 109 with azure blue, burnt umber and white to make a grey. Use the dry scumble technique to create the top of the distant tree canopies.

20 Before the previous work has dried and left an uneven surface to paint over, draw down some fine lines with the edge of the knife to create some tree trunks further within the woodland.

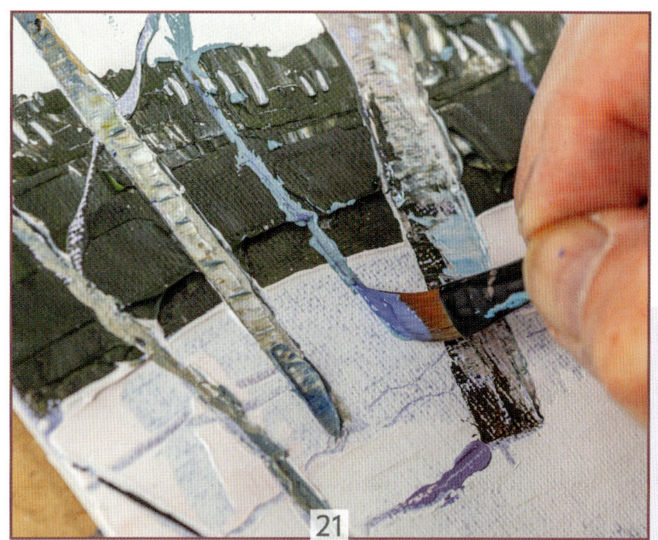

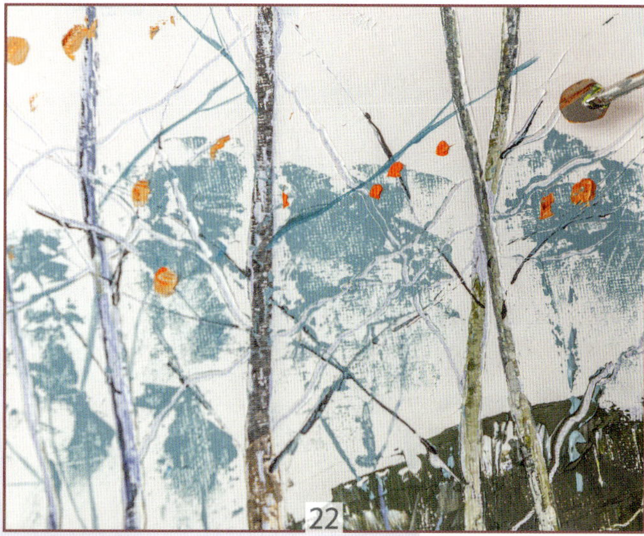

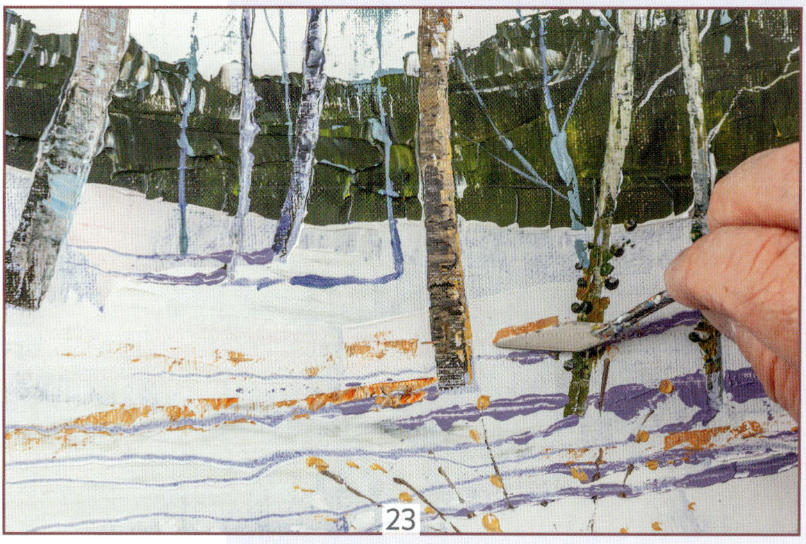

21 Use the size 12 Zhu Ting angled brush to paint in the distant tree trunks using the same colour mix.

22 Suggest a few dead leaves by dabbing cadmium orange marks into the tree canopy with the small round.

23 Finally, switch to the RGM 41 and, using cadmium orange, dab the edge on the surface to suggest dead leaves fallen onto the woodland floor.

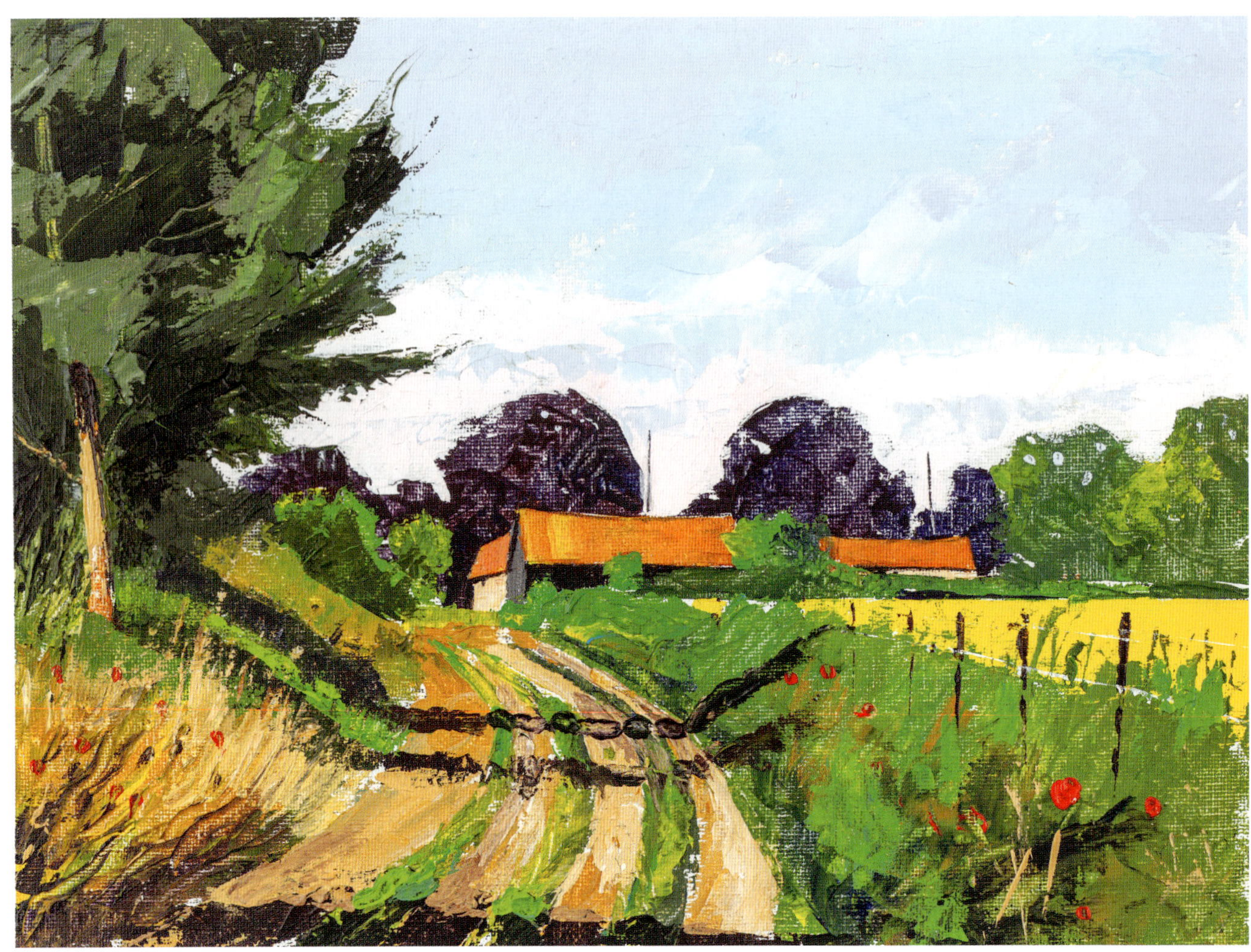

Sunlight and Shadow, Newbourne Country Lane, UK

33.5 × 25.5cm (13¼ × 10in)

This painting shows a number of different foliage types. The large tree on the left
was created using the broad edge of the RGM 109 to create those specific leaf
shapes. Some *sgraffito* helps to suggest branches set against a dark background.

Morning Light, Alstonefield, UK

44.5 × 35.5cm (17½ × 14in)

There are numerous trees present in this subject. Most of the foliage was completed using just two knives: the RGM 6 and the RGM 41. I also employed the use of a little marble dust to denote the finer leaf textures for the tree on the right.

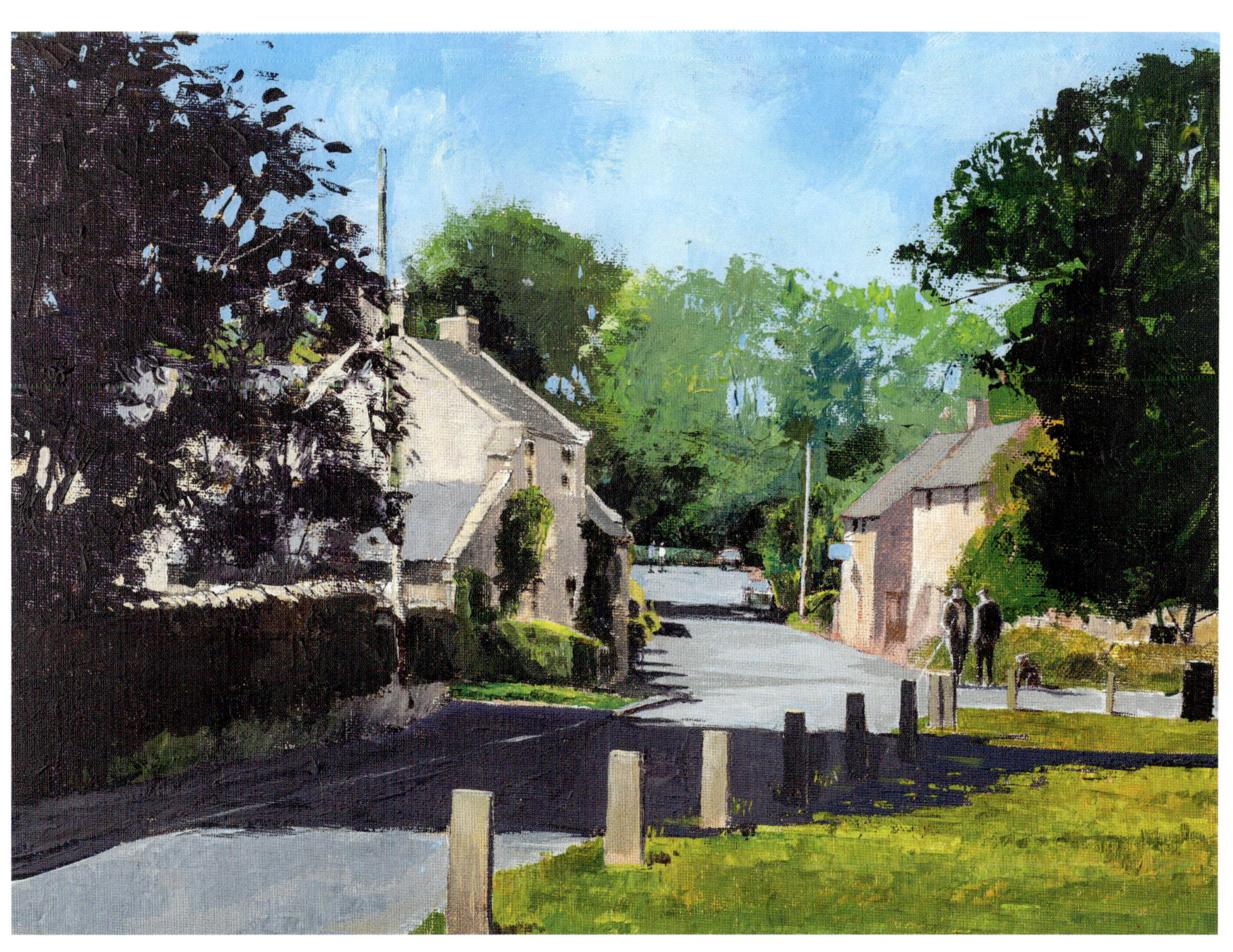

SALTY SEASIDE LOBSTER

Working with collage is interesting and challenging. Combining elements of objects and knife marks creates a subject that will help convey a message or idea. Working this way helps to develop creativity, imagination and problem solving. When on holiday, I collect objects and literature that give a sense of place, and incorporate these into paintings combined with knives and acrylics.

This project helps to develop knife skills when infilling or working around complex shapes. The type of knife and the way it is held will hopefully start to become much more natural when applying paint. Collage sometimes includes just fabric and paper cuttings, but in this instance I have also combined heavier objects such as shells and sand, to get you used to combining different knife strokes with a variety of bulkier found materials.

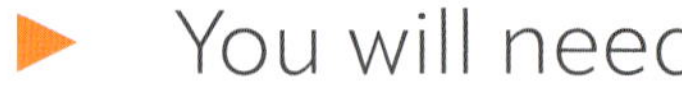

► You will need

SURFACE:

Plain white primed canvas board, 40.5 × 30.5cm (16 × 12in)

KNIVES:

RGM 6, 41, Pastrello 38 and bull nose.

PAINTS:

Titanium white, yellow ochre, cadmium red light hue, cadmium orange, burnt umber, azure blue and purple.

OTHER TOOLS AND MATERIALS:

Wolff carbon pencil, black finepoint pen (permanent marker), Mod Podge®, Golden heavy texture gel, Golden crackle paste and 2.5cm (1in) flat brush.

Found objects from the beach.

Printed papers (brochures and magazines).

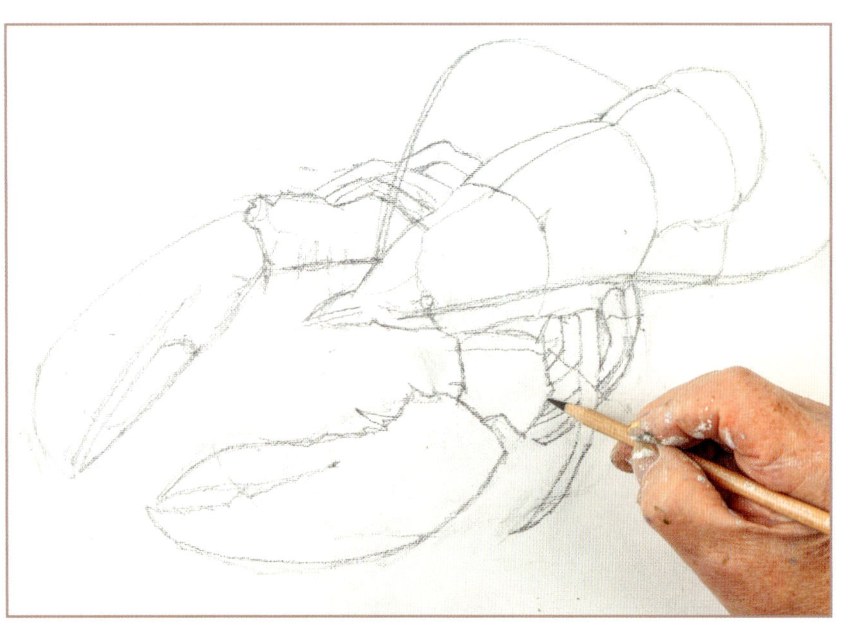

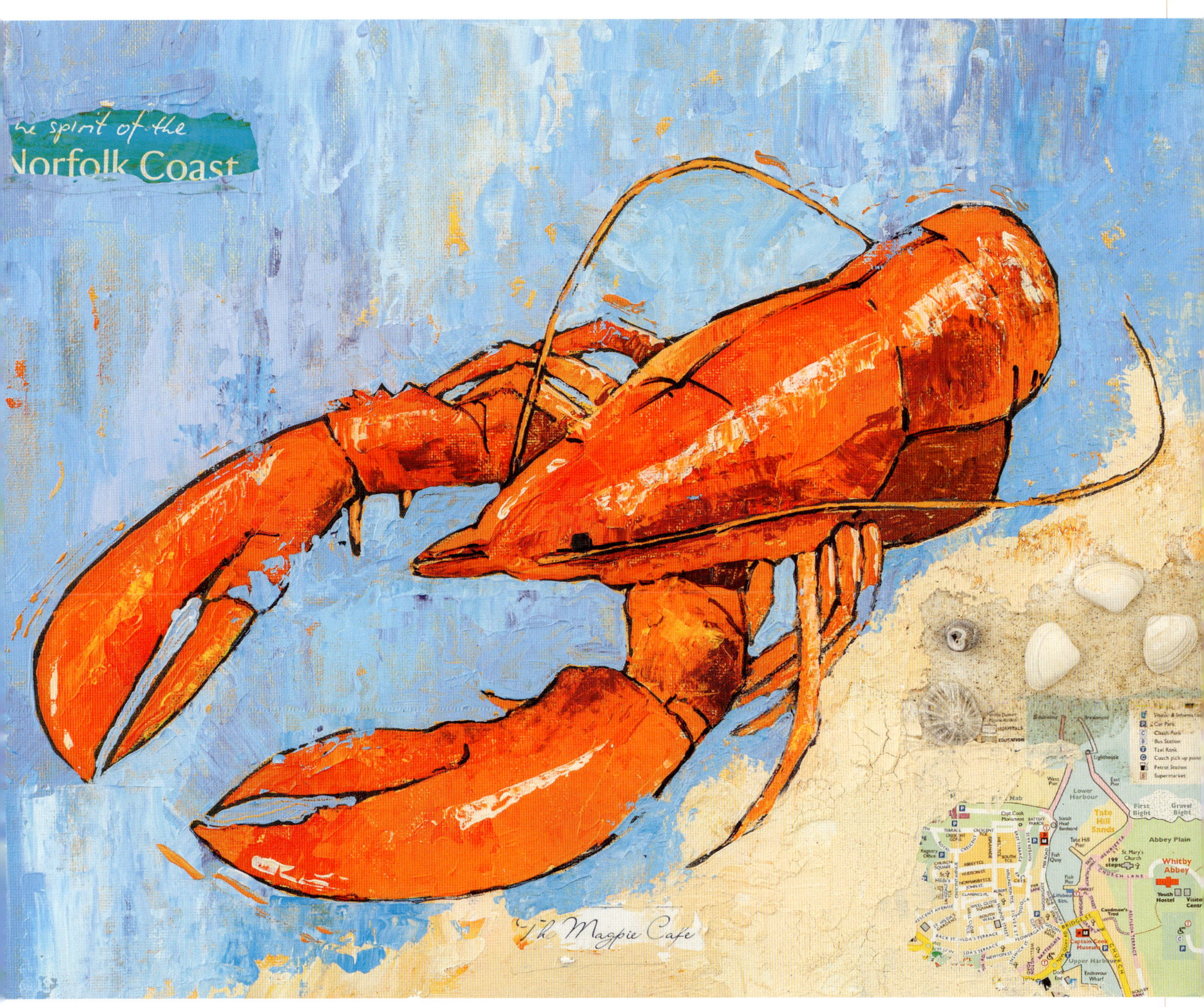

Salty Seaside Lobster

40.5 × 30.5cm (16 × 12in)

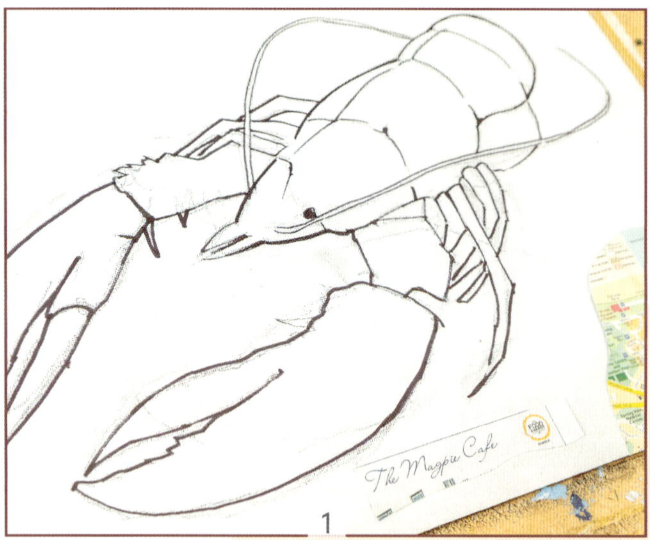
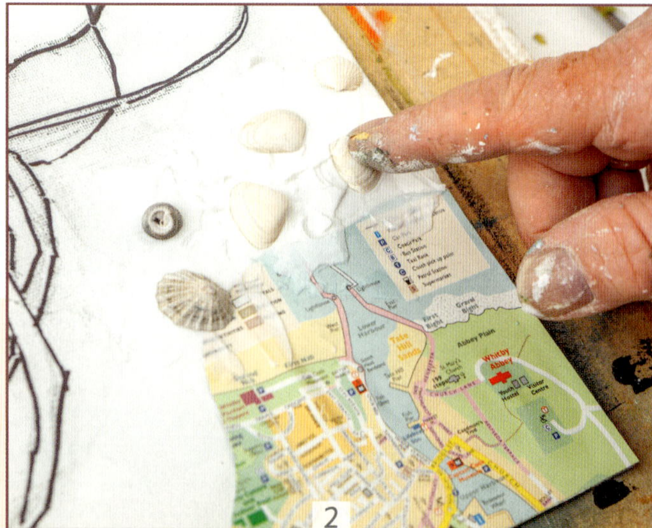
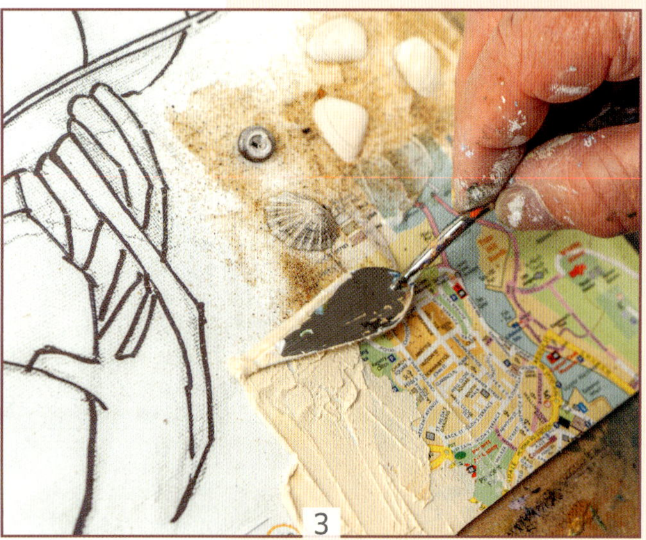
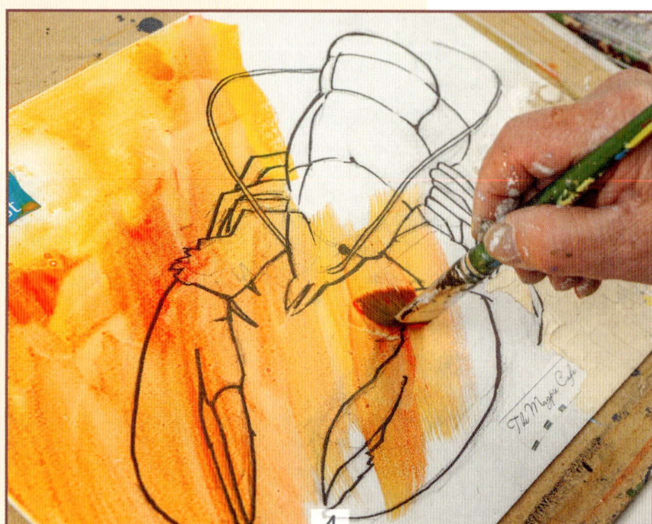

1 Using a Wolff carbon pencil, draw in the lobster design. Any mistakes at this stage can be gently removed by dabbing the surface with a soft putty rubber. Once you are happy with the design, strengthen the edges with the black permanent marker pen. Cut out and apply paper collage around the painting using Mod Podge® as the adhesive.

2 Add found objects next. Use heavy texture gel to glue these to the surface and allow the gel to dry.

3 Make a homogenous mix of yellow ochre and titanium white and add crackle paste to the mix. Sweep this over the lower half of the board with the RGM 6 knife. Allow to dry and let the crackle shapes form.

4 Dilute yellow ochre and cadmium red light hue and wash over any remaining white canvas showing with a 2.5cm (1in) synthetic/nylon brush.

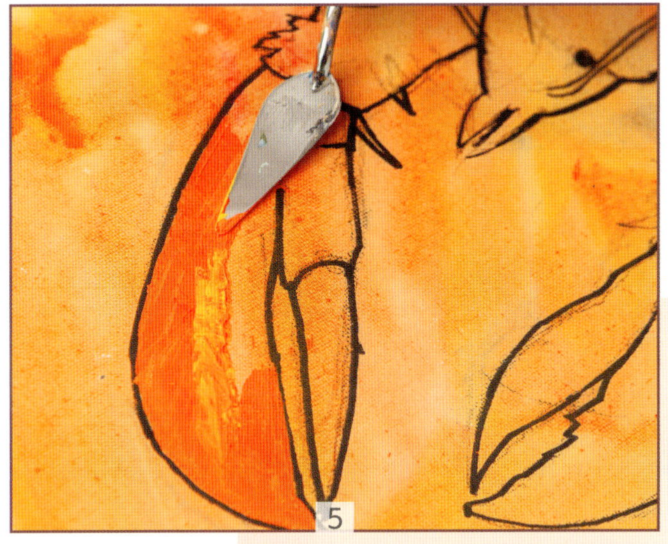

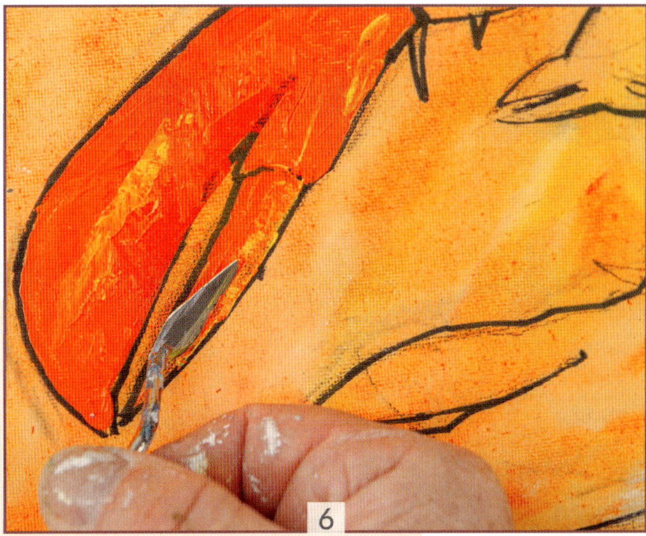

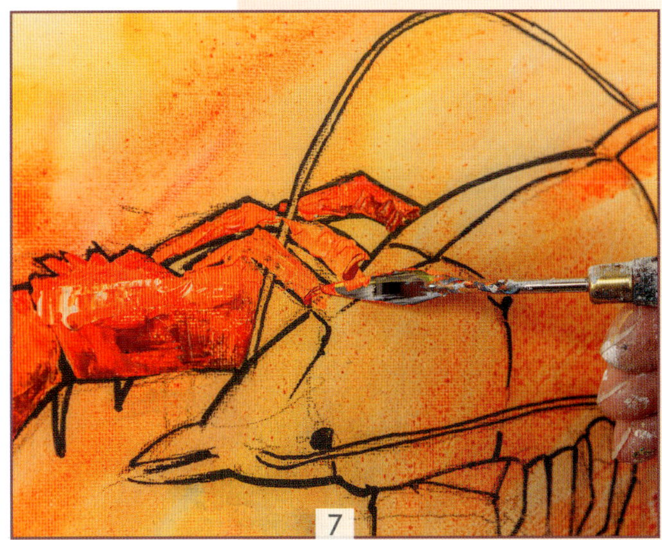

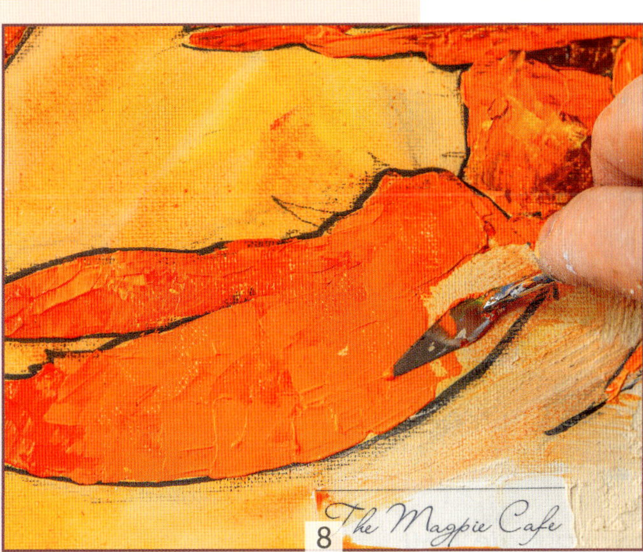

5 The drying time of the wash can be sped up with a hairdryer, after which some of the lobster shapes can be filled in. Starting with one of the large claws, add a mix of cadmium orange and cadmium red light hue using the RGM 6, keeping the knife edge parallel to the outside edge of the claw and working inwards. Add a highlight by mixing titanium white into the orange-red mix.

6 Infill the lower claw; switch to the RGM 41 and use the same colour combination.

7 Darken some shadow areas by mixing in a little burnt umber.

8 Continue to fill the claws; use the knives that feel most comfortable for working in a particular area – in this instance I'm using the RGM 41.

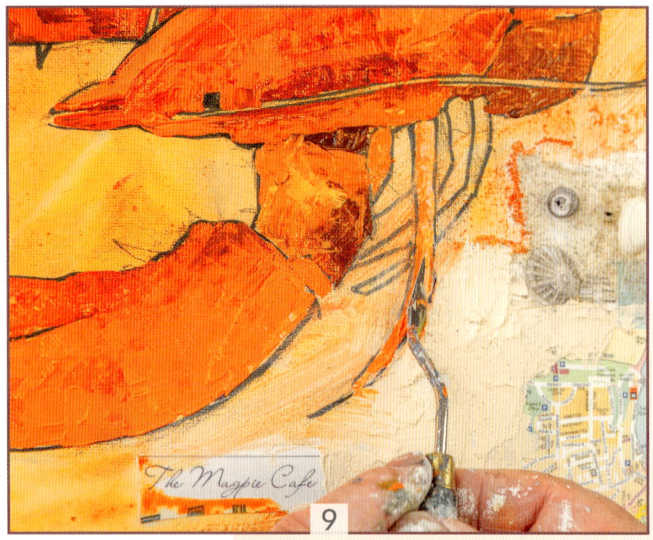

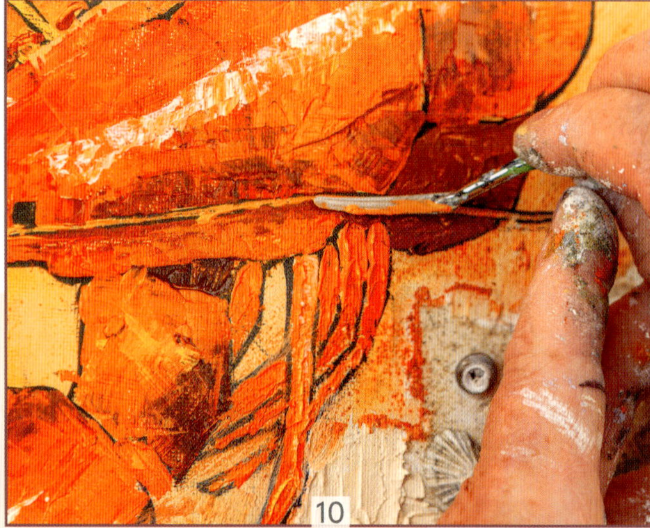

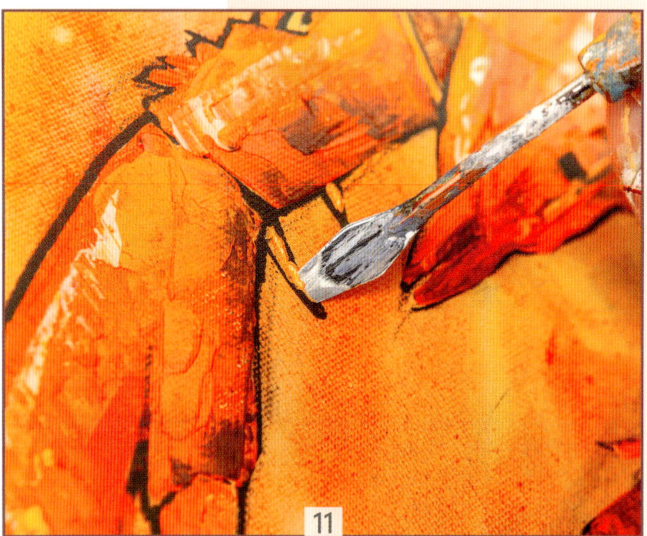

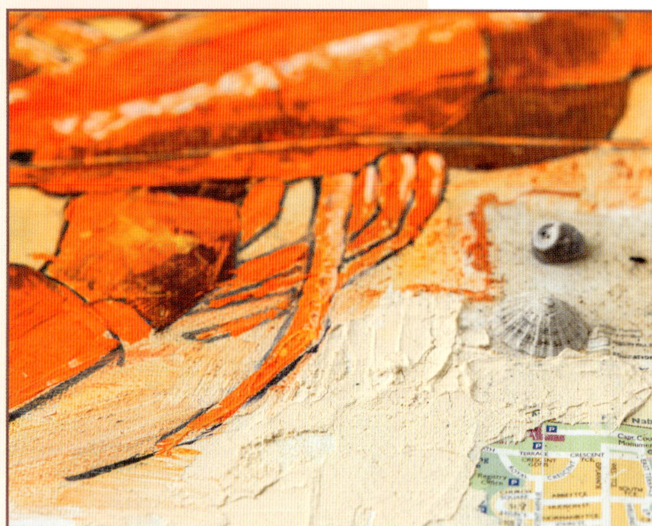

9 Add highlights onto the legs using the side of the same knife and a mix of cadmium orange and titanium white.

10 For the fine antennae, use the RGM Pastrello and add a little pouring medium to aid flow when producing thinner lines.

11 Add the last of the highlights. For the trickier areas, use the tip of the bull nose, then allow to thoroughly dry.

The now-dried crackle paste has taken on the texture of a sandy surface and sits well against the lobster's legs and the collage.

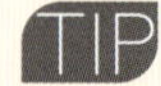

TIP

You will start to develop an instinct for which knife shape is best to use. When infilling broader areas requiring larger marks, the RGM 6 should be perfect. For more detailed areas, the RGM Pastrello or bull nose may become the knife of choice. Keep doing this until you naturally start changing the size and shape of the knife to accommodate the space you need to fill in.

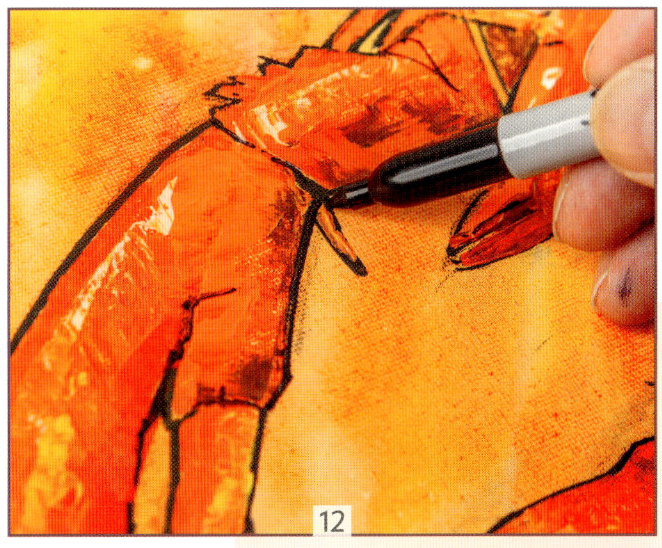

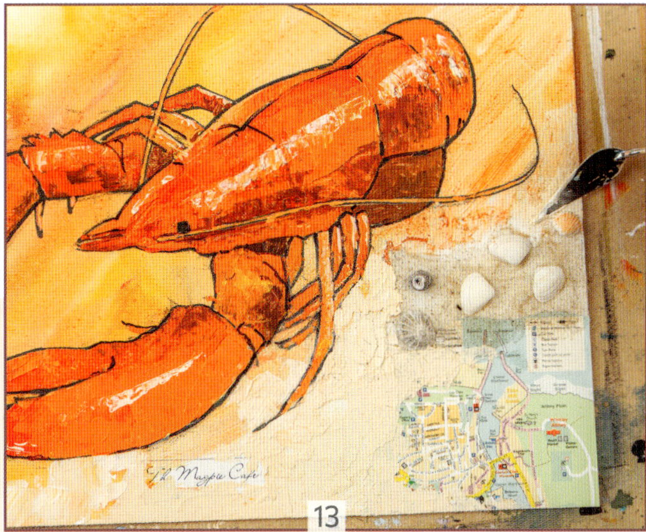

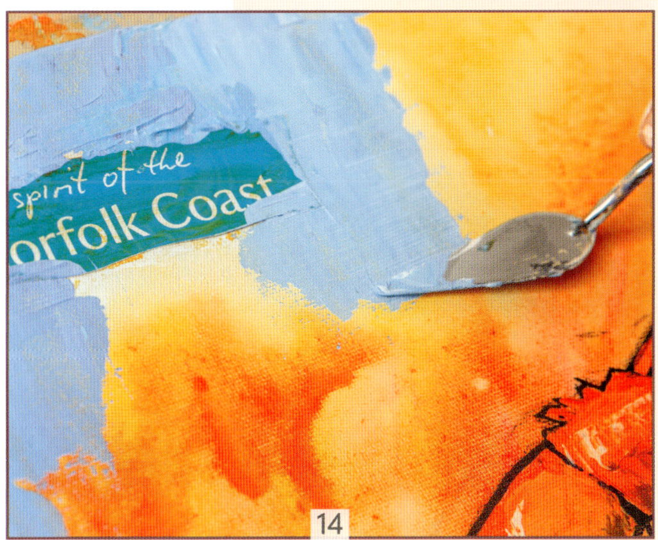

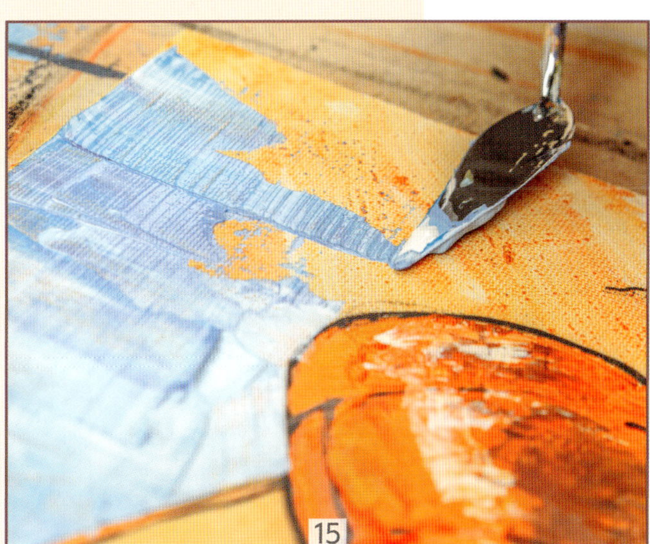

12 Return with the permanent marker and improve the definition of the lost edges in places. This works more successfully if an intermittent line is added, rather than a thick continuous one.

13 Extend the sandy area around the found objects using a uniform mix of titanium white and yellow ochre with the RGM 6 knife.

14 Mix azure blue, purple and white and start to add to the upper-left corner, working down towards the lobster.

15 Work around the outside of the left antennae, touching the edge of the knife onto it, then dragging away until the entire outer curve is complete.

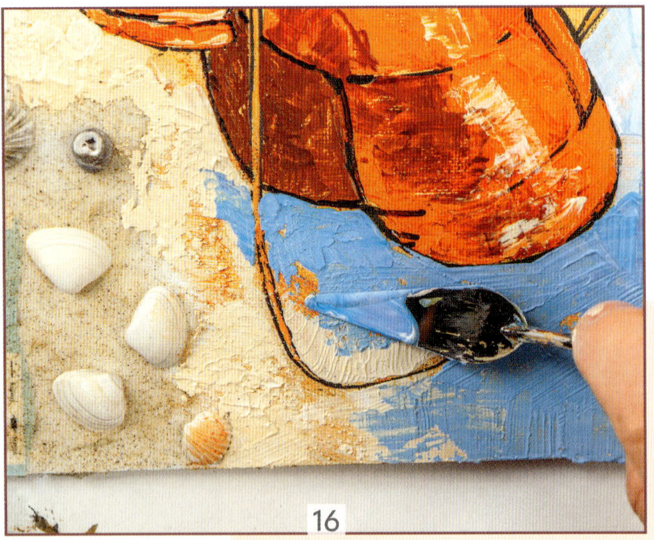

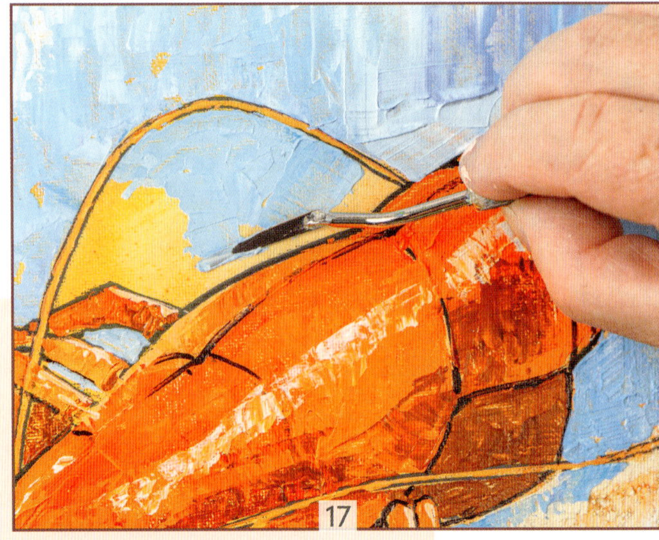

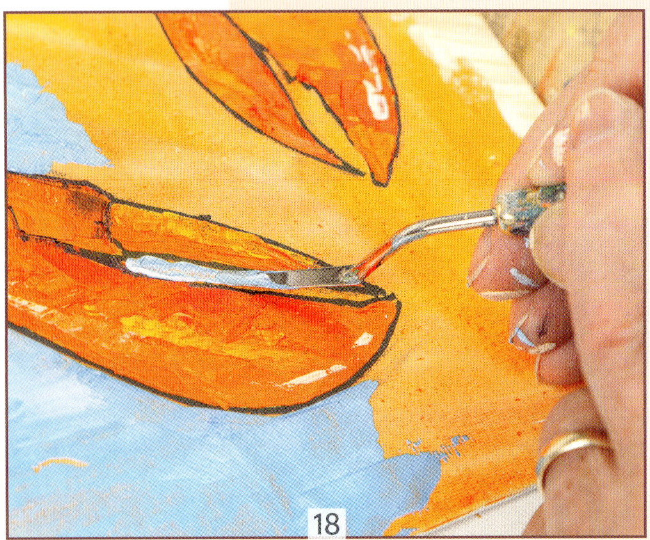

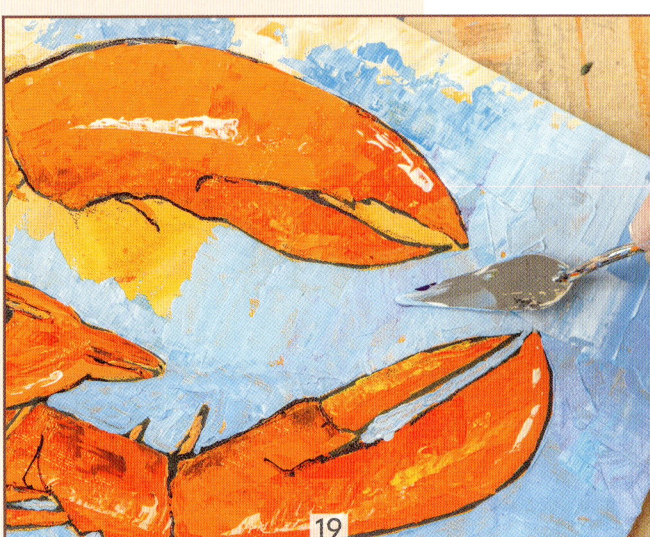

16 Repeat the process around the right antennae breaking up the blue to reveal some of the sandy colour in places.

17 For the internal curve made by the left antennae, switch to the RGM Pastrello to gain more accuracy when applying the paint.

18 For the gaps between the pincers, double-load the RGM Pastrello and apply pale blue into this space.

19 Swap back to the RGM 6 to complete the remaining portion of the upper blue area. Keep turning the board to make the process of cutting around the shape easier.

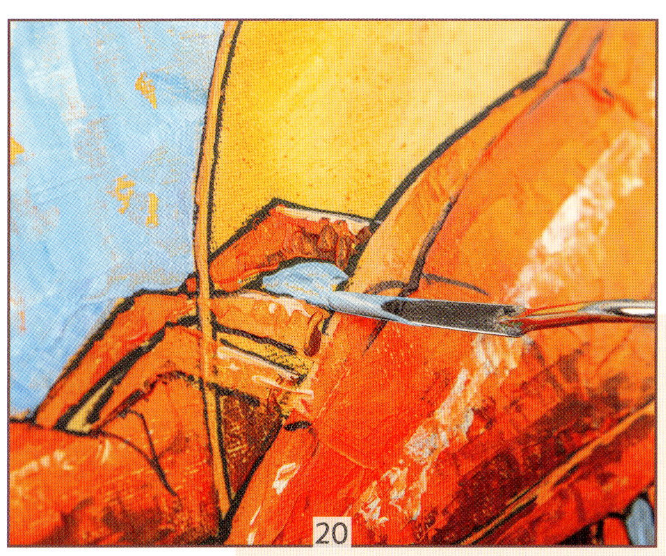

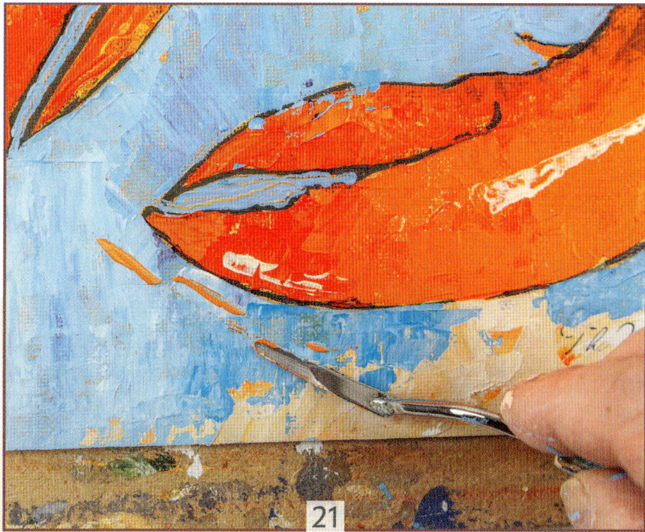

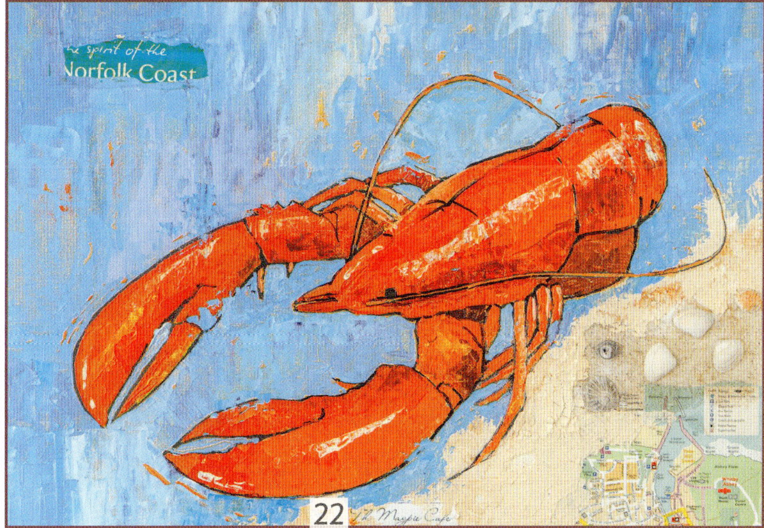

20 Use the RGM Pastrello for the small areas where the legs overlap each other. It may be necessary the revert to the RGM 41 for the really small gaps.

21 Using cadmium orange and the RGM Pastrello, add a few flashes of colour that echo the shape of the lobster around some of the edges.

22 Finally, when the work is dry, work around the painting and recover some of the dark pen lines with the permanent marker pen that have become obscured during the painting process.

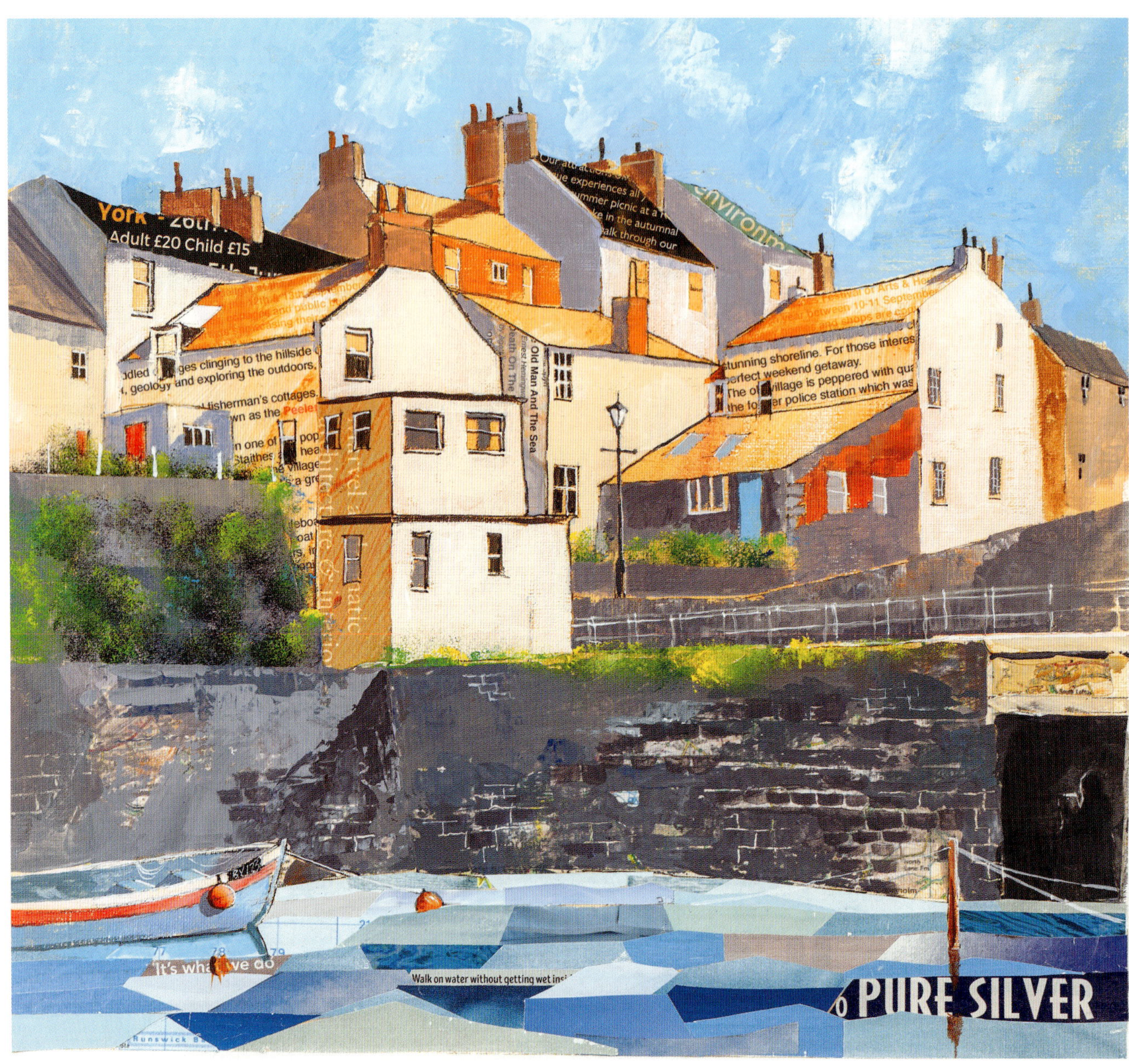

Staithes Splendour

30.5 × 30cm (12 × 11¾in)

This image uses cuttings from holiday brochures of the area depicted. I selected text that fitted in with the old fisherman's cottages. Once the collage was applied, acrylic was added with an RGM 6 knife over the sky and harbour wall.

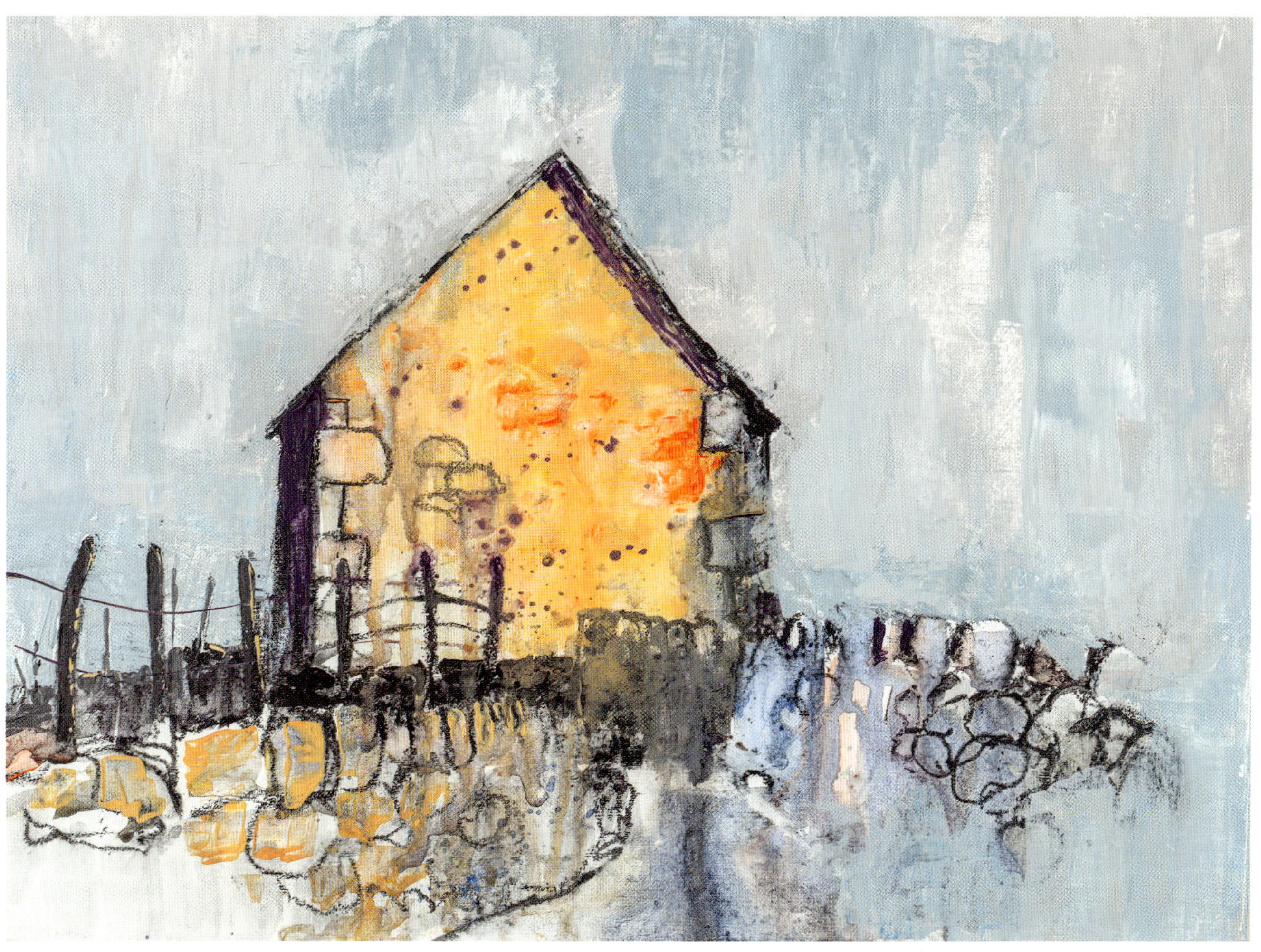

Hartington Barn, Derbyshire, UK

40.5 × 30.3cm (16 × 12in)

This is a mixed-media painting, in which I have used Neocolor II water-soluble pastels to draw in the outline of the barn and the foreground stone wall. Diluted washes of acrylic have been added over the drawing of the building and walls, allowing the pastel to bleed in places. The sky has been added last using downward strokes to break up the edges.

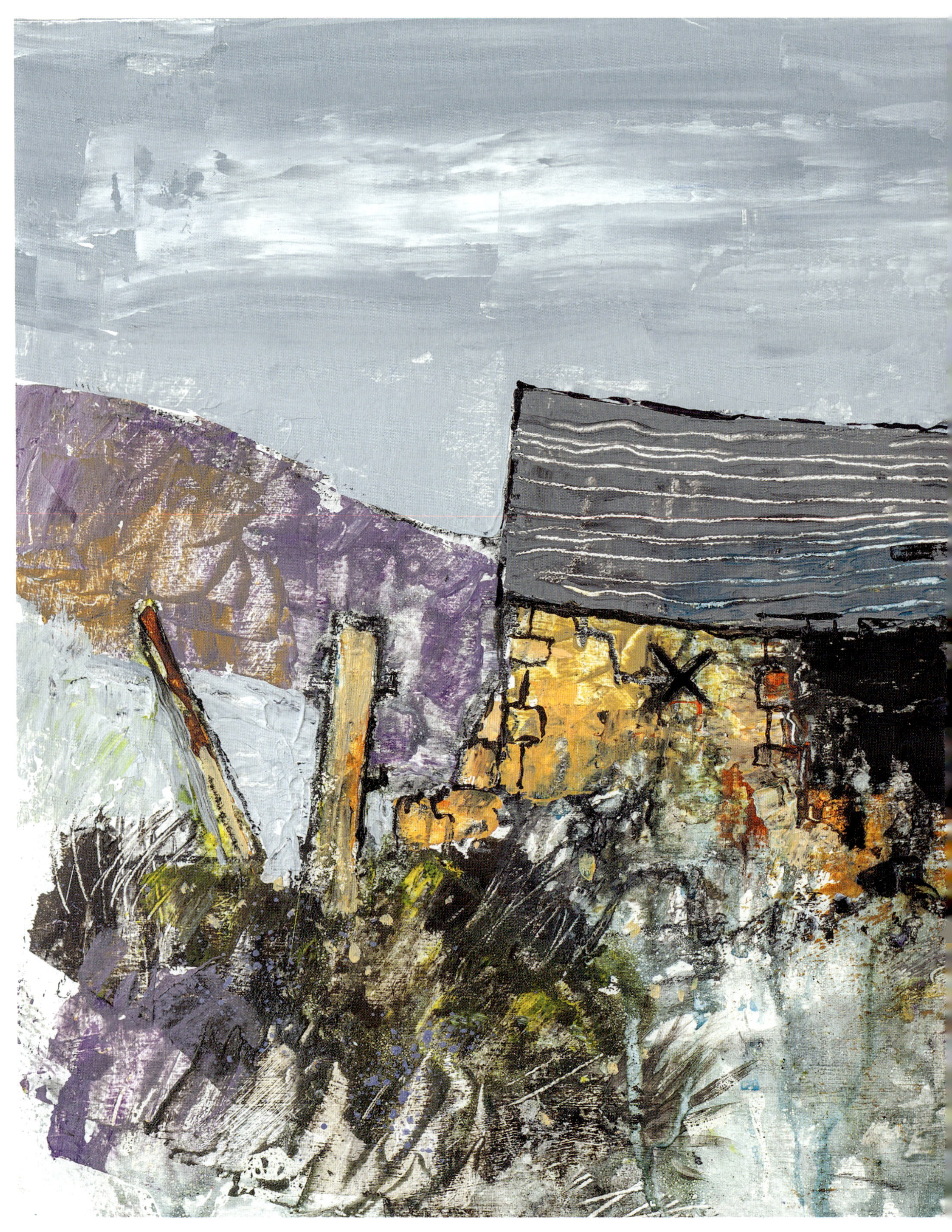

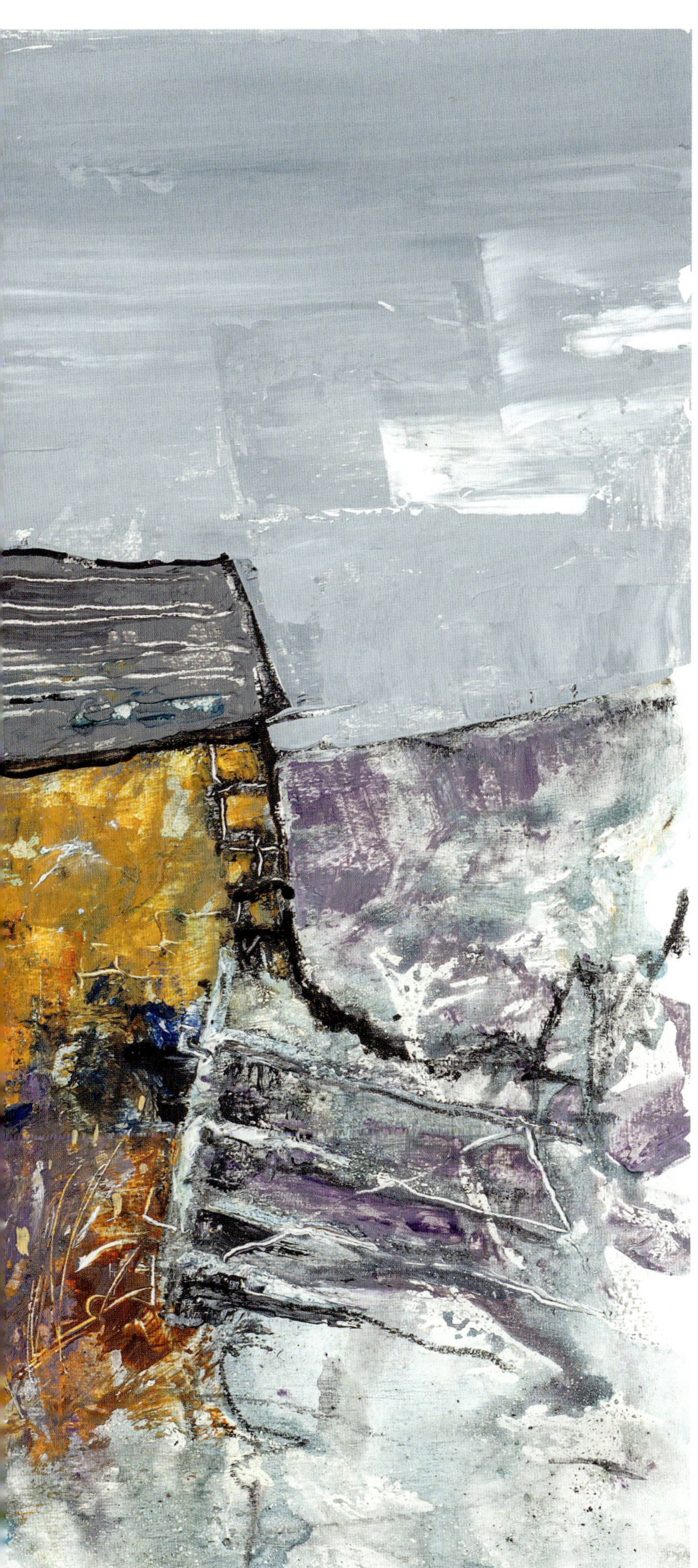

Derelict Barn, Wetton Mill, Derbyshire, UK

40.7 × 30.5cm (16 × 12in)

I used the permanent marker pen quite extensively to describe the forms within this subject. This was followed by heavy applications of acrylic, into which shapes and forms were scratched out. Within the centre foreground I experimented by adding a little linseed oil to very diluted acrylics to add texture. Finally, I added some Neocolor II pastel marks to add further texture to the foreground.

Taking it FURTHER

By now, if you have worked through the projects, your skill level in using knives should have increased considerably. This opens up the opportunity to take things further and experiment with a few other techniques that should help to make you a competent palette knife painter. The next series of projects should hopefully stimulate new ideas and ways of working, such as the advanced technique of working wet-into-wet, as well as using brushes in partnership with the knife in such a way that both styles will merge seamlessly within the finished painting.

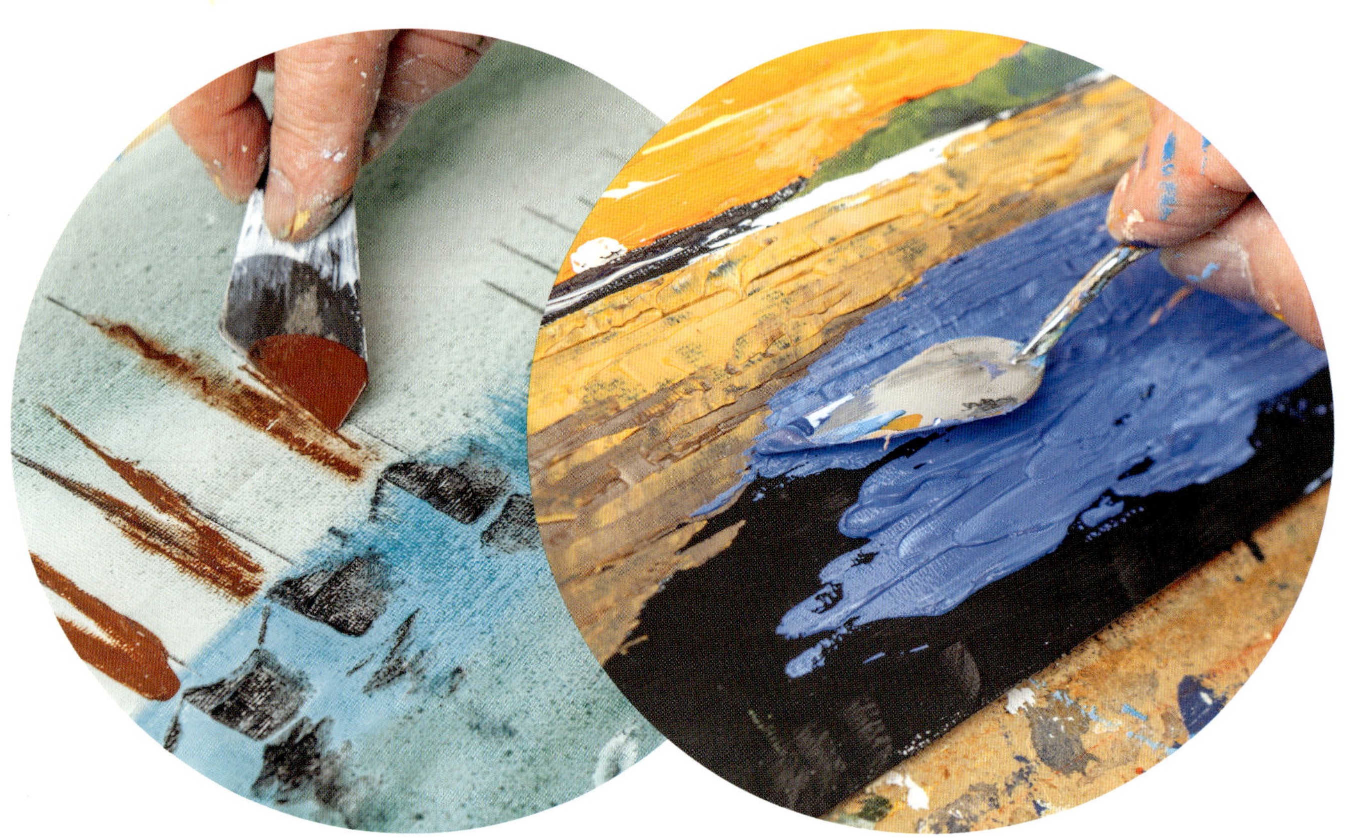

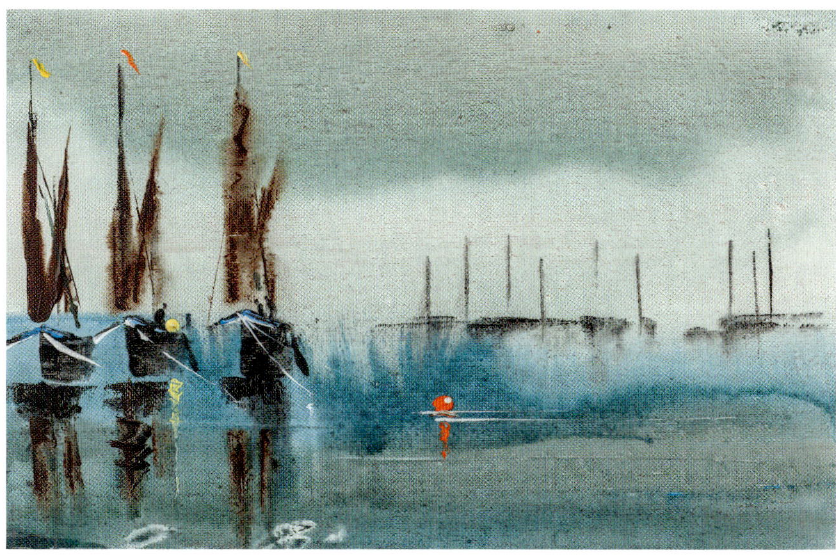

{ Barges on the Blackwater | page 98 }

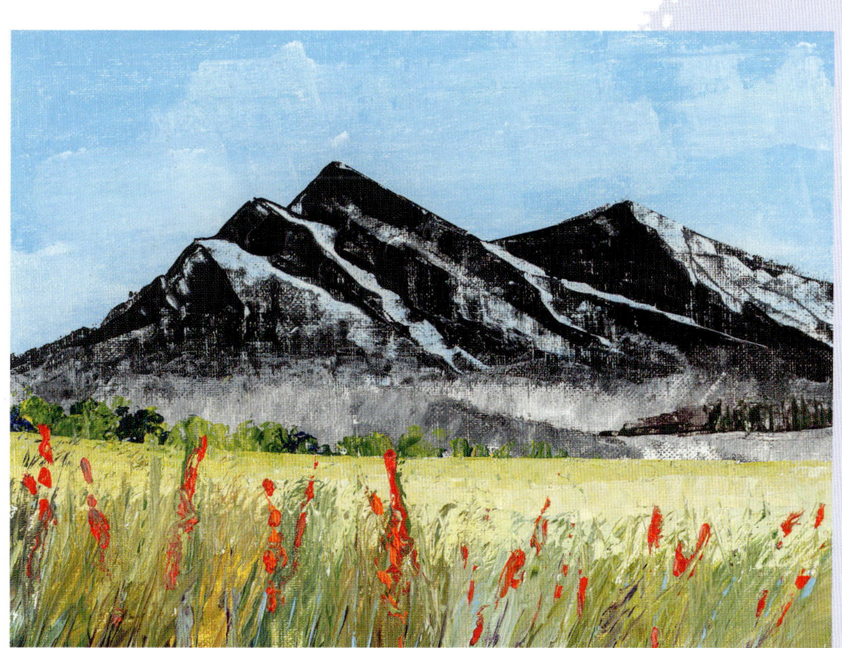

{ Alpine Pinkweeds | page 106 }

{ Bamburgh Sunset | page 114 }

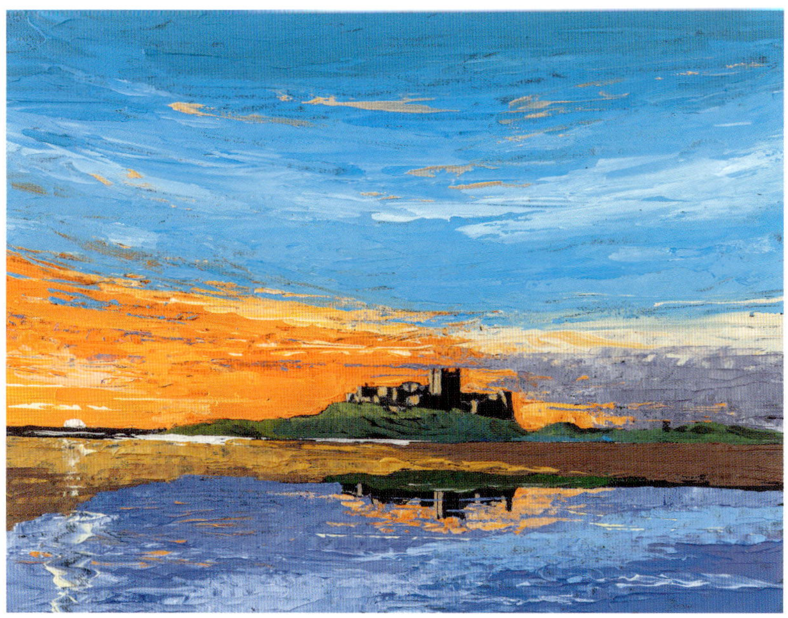

BARGES ON THE BLACKWATER

I am constantly experimenting and thinking of new ways of working. The effect that can be achieved by pulling a loaded knife through a very wet layer of acrylic is quite intriguing and is a way of working that should be explored further.

We push the envelope with this project by creating simple shapes on a wet surface. A limited acrylic palette lends itself particularly well to this approach and the bleed is minimized by the consistency of the paint. Most of the key shapes are produced with just the RGM 109. The broad edge combined with acrylic paint allows hard and soft edges to be produced. The experience of working wet-into-wet is one I would strongly recommend, as the process significantly differs from some of the previous techniques used.

▶ ## You will need

SURFACE:
Plain white primed canvas board, 30.5 × 20cm (12 × 7¾in).

KNIVES:
RGM 109 and 41.

PAINTS:
Burnt umber, azure blue, Mars black, cadmium red light hue, primary yellow, titanium white and cadmium orange (Golden).

OTHER TOOLS AND MATERIALS:
2.5cm (1in) flat brush and pouring medium.

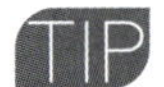

Don't be afraid to use lots of water when applying paint in the early stages.

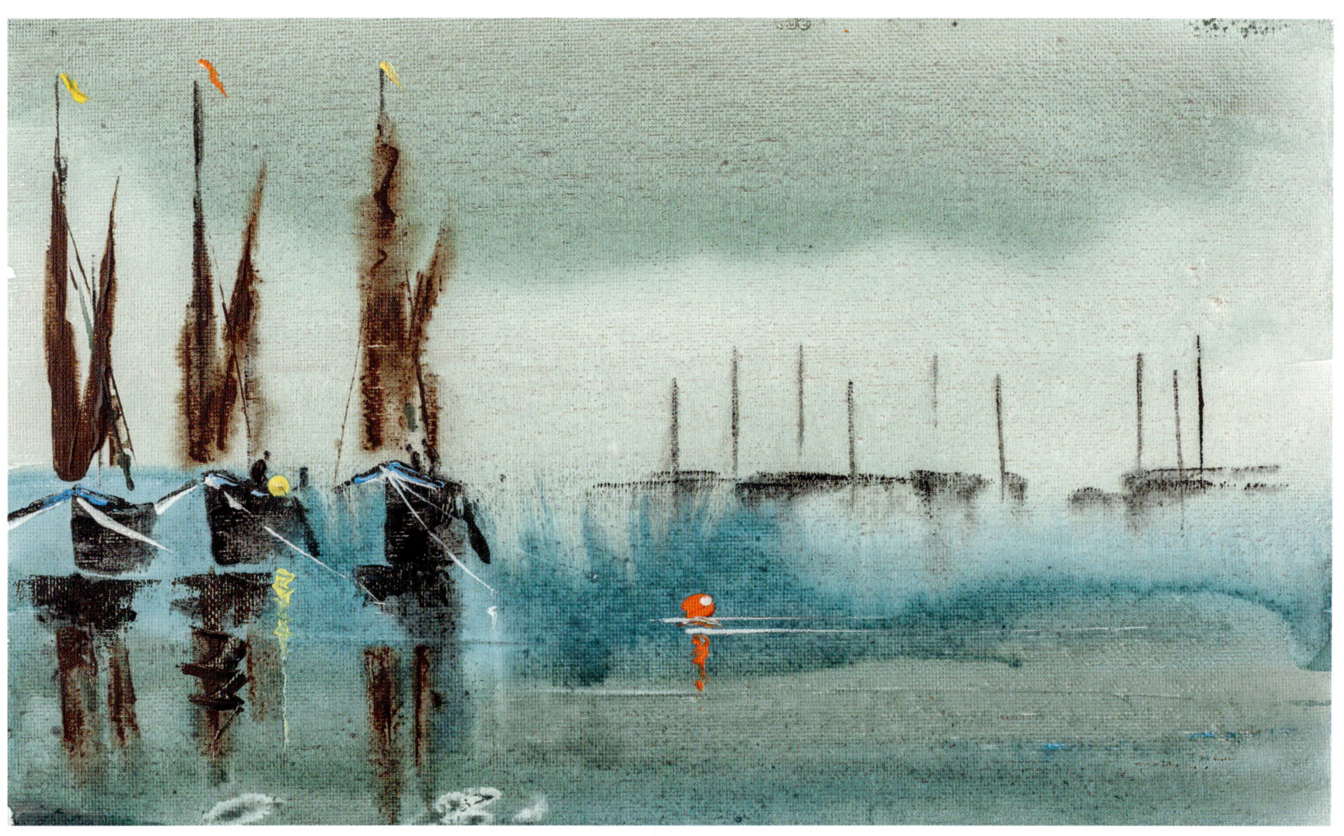

Barges on the Blackwater

30.5 × 20cm (12 × 7¾in)

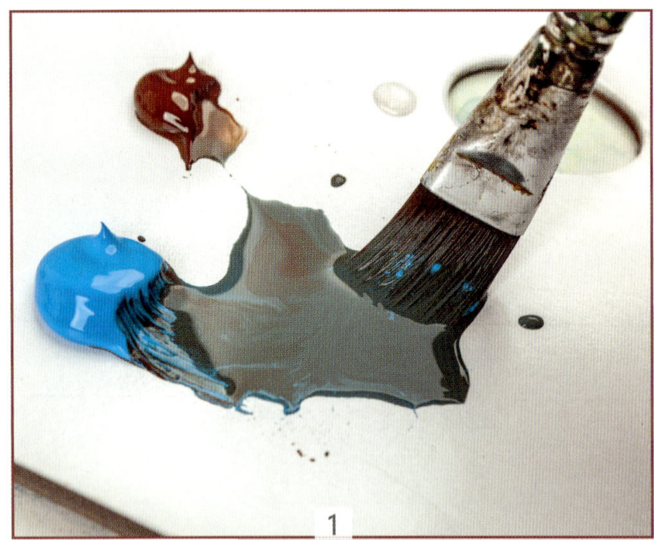

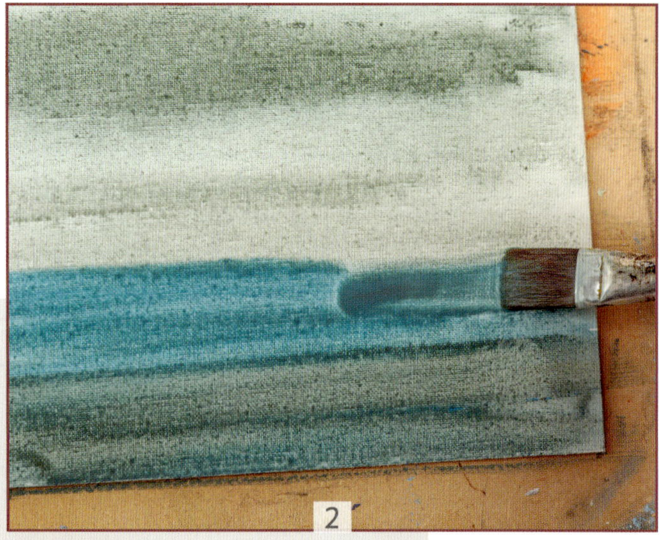

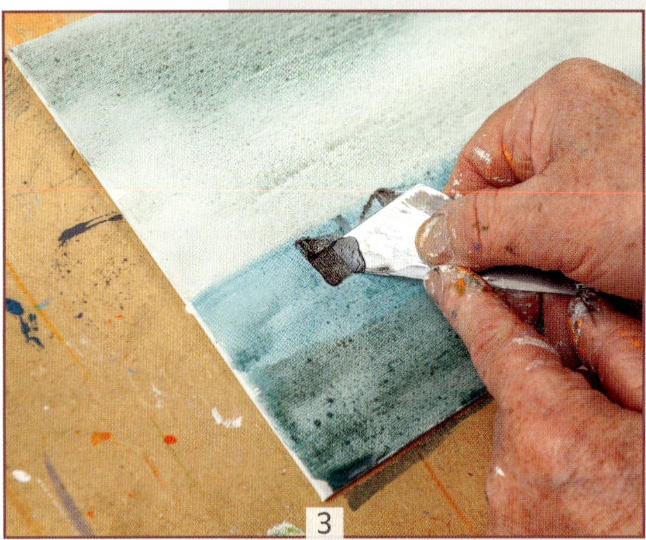

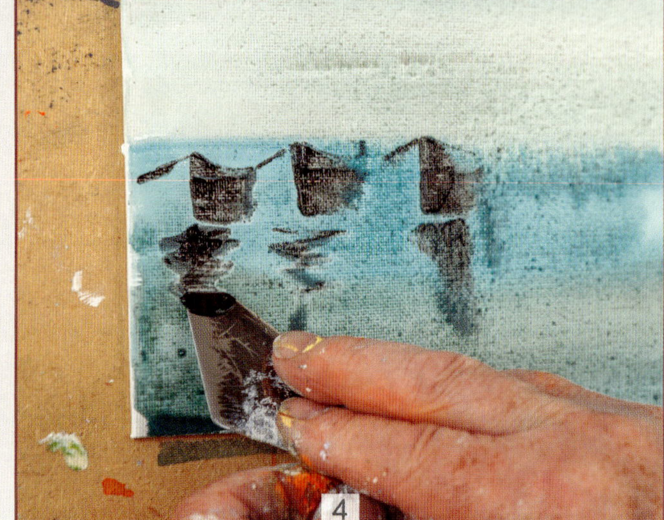

1 Using a 2.5cm (1in) flat brush, mix burnt umber and azure blue with plenty of water and apply to the upper regions of the board for the sky.

2 Add more azure blue for the water and apply this using horizontal strokes across the board. A hazy line should appear where land meets the sky.

3 Create the hull shapes on the left by adding a roll of black from the narrow edge of the RGM 109 into the wet wash.

4 Use the same edge of the blade and slightly less black to create the reflections in the water.

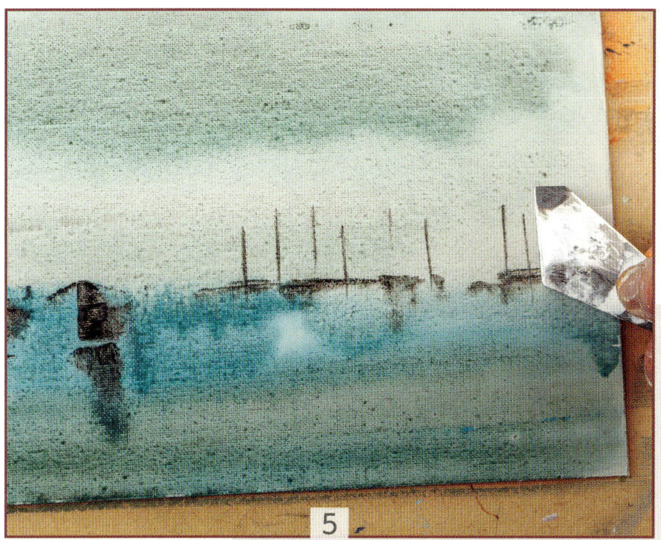

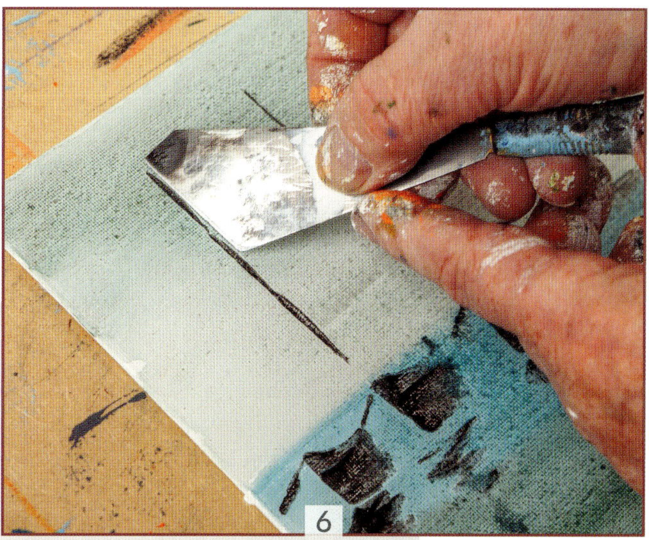

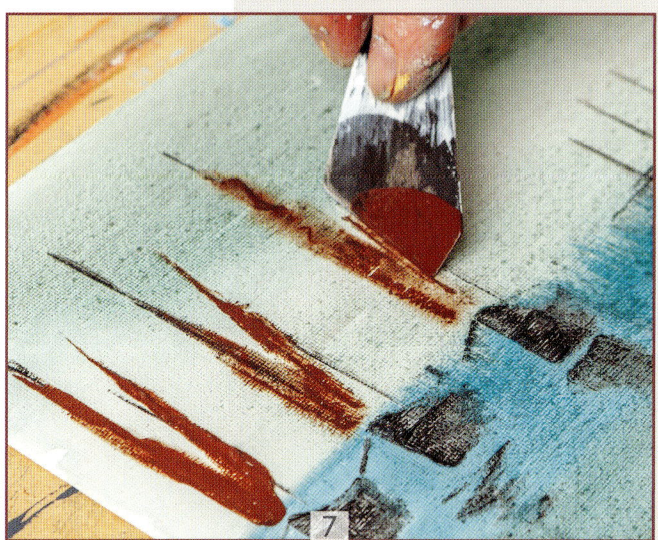

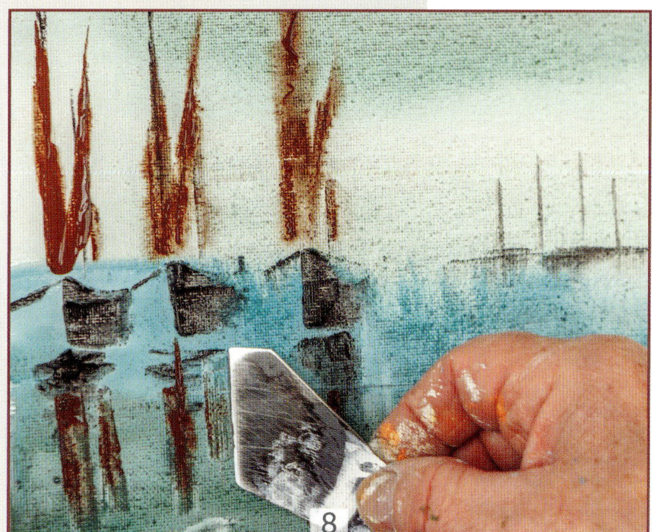

5 The distant boats are added next using the same colour. Add some horizontal marks to suggest moored boats, then add a fine vertical mark for the masts.

6 Add more fine vertical masts for the moored boats on the left.

7 With a mix of burnt umber and cadmium red light hue, add the furled sails onto the foreground boats.

8 With the remaining paint on the knife, add the reflections. Allow the knife to run out of paint for each mark creating a scumble. The length of the reflection should be long enough to run off the base of the painting.

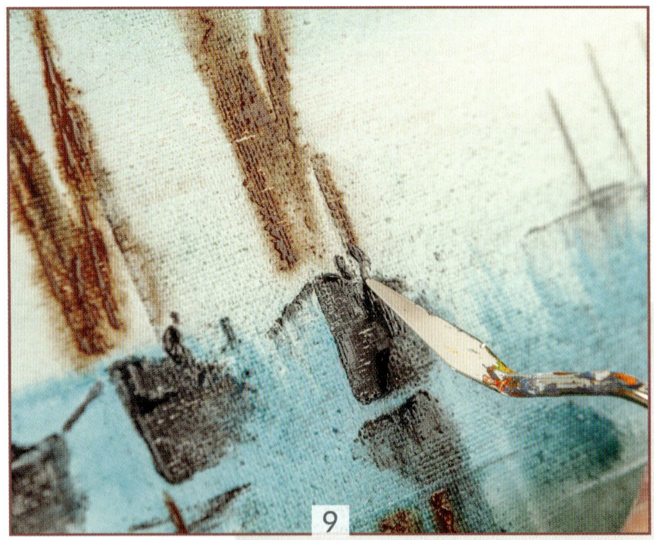

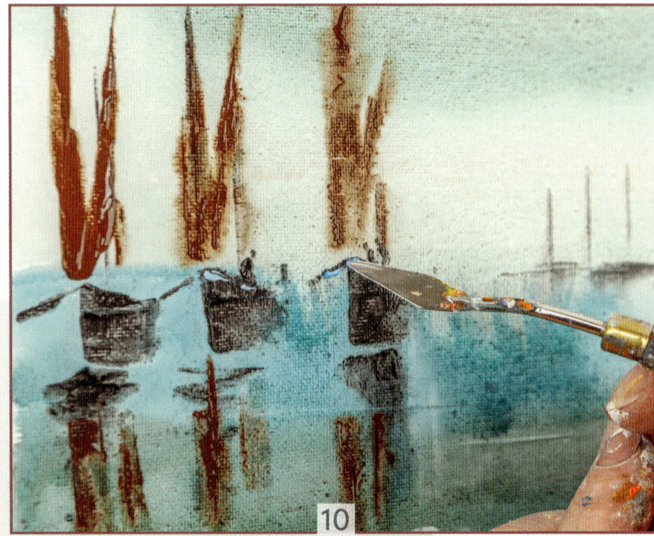

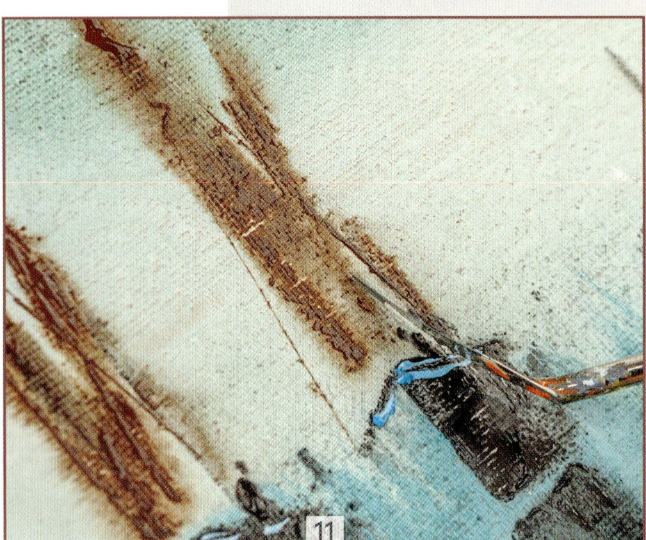

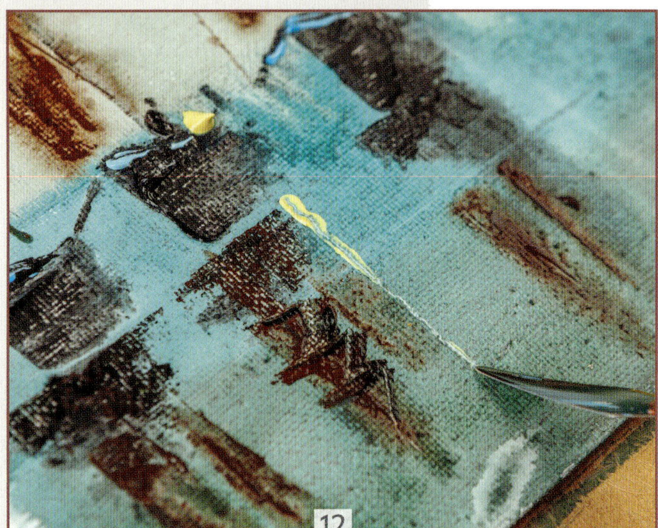

9 Using the tip of the RGM 41, add figures with the mix of azure blue and black. Start with a button for the head, then make a slightly larger mark for the shoulders.

10 Use azure blue to paint the stripe along the upper part of the ship's hull on the left (this is a cove stripe).

11 To suggest rigging, add fine straight marks through the furled sails.

12 Using primary yellow, add a button of light to the second boat, then add an elongated reflection into the water with a vertical fine stroke.

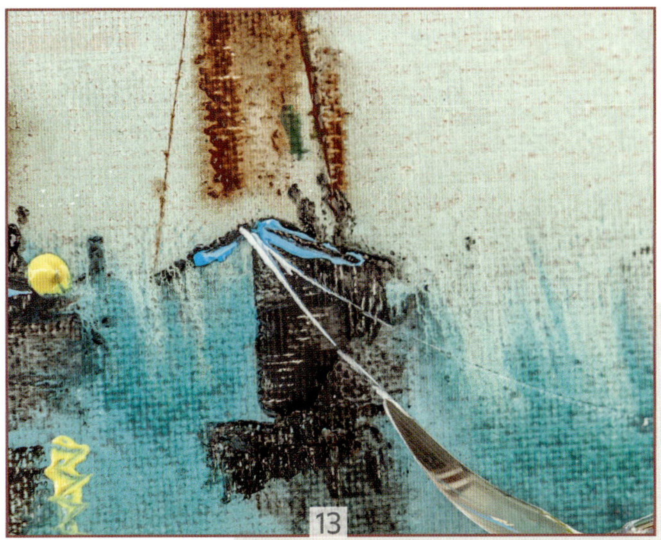

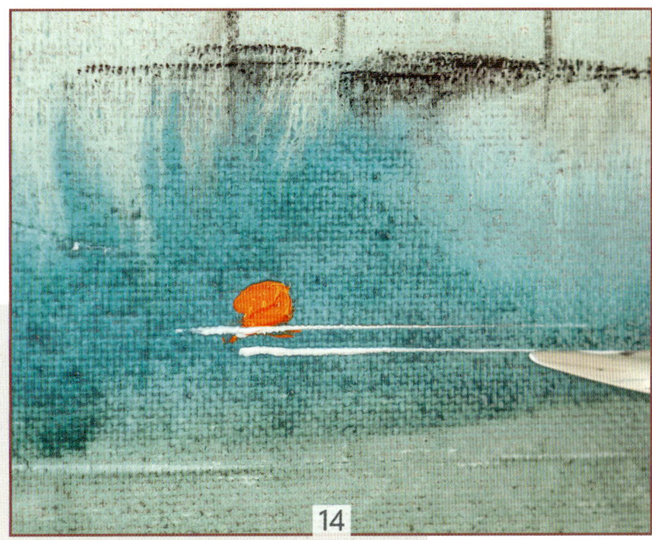

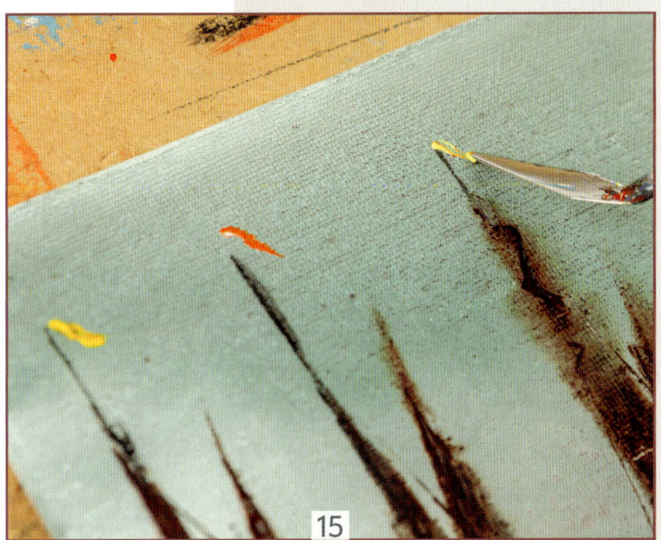

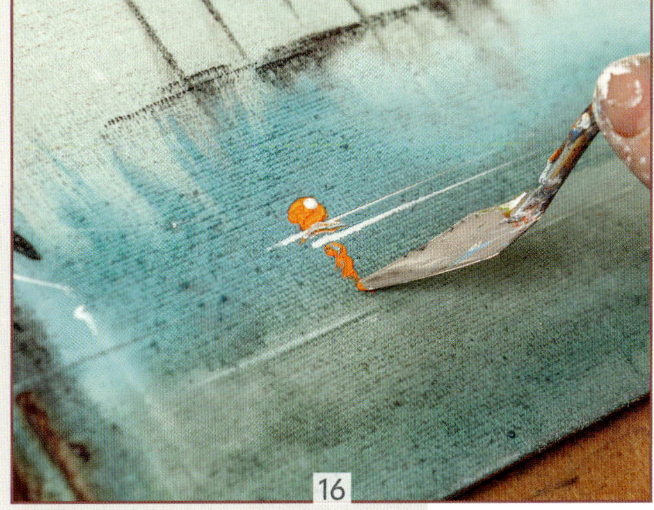

13 Prepare a mix of titanium white and pouring medium. Using a clean RGM 41, add the mooring ropes in front of the boats.

14 Add two fine parallel lines onto the surface of the water below and to the right of the moored boats. On top of the first line, add a button of cadmium orange to represent a buoy.

15 Introduce the individual colours of flags to the top of the masts using primary yellow and cadmium red light hue, mixed with a little pouring medium. Drag the shape of the flag from a small blob of paint applied to the top of each mast.

16 Finally, add a tiny button highlight of white to the buoy, then drag more orange down below for its reflection.

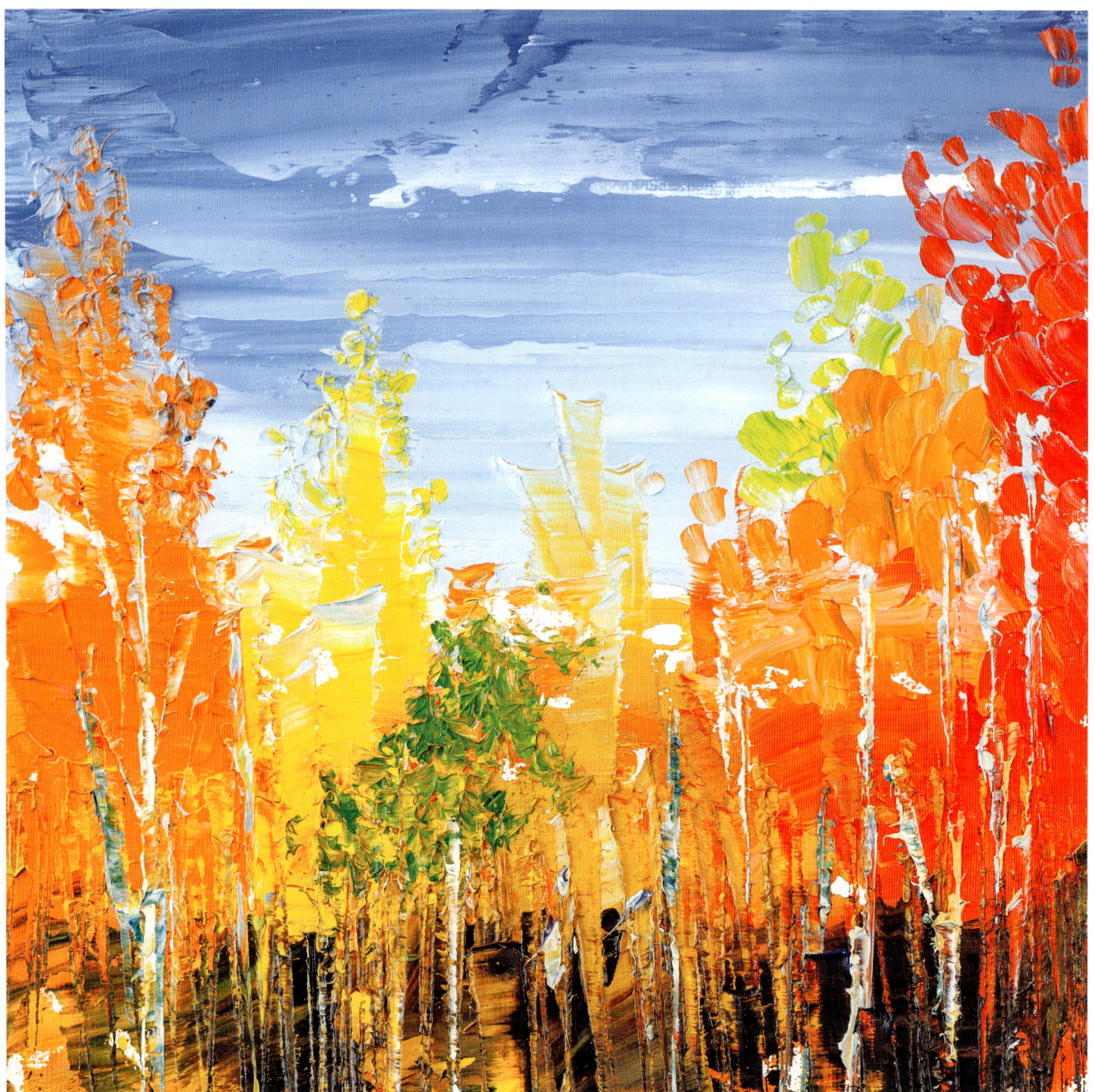

Autumn Glory

17.5 × 17.5cm (7 × 7in)

Although not strictly wet-into-wet, I used gloss glazing liquid to keep the colours
workable for longer and to remain, as far as possible, pure colours. Using a set of
nozzles screwed onto the acrylic pouch, I squirted colour into the rough forms of
the autumn trees, added glazing liquid on top, and then blended the painting into
the tree forms using the RGM Pastrello and small round knife.

Wet Evening in the City

29.5 × 20.5cm (11½ × 8⅛in)

This early nocturne is mostly Mars black and titanium white and was probably the trigger that inspired me to try wet-into-wet painting. I wanted to create a soft amorphous effect using knives and found, after some experimentation, that wet-into-wet was the way to go.

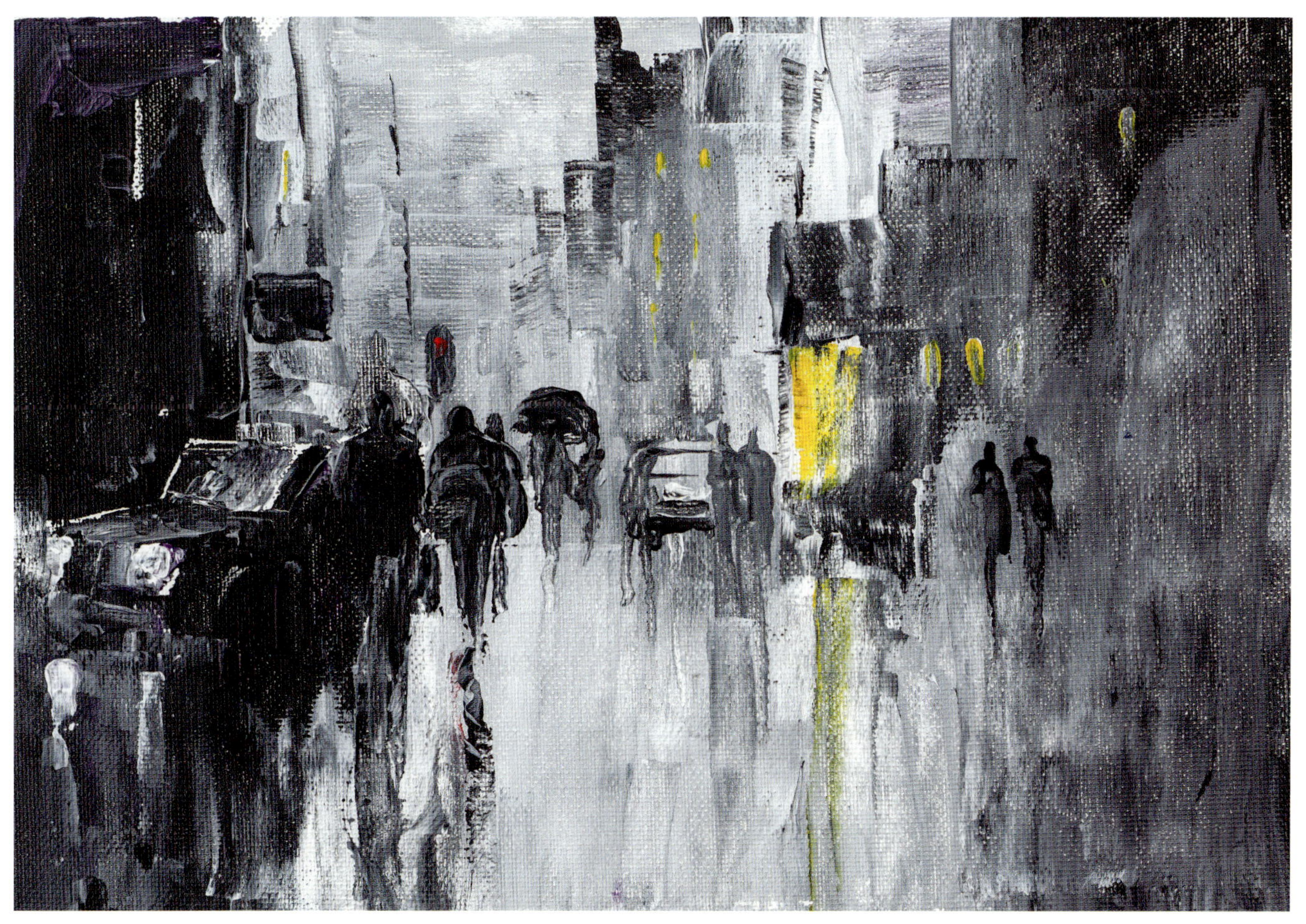

ALPINE PINKWEEDS

At this stage in the book, you have already accrued a lot of useful, fun techniques – now's your chance to revisit some more of the techniques carried out earlier.

I have chosen to paint a set of majestic mountains from my imagination and will introduce you to the technique of forming peaks and fissures in rocks, as well as using masking techniques to form a horizon. This is something I do frequently when producing a landscape painting. To add interest to the painting, I've added some Persicaria or pinkweeds for a colourful foreground.

▶ ## You will need

SURFACE:

Plain white primed canvas board, 30.5 × 24cm (12 × 9½in).

KNIVES:

RGM 109, small round, RGM 6 and Pastrello 38.

PAINTS:

Titanium white, azure blue, Mars black, ultramarine blue, burnt umber, primary yellow, sap green, yellow ochre, purple and cadmium orange.

OTHER TOOLS AND MATERIALS:

2.5cm (1in) masking tape and marble dust.

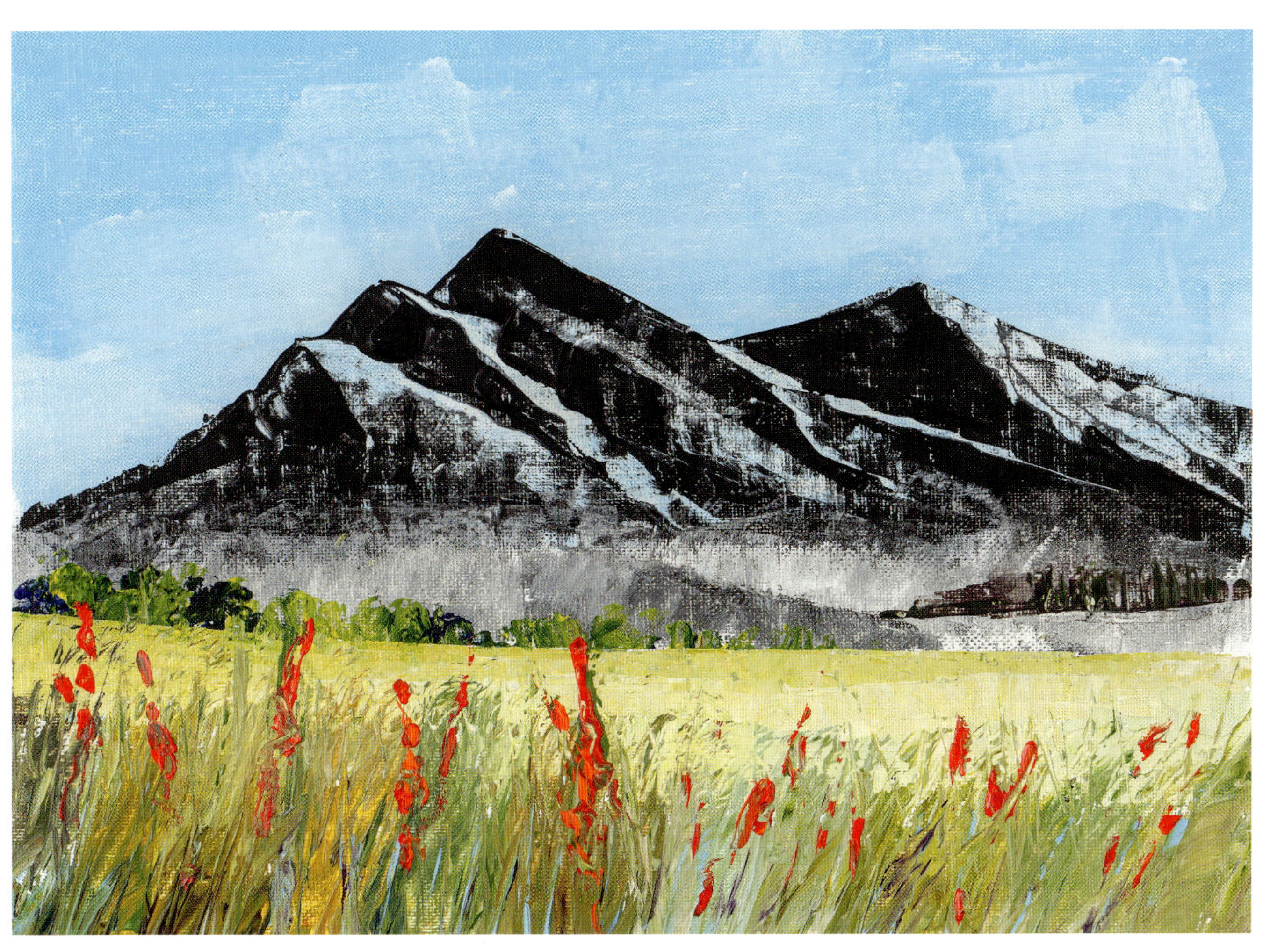

Alpine Pinkweeds
30.5 × 24cm (12 × 9½in)

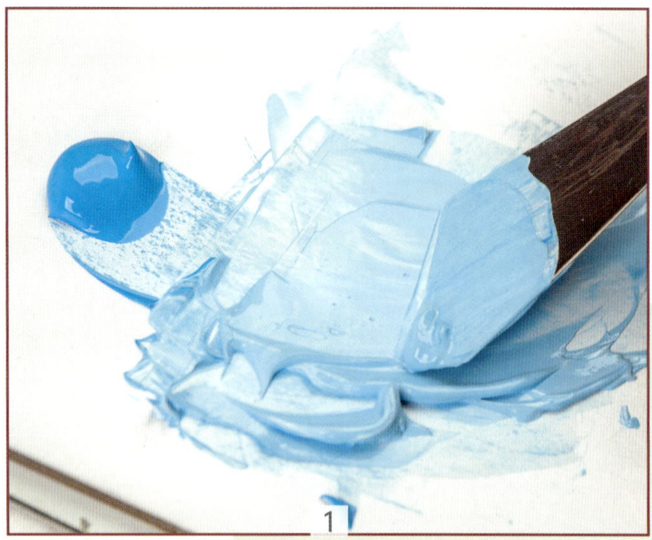

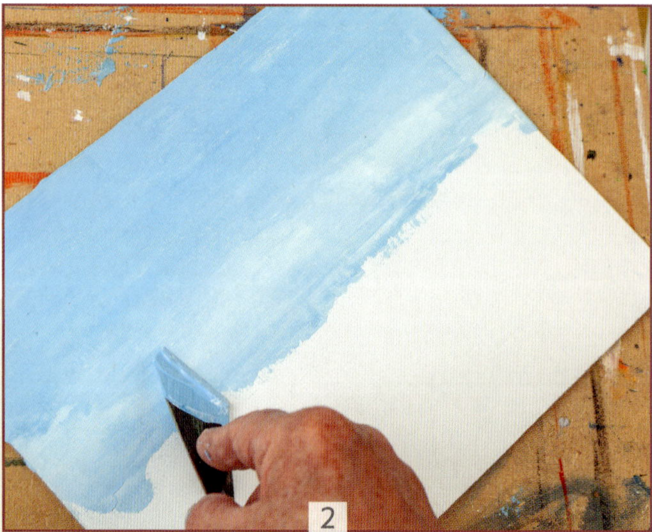

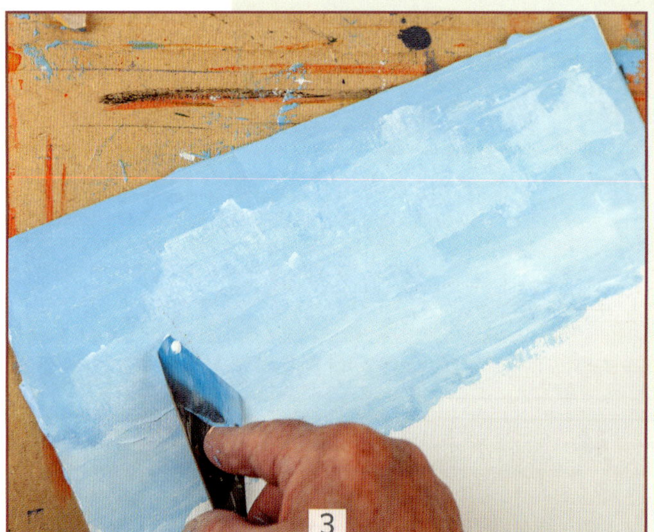

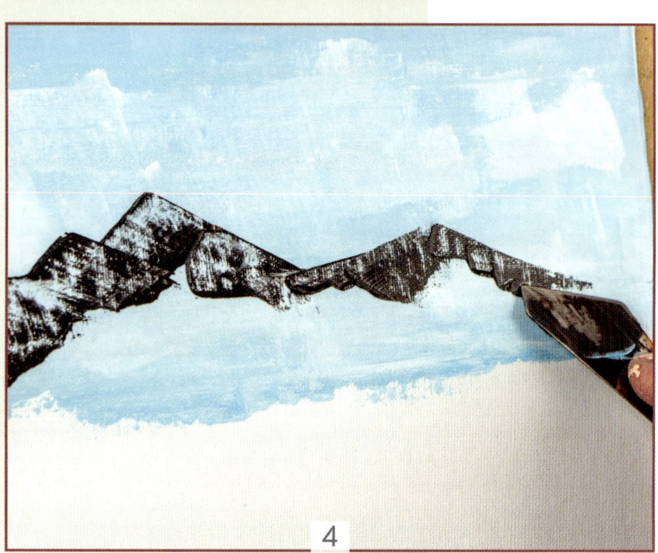

1   Make a homogenous mix of azure blue and white.

2   Piggyback the strokes going from one side of the canvas board to the other. Add a little pressure when applying the paint to keep the surface flat and smooth ready for adding the mountains. Proceed down the board and gradually add more white to the mix so that the sky becomes lighter nearer the horizon.

3   Suggest clouds by scumbling over a little white paint onto the wet surface. Remove any ridges of thick paint near the horizon and allow to dry.

4   Mix ultramarine blue, burnt umber and Mars black. Using the RGM 109, add a roll of paint to the wide part of the blade and start to form the ridge of the mountains, pulling the paint downwards. Use the narrow edge of the blade to scrape out any light areas (*sgraffito*) revealing the previously painted sky below.

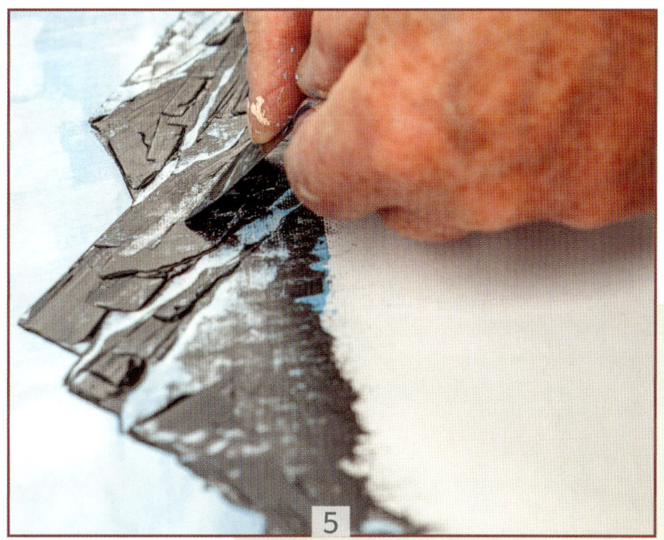

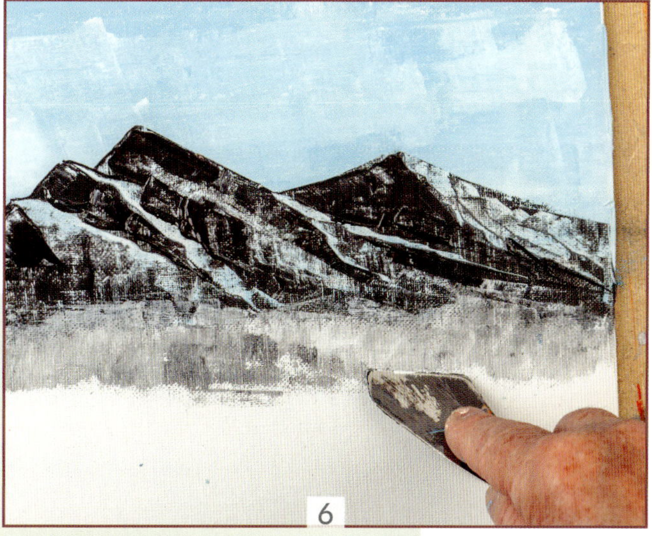

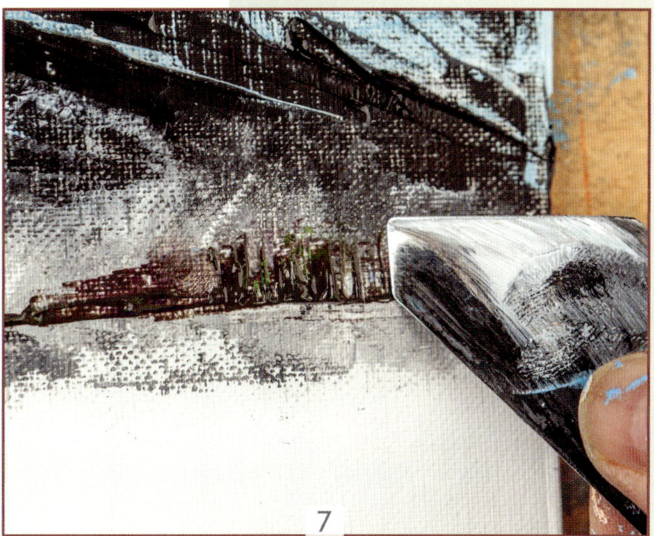

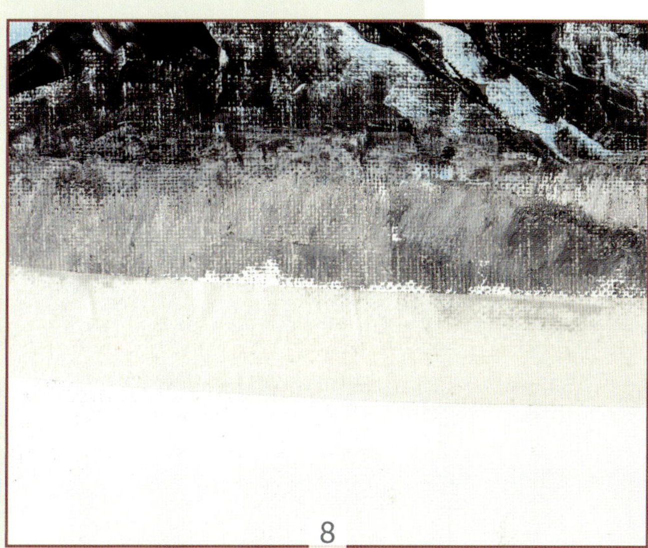

5   Add more paint to build up the shape of the mountains, then sculpt the mountain shapes by scraping out some areas of the wet paint.

6   Using a clean knife, drag the base of the mountain downwards to create a soft, misty effect.

7   Add some distant trees using a striated mix of purple and sap green.

8   Using masking tape, add a slightly curved horizon at the base of the mountains.

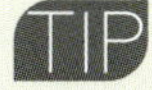
TIP

Don't apply tape onto wet paint.

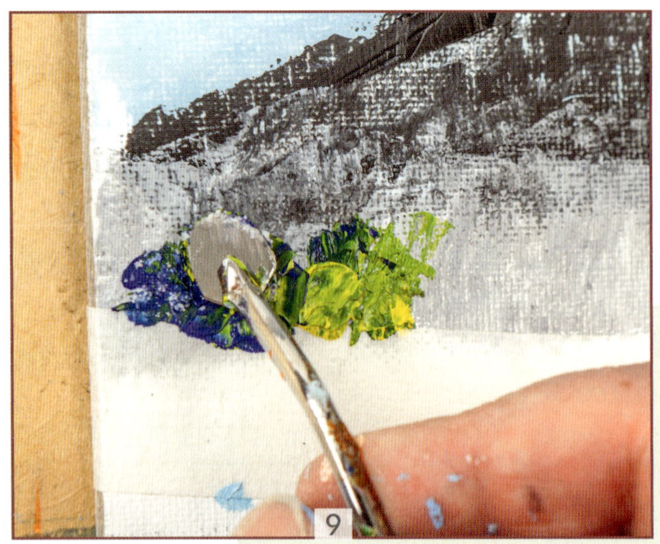

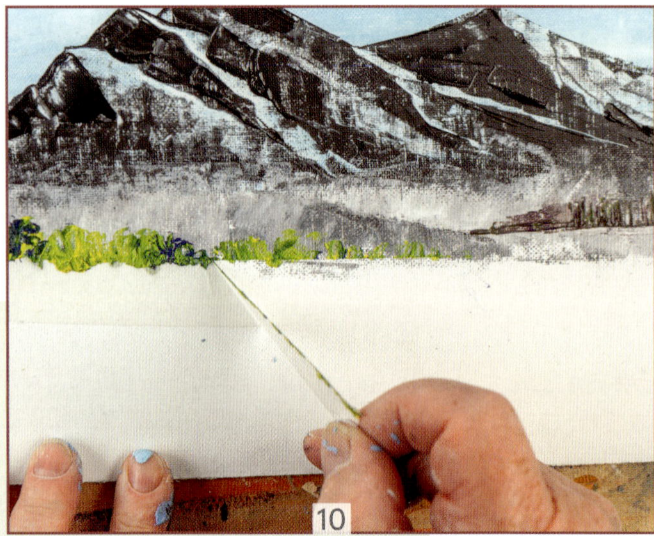

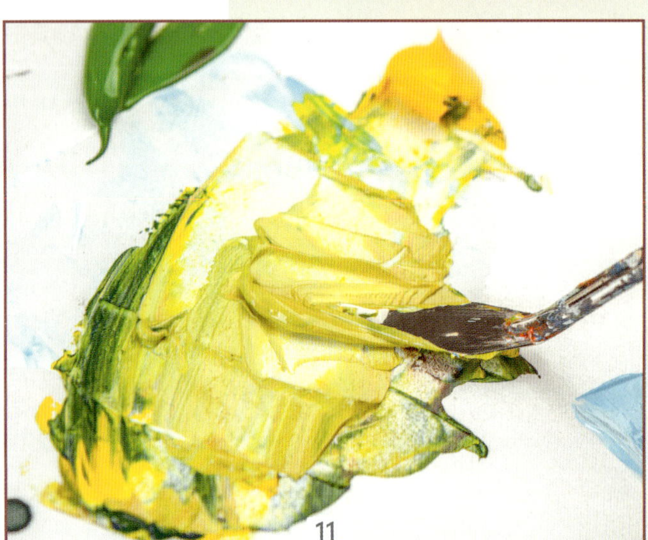

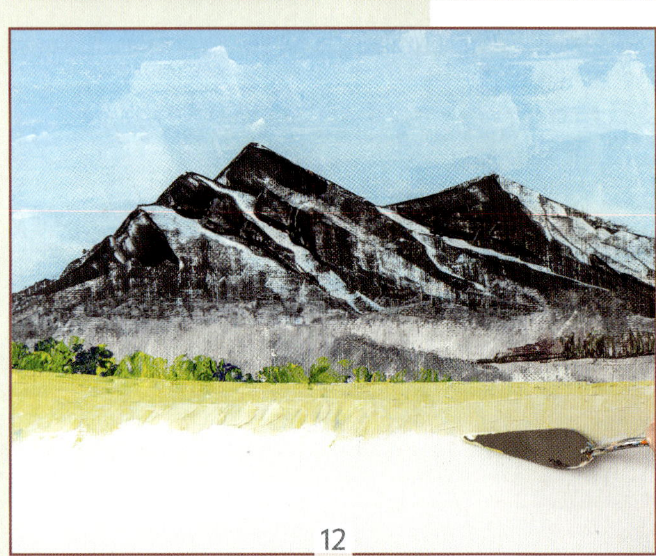

9   Mix a green using primary yellow and ultramarine blue. Using the small round, pick up some paint and then dab onto the marble dust. Place the knife just above the masking tape and, using a circular motion, start to create the tree shapes. Allow some of these marks to overlap the tape.

10   Peel off the tape to reveal a crisp horizon below the tree line.

11   Change to the RGM 6 and mix the colour for the meadow using titanium white, primary yellow, sap green and yellow ochre.

12   Using the edge created by the masking tape carefully paint along the line using the edge of the knife, dragging the paint downwards. Work down until about one-third of the meadow has been painted.

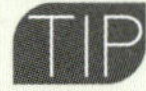

If the tape won't peel off, use a hairdryer to soften the adhesive under the tape.

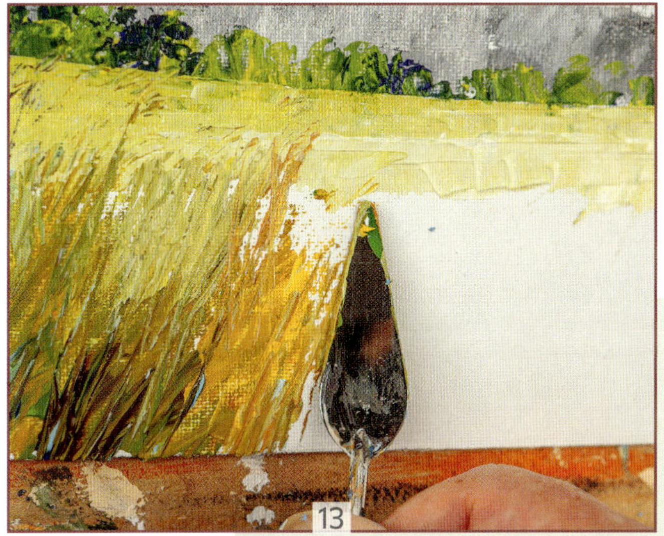

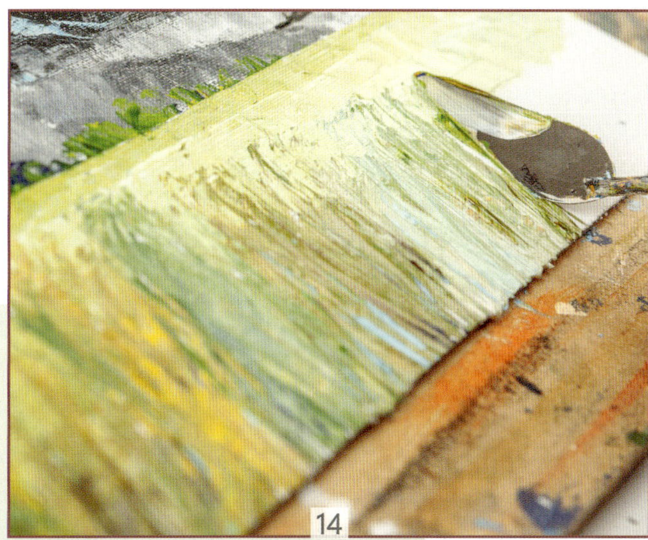

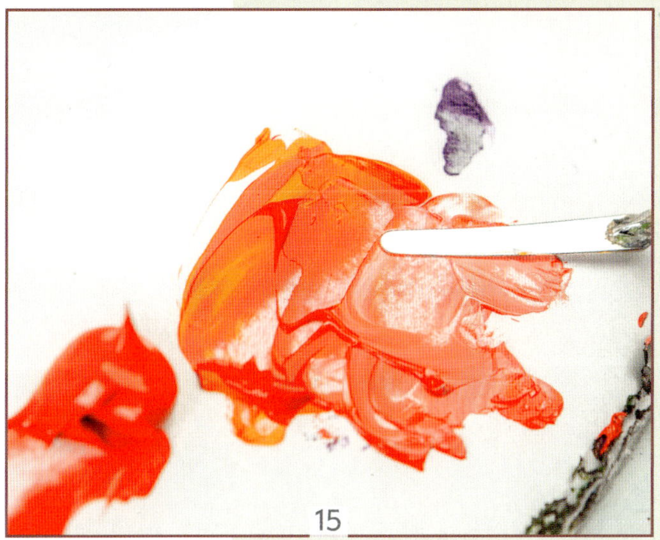

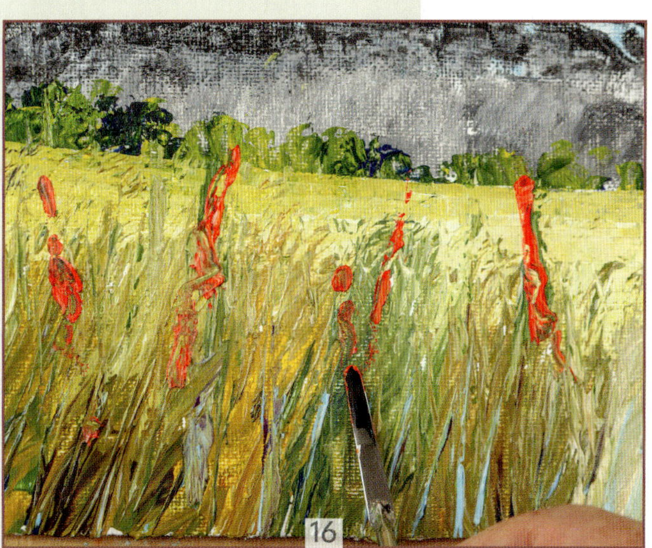

13 Add the grassy foreground next using the same technique as for the *Summer Meadow* foreground (see page 61) with a mix of burnt umber and ultramarine blue.

14 With the side of the knife held at an angle, slide the blade upwards to create the individual grass stems. For the deeper colours near the base, add azure blue and purple. Scratch out some of the lighter stalks with the knife tip.

15 Use the RGM Pastrello to mix cadmium red light hue with a touch of cadmium orange.

16 Add the flower spikes for the pinkweeds. Finally, work quickly across the meadow, adding flower spikes as randomly as possible.

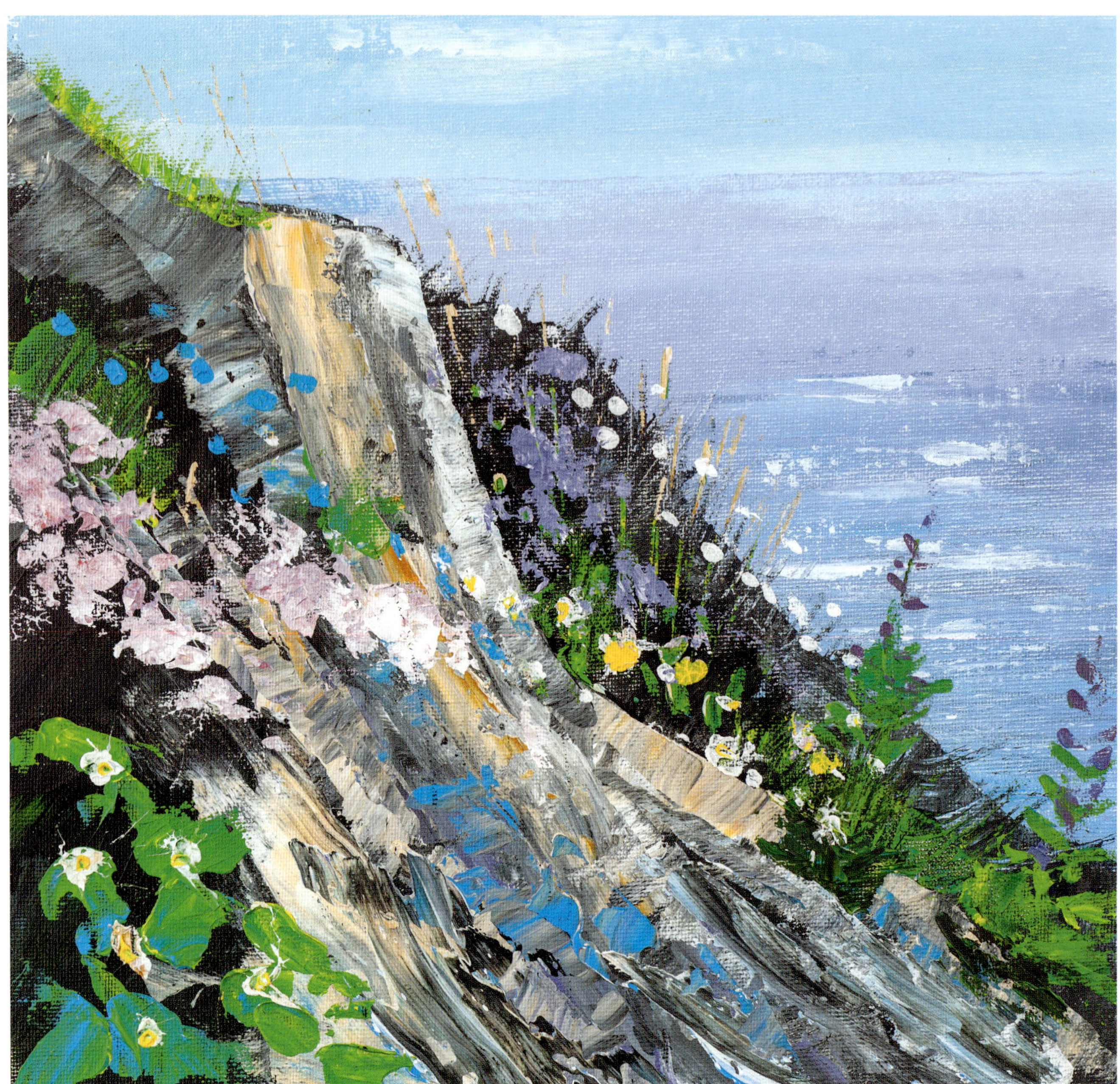

Strumble Head, Pembrokeshire, UK

30.5 × 30cm (12 × 12in)

Not mountains but a close-up of a cliff edge. Here, there is an opportunity to depict rock textures using the RGM 109, as well as using different knives for the huge variety of flowers clinging to the rocks.

Poppyfields

29.5 × 19.5cm (11⅝ × 7¾in)

The distant hills have been suggested by scumbling a violet
grey over the sky area. The curved horizon was created with
masking tape. Curves much greater than this are difficult to
produce using tape. The line of trees on the horizon was created
using ultramarine blue, primary yellow and marble dust. The
poppies in the foreground were painted using cadmium red
light hue and the small round.

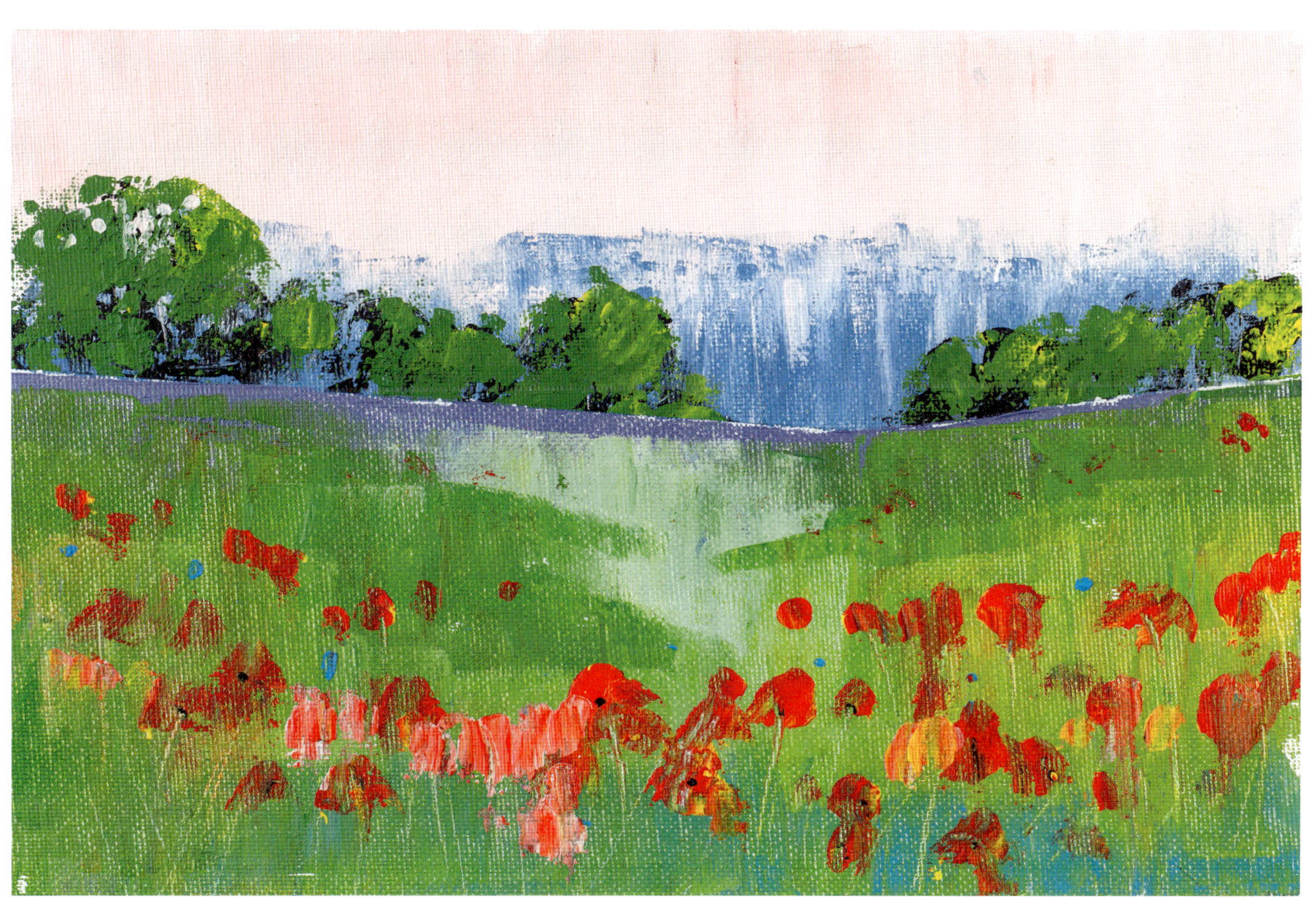

BAMBURGH SUNSET

For the final project, we look at painting on a black background. This offers a whole new dimension when painting, as the dark ground gives a certain vibrancy to the colours applied. We also look at combining brushwork with knifework. This usually happens when the desire for detail exceeds the ability to make the required marks with a knife. The marks made with the brush must sit comfortably with the knife marks, to ensure that the painting works well as a whole. This is usually achieved by learning to apply striated paint in small slabs with a brush and avoiding the feathered marks that brushwork can easily achieve.

The benefit of painting on a black background is that hot colours such as cadmium orange will really 'pop'. Also, shadow areas of buildings and other objects can be left as the black underpainting.

You will need

SURFACE:

Plain white primed canvas board tinted with a flat coat of Mars black, 40.5 × 30.5cm (16 × 12in).

KNIVES:

RGM 6, Pastrello 38 and bull nose.

PAINTS:

Cadmium orange, Naples yellow, titanium white, azure blue, Mars black, burnt umber, light violet, purple, primary yellow, ultramarine blue, yellow ochre and Chinese blue.

OTHER MATERIALS:

Neocolor II white water-soluble wax pastel, System3 filbert, size 4, and Zhu Ting angled flat brush, size 7.

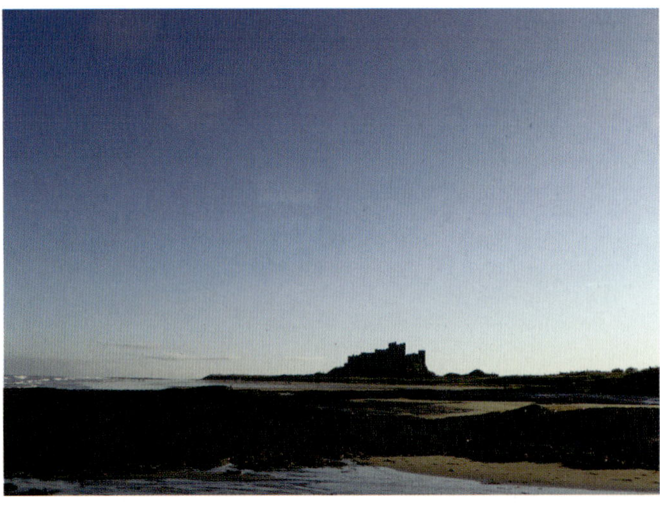

The reference photograph.

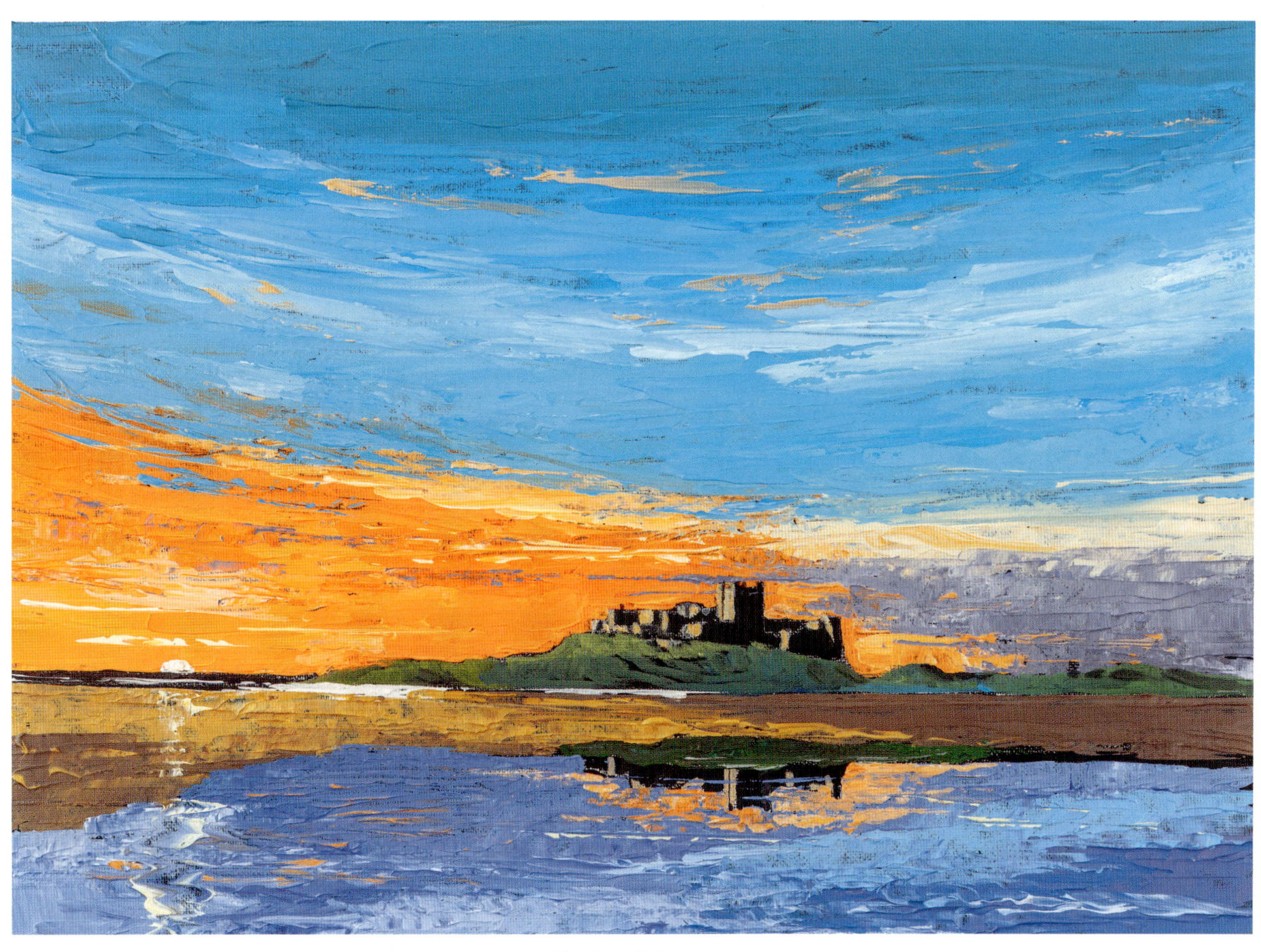

Bamburgh Sunset

40.5 × 30.5cm (16 × 12in)

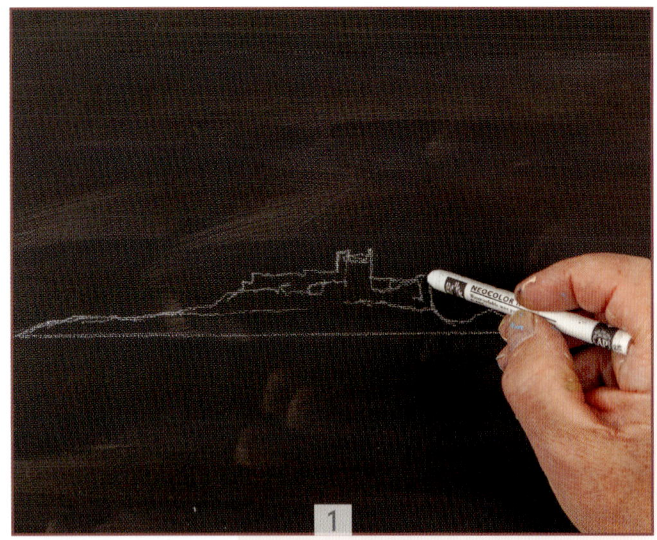

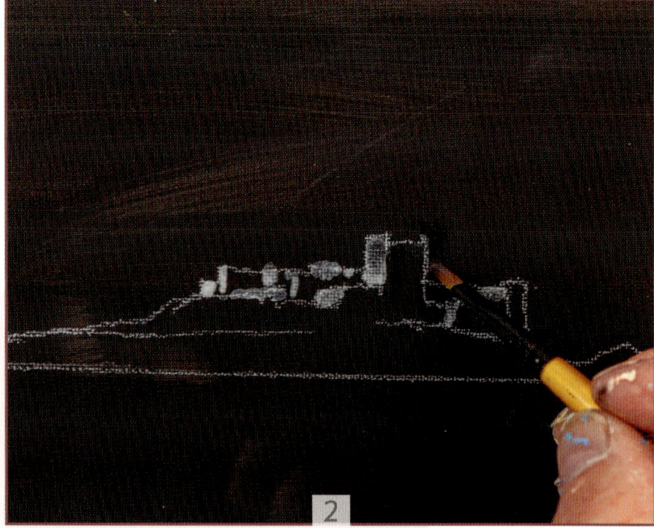

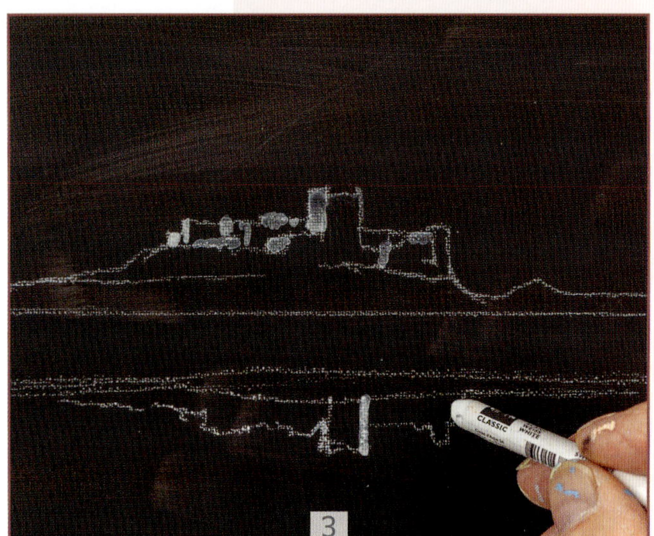

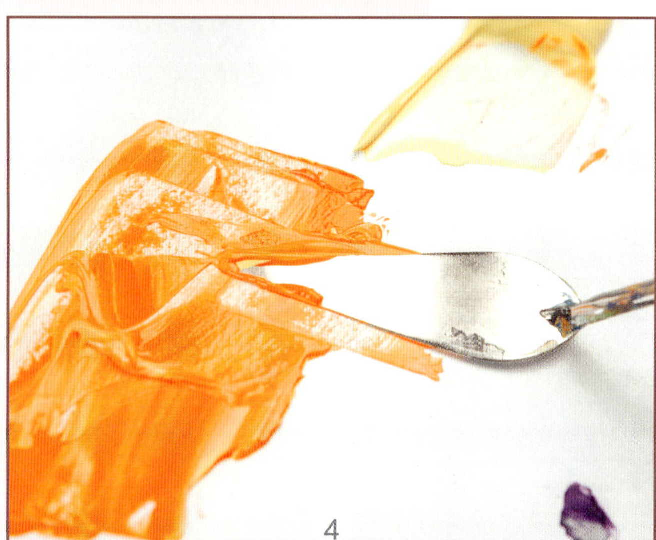

1 Draw in the horizon line about one-third up from the base of the board using a straight edge. Draw the profile of the castle on the embankment above this, using a white Neocolor II water-soluble wax pastel.

2 Use a damp brush to dilute the pastel and wash in the sunlit sides of the castle.

3 Create the reflection in the water below. This should be done quite simply without detail to just suggest the position of the buildings in the water.

4 Mix cadmium orange and Naples yellow with the RGM 6 knife.

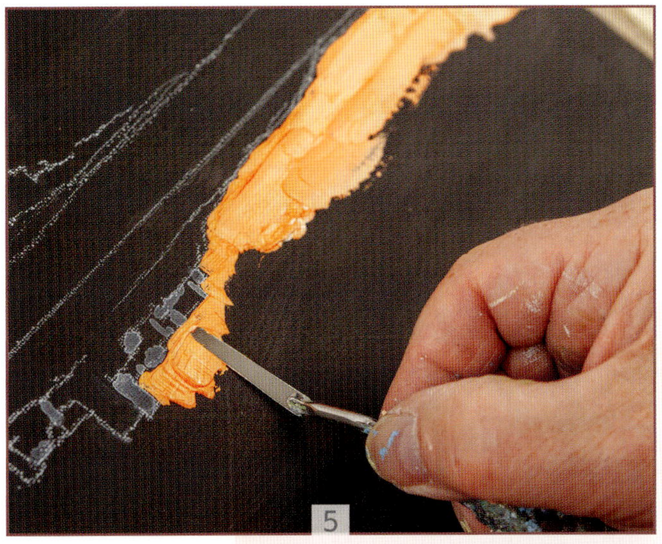

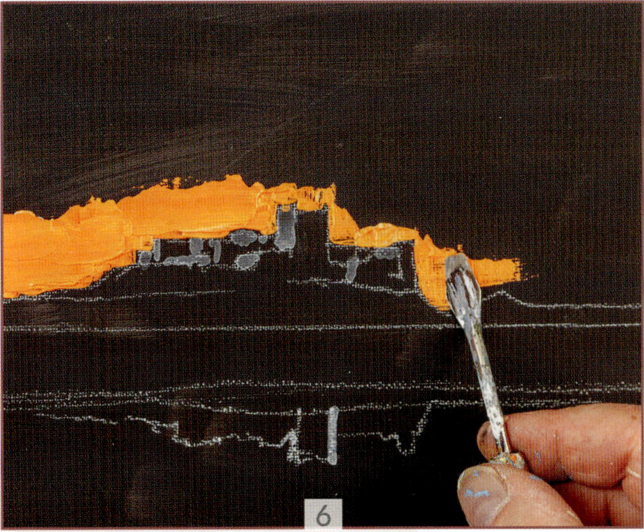

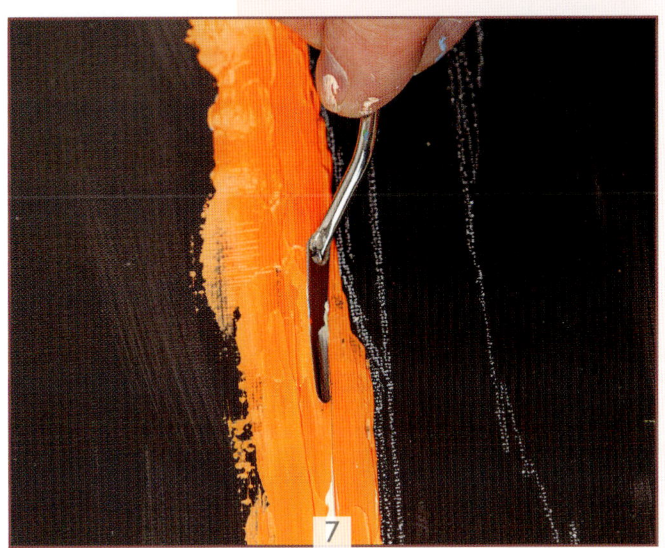

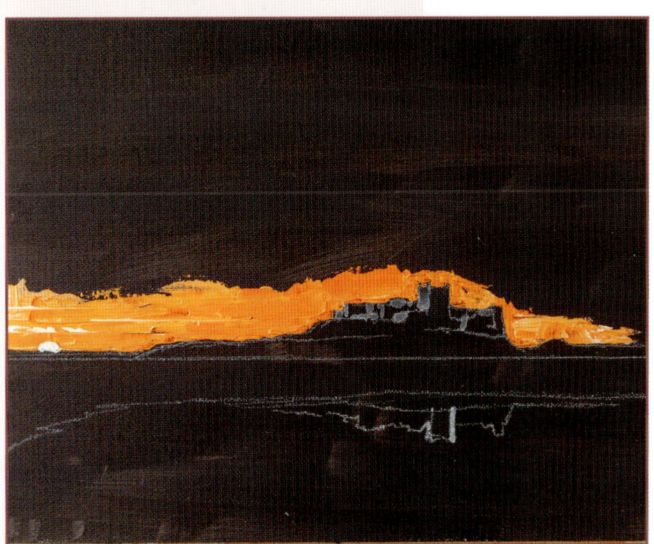

5 Start adding the sky quite thickly to the left moving towards the castle. As the castle is a complex shape, it's necessary to turn the work upside down and switch to the RGM Pastrello. Don't press down too hard as you need to avoid too much black showing through.

6 Turn the work the correct way up. For the really tight areas around the castle, use the bull nose.

7 Add a couple of horizontal slivers of Naples yellow mixed with titanium white to the lower horizon, as well as a small button of white to represent the setting sun.

A painter should begin every canvas with a wash of black, because all things in nature are dark except where exposed to the light.
– Leonardo da Vinci
(1452–1519)

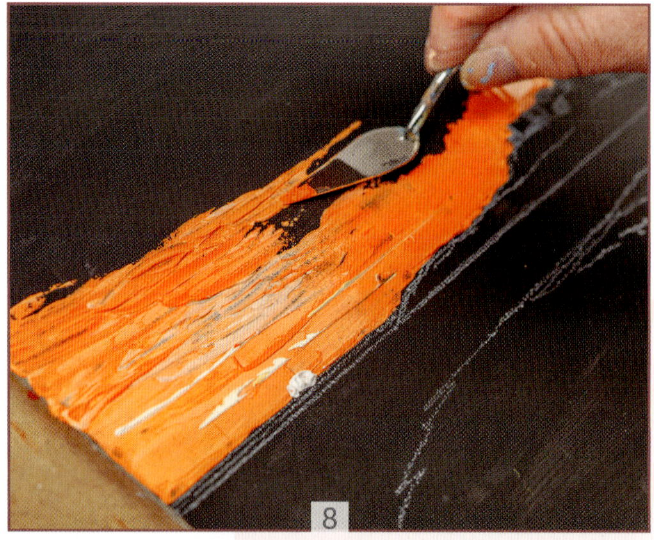

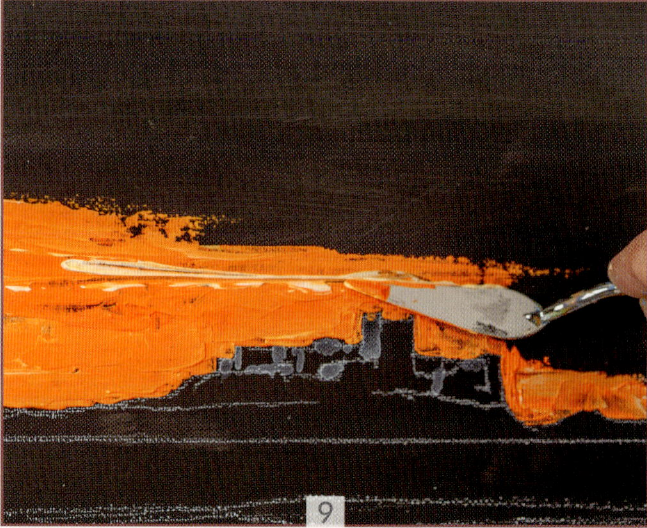

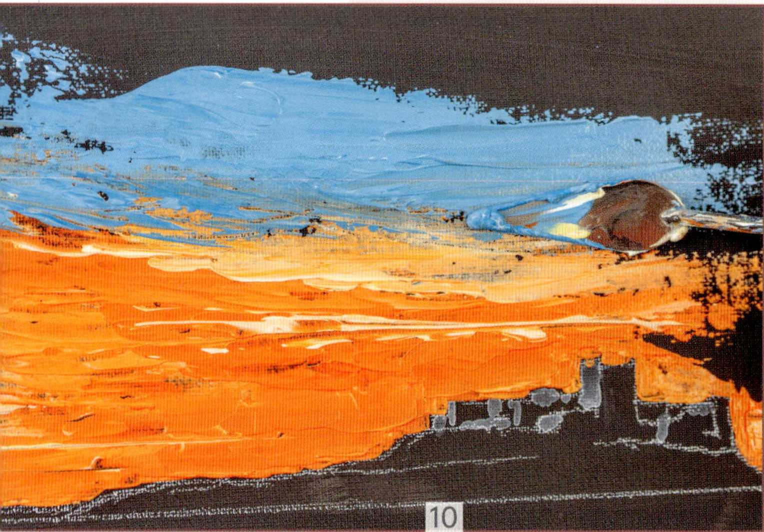

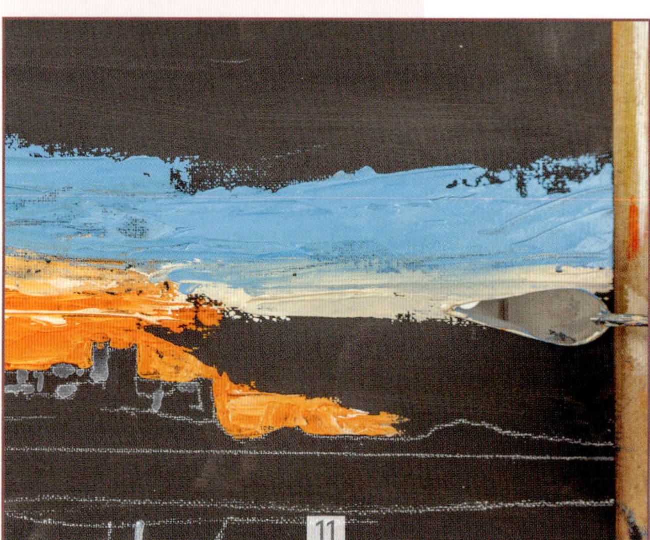

8 Make a striated mix of cadmium orange and white. Apply this with the RGM 6 above the castle using quite heavy applications of paint to get good coverage over the black, allowing the colours to split apart on the surface to suggest horizontal strokes of layered cloud.

9 Add some thin horizontal slivers of Naples yellow and white with the RGM 6 above the castle.

10 Using azure blue lightened with white, piggyback over the orange and gently blend the two colours together without too much mixing to avoid making a grey/green.

11 Add a mix of Naples yellow and titanium white to the right-hand side of the castle, gently blending with the applied blue mix.

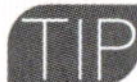
TIP

When I push the blue through the wet orange it tends to pick it up, so wipe the knife after every stroke to get a good distinction between the two colours.

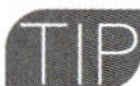
TIP

Choose a yellow such as yellow ochre or Naples yellow for the sky area and there's less chance of the sky turning green, as would happen if a purer colour such as primary yellow were used.

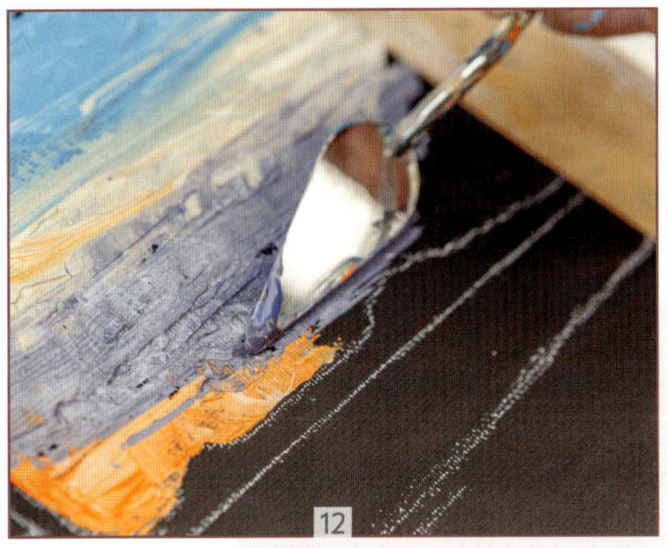

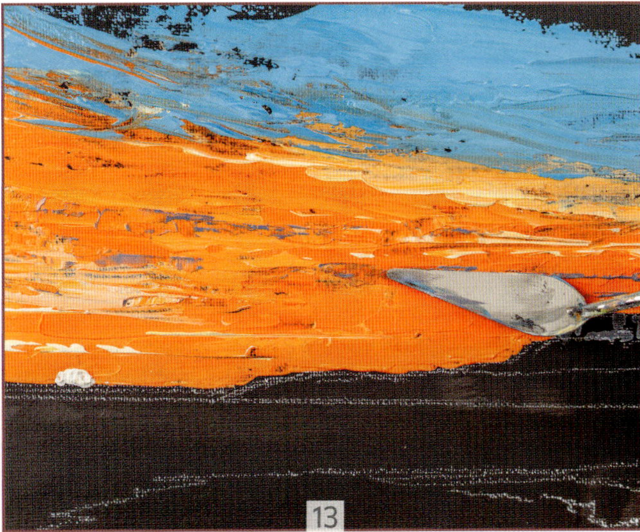

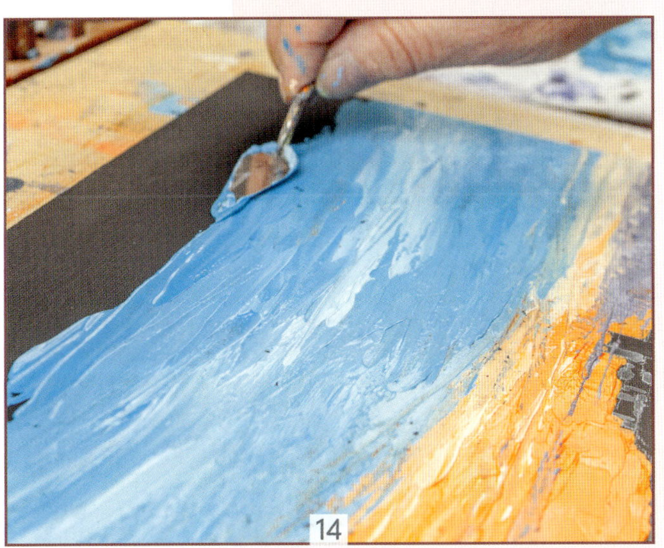

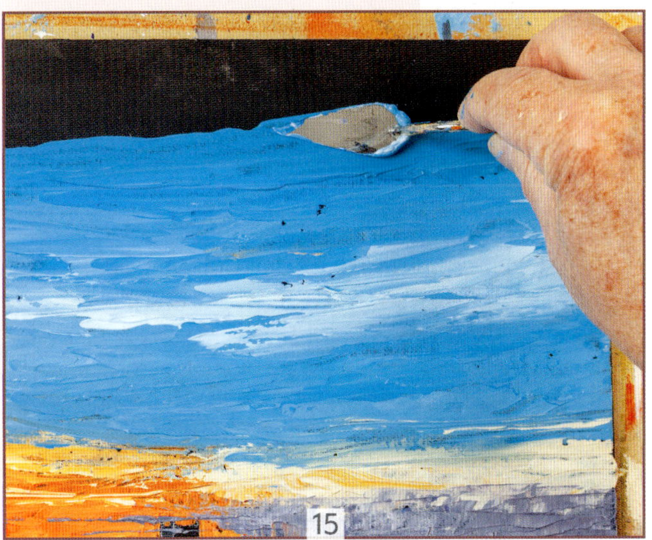

12 Add a little violet grey into the lower sky by mixing light violet with a little burnt umber; carefully work around the profiles of the distant hills.

13 Add flecks of the same colour into the sky on the left-hand side to suggest cloud shadows.

14 Continue to build up the sky above the castle using azure blue and white towards the top of the painting. Use the RGM 6 and thicker paint to get some good textures in. Occasionally apply a much lighter colour into the wet paint to suggest some stratus clouds near the top of the painting.

15 Darken the sky slightly near the top by adding a little burnt umber.

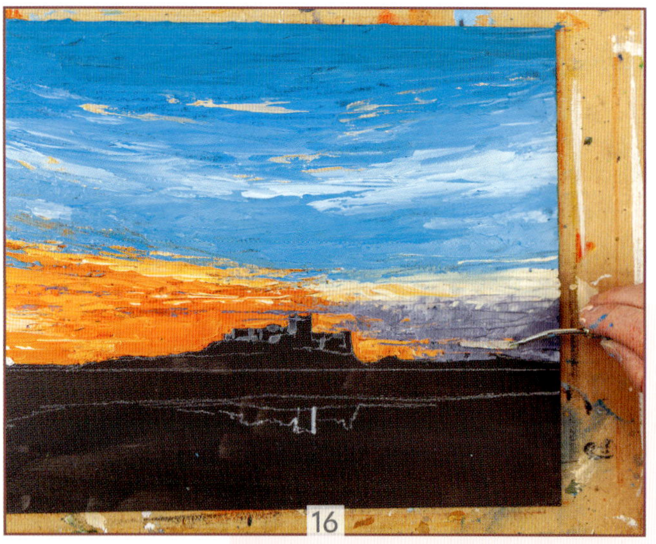

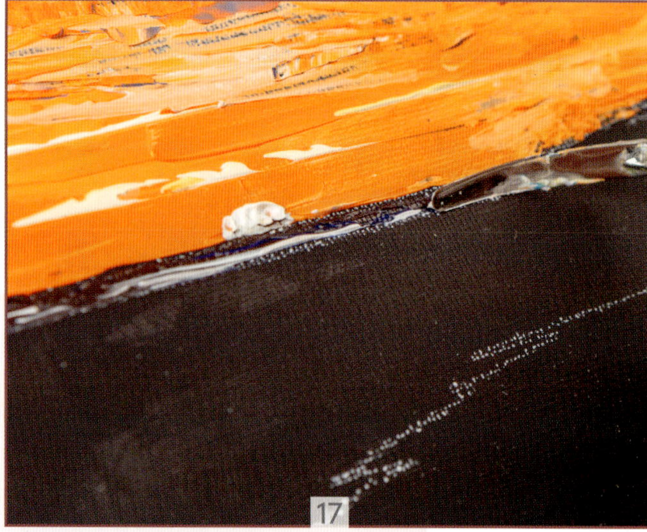

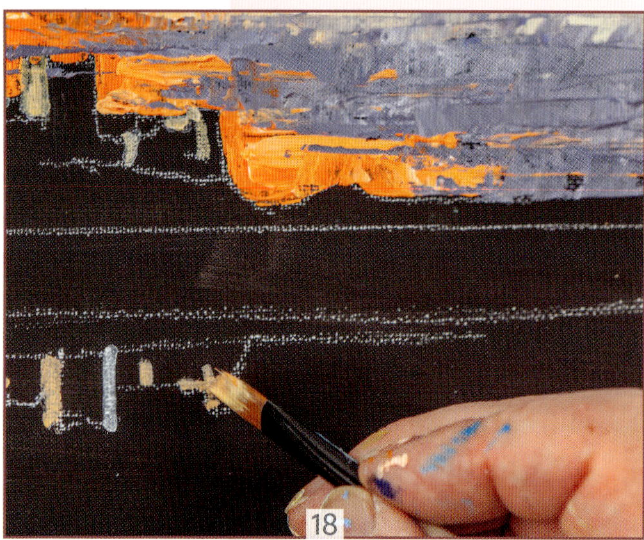

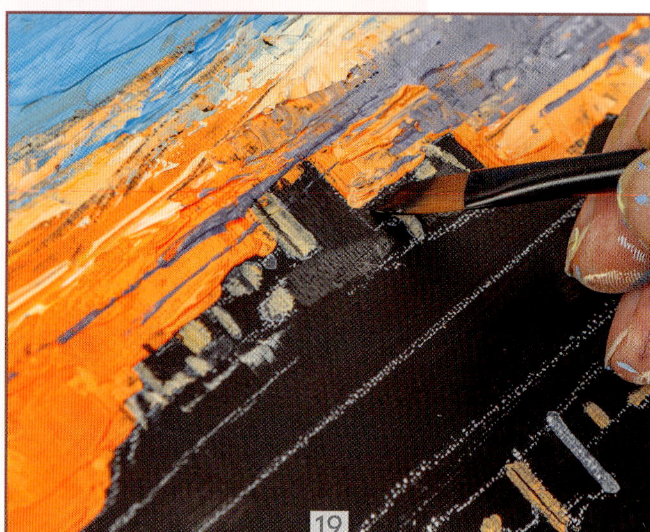

16 Finish the sky by working over it with the RGM Pastrello to cover up any parts where too much black is showing through.

17 Add a strip of purple with a double-loaded RGM Pastrello, then add a sliver of white through the wet paint to suggest crashing waves on the distant shore.

18 Using the size 7 Zhu Ting angled chisel brush, paint in the sunlit walls of the castle using a mix of titanium white and yellow ochre. The dark shadow sides can be left as the black underpainting. Add a slightly darker mix to the corresponding reflections below in the water.

19 Correct any mistakes around the castle walls by applying more Mars black with the chisel brush.

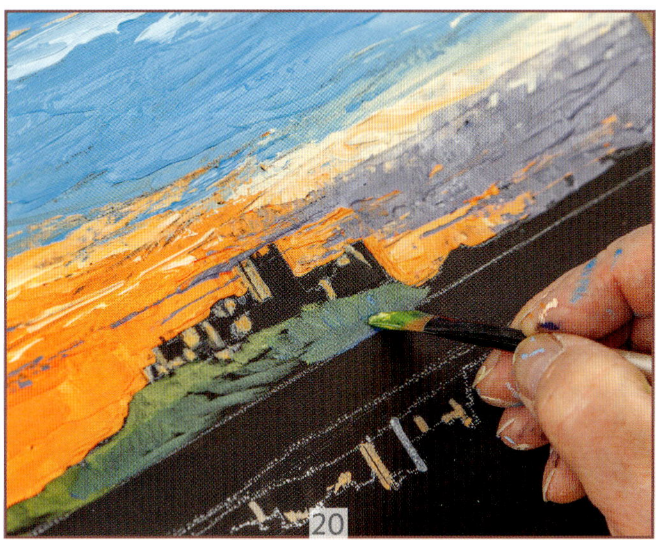

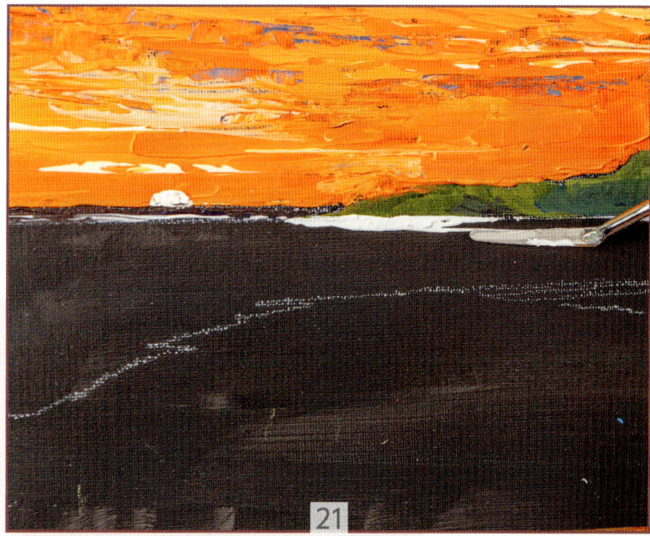

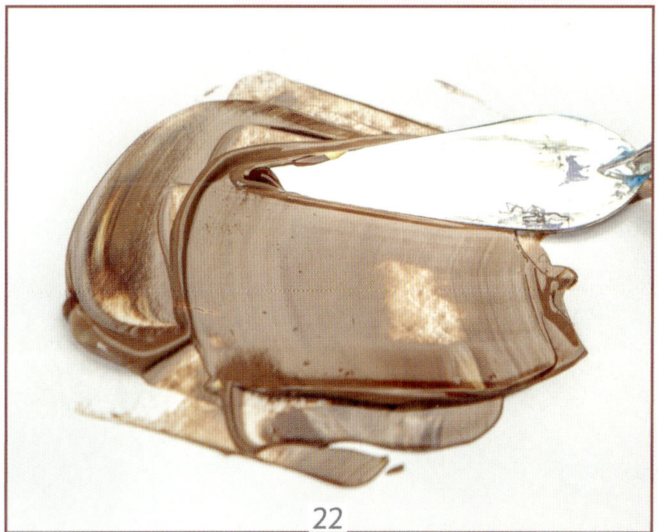

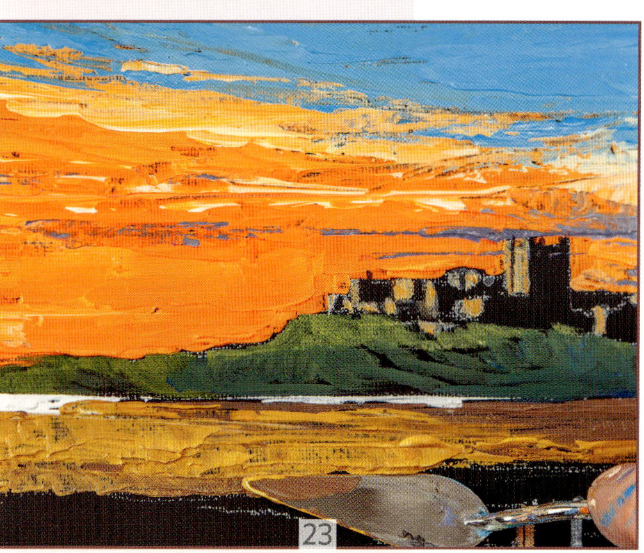

20 Switch to the filbert. Push a little orange into the sunlit castle walls around the keep, then paint the embankment green with a mix of ultramarine blue and primary yellow. Lighten some areas by adding more yellow and titanium white and darken others by introducing Mars black. Apply paint carefully down to the drawn line.

21 Switch back to the RGM Pastrello to add the pale blue water surrounding the base of the embankment using a mix of ultramarine blue and titanium white.

22 For the large area of sandy beach below the castle, start with burnt umber and then add a loose mix of Naples yellow and yellow ochre to it. Apply this striated mix using horizontal strokes with the RGM 6 knife.

23 Continue down to the foreground using smoothing strokes to blend the colours together.

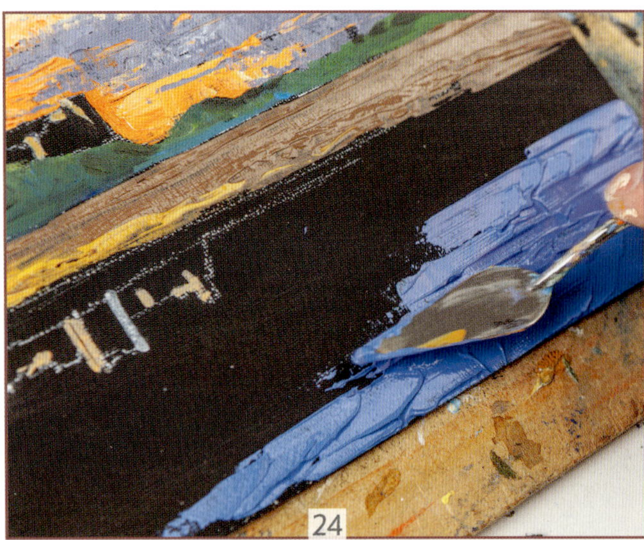

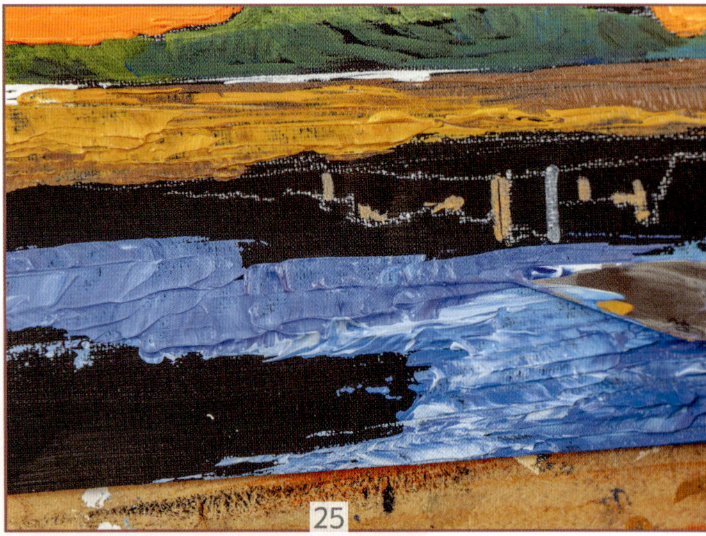

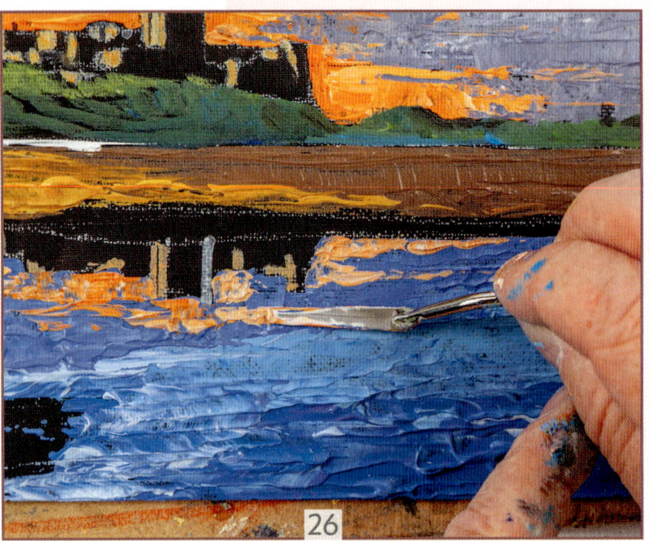

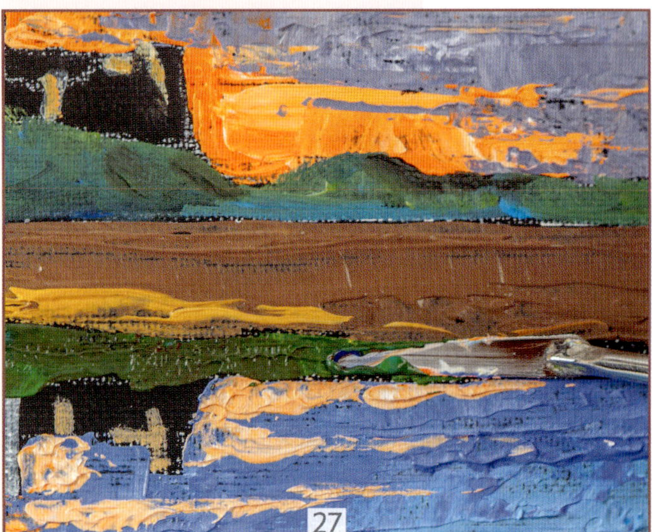

24   Mix light violet, Chinese blue, ultramarine blue and titanium white and add to the foreground sea/water area. Apply quite thickly to suggest the ripples in the water. Add a little azure blue with the double-loaded RGM Pastrello for the paler ripples.

25   To add more texture, touch the wet surface with the sole of the knife, then lift to create a few suction marks.

26   Add the remaining reflection shapes with the RGM Pastrello, adding a slightly darker version of the colours in the water, finishing with cadmium orange with a touch of titanium white. Drag these colours over the surface to create a broken texture. Keep turning the board to access the more difficult areas.

27   The reflections of the embankment can just be seen beyond the layer of sandy beach. Add these with a mix of ultramarine blue, primary yellow and burnt umber.

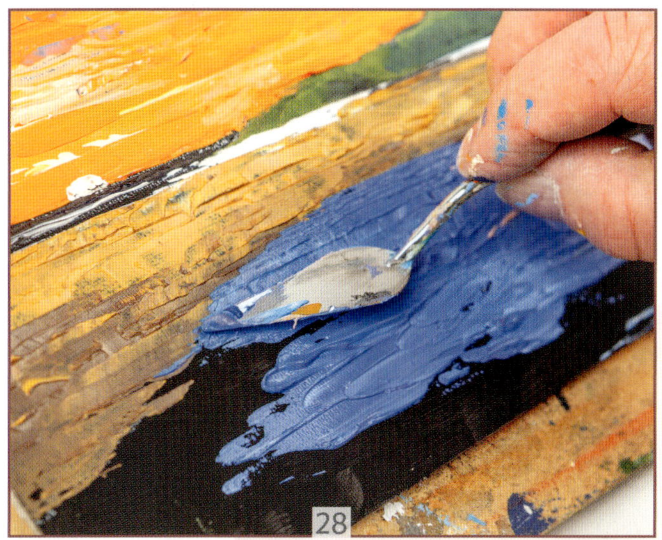

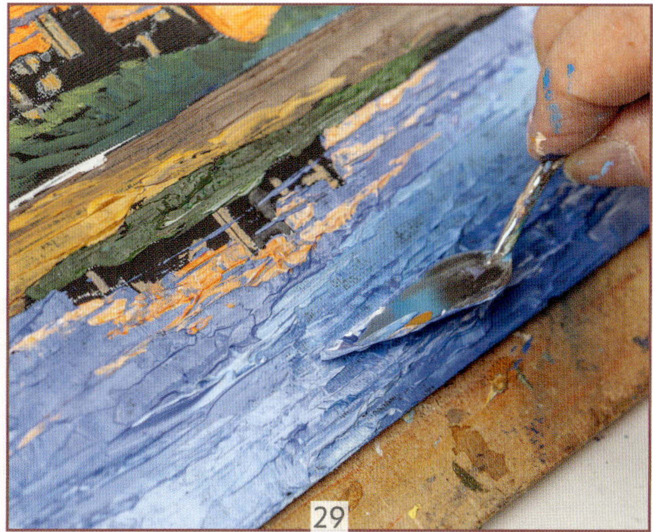

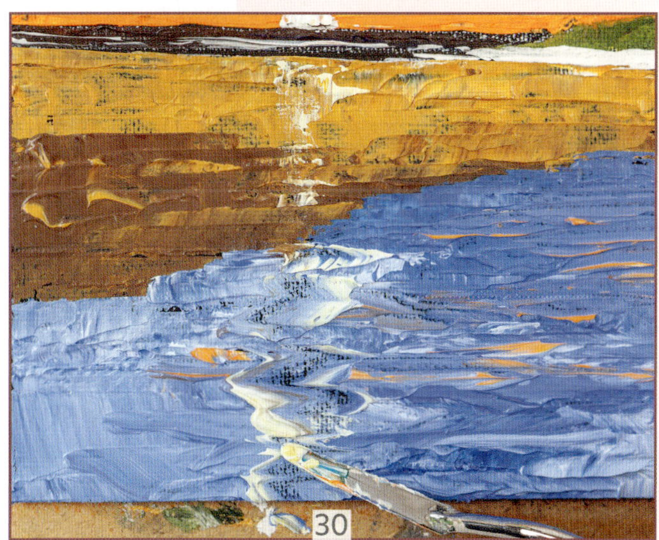

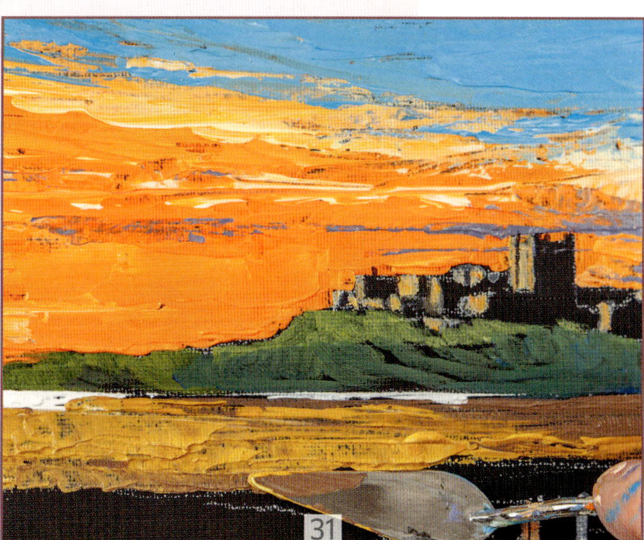

28 Continue to paint the water along the shoreline using ultramarine blue mixed with light violet using the RGM 6 knife.

29 Tap and lift the side of the knife into the wet paint to generate more ripples and texture effects.

30 Using Naples yellow and a double-loaded RGM Pastrello, make a wobbly vertical mark through the wet paint to suggest light reflections in the water. Add a few flecks of cadmium orange also.

31 Complete the painting by tidying up the foreground, covering up any larger black gaps that don't sit correctly with the finished painting.

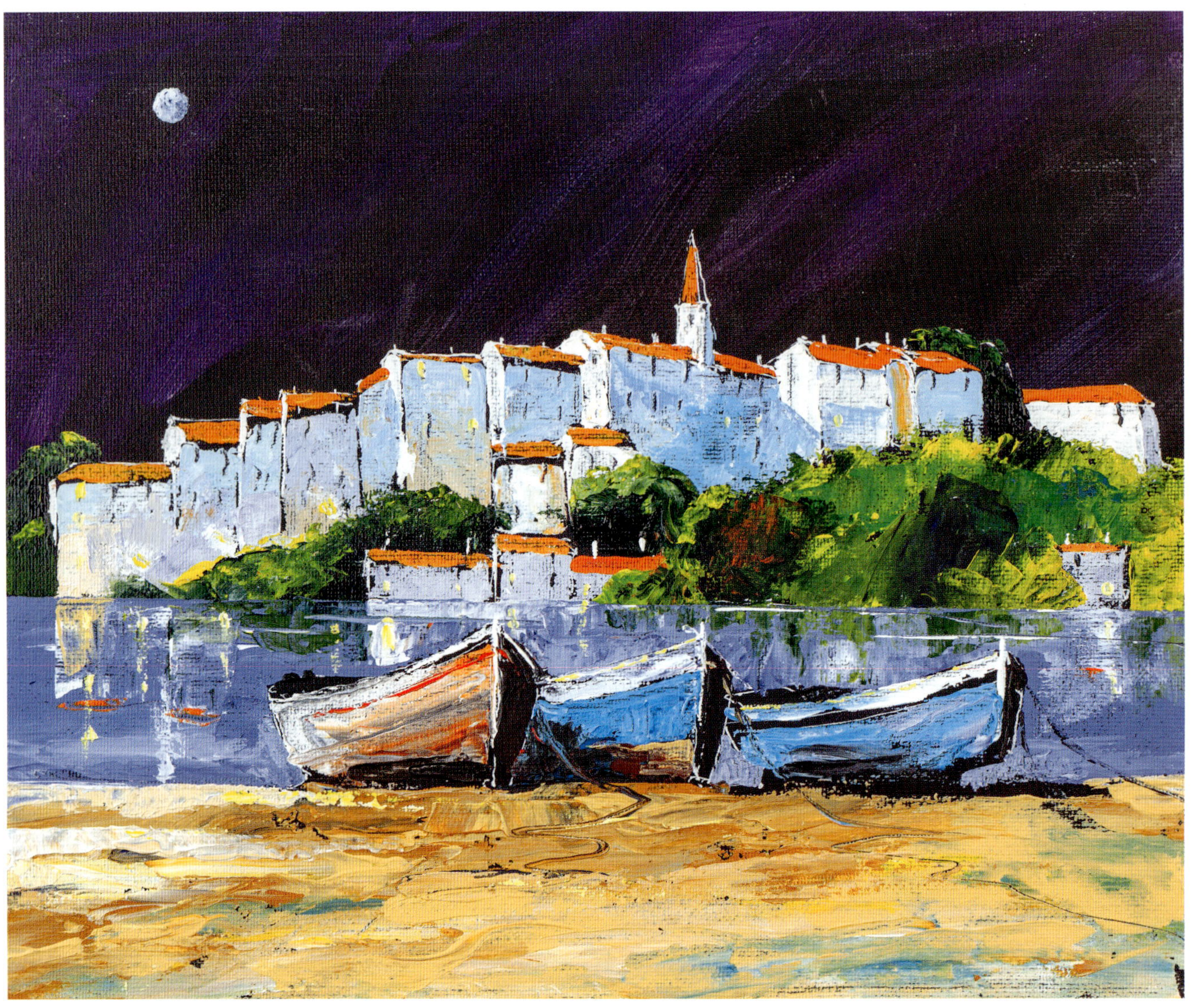

La Cadière d'Azur Nocturne, Provence, France

30.5 x 25.5cm (12 × 10in)

La Cadière d'Azur Nocturne is a painting I greatly enjoyed creating. The original subject had a different setting. After playing with the composition, I decided to place the town above a harbour scene. As the painting developed, the black surface started to suggest a nighttime scene and slowly developed into a moonlit evening.

Cley Windmill, Norfolk, UK

40.5 x 30.5cm (16 × 12in)

The entire painting, including the sky, was painted with knives, using marble dust for the foliage textures. Over this, the mill, buildings and boats were painted with a brush. There was quite a lot of texture on the surface, so it was much easier to add the mill sails and the mooring lines and detail with a fine brush.

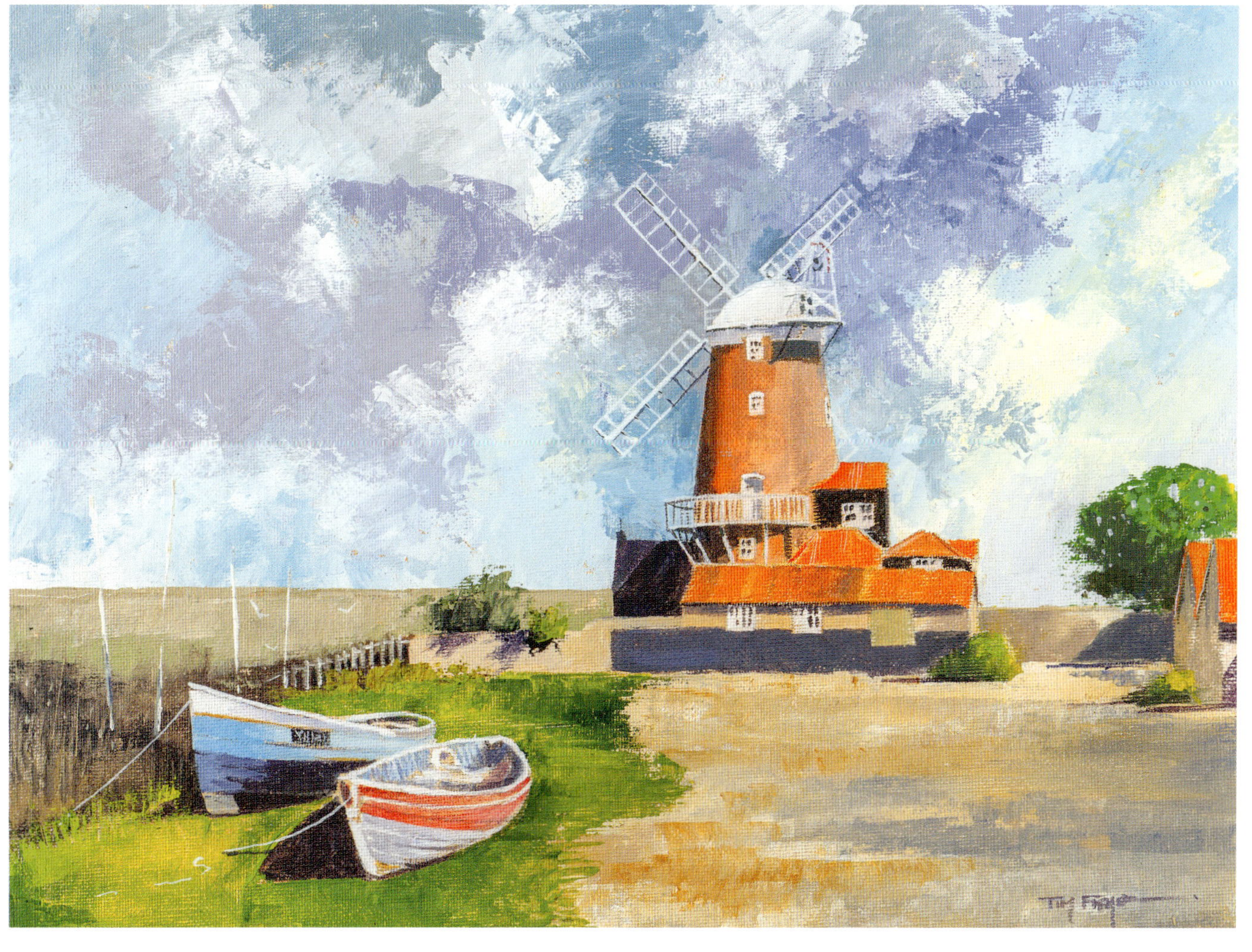

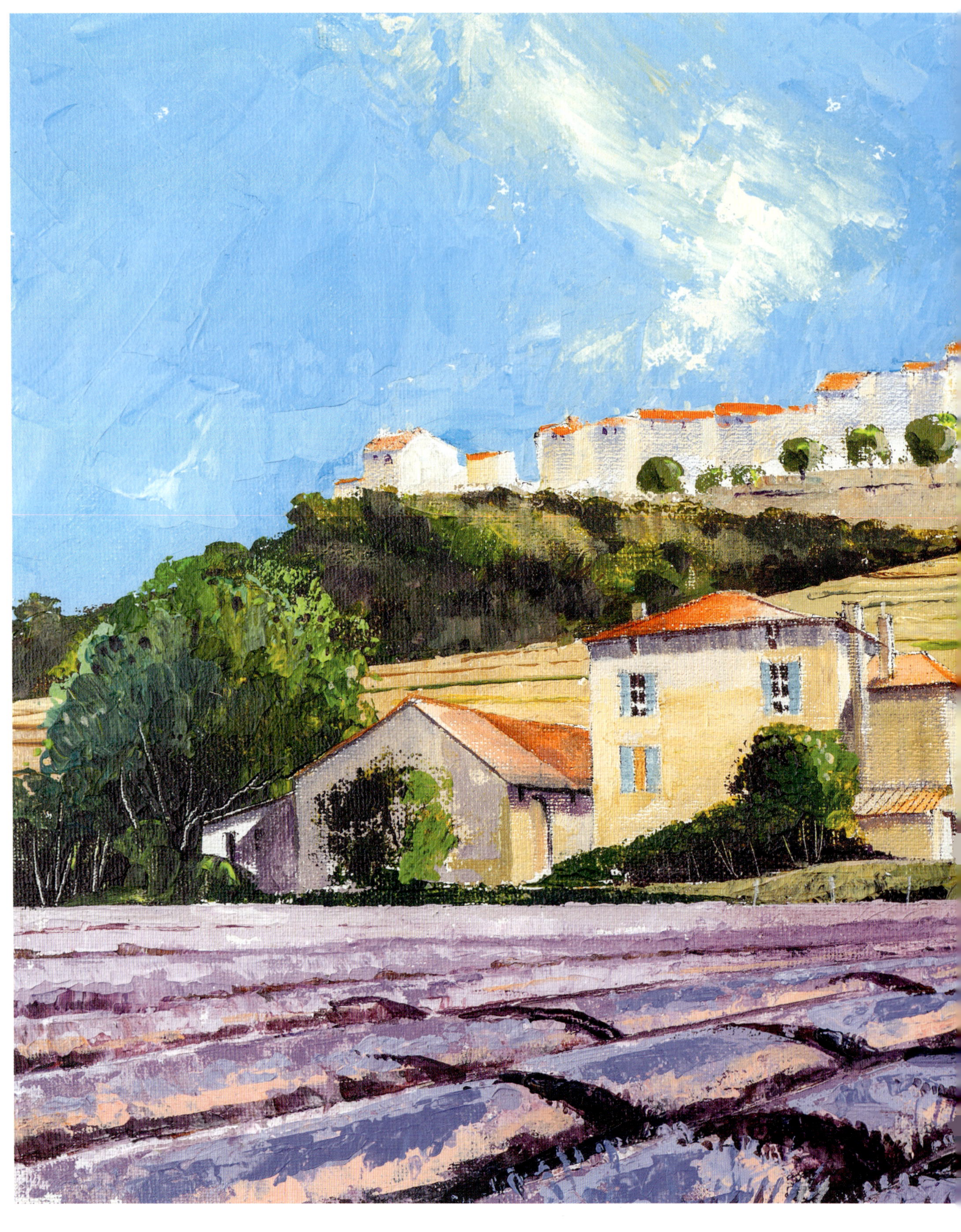

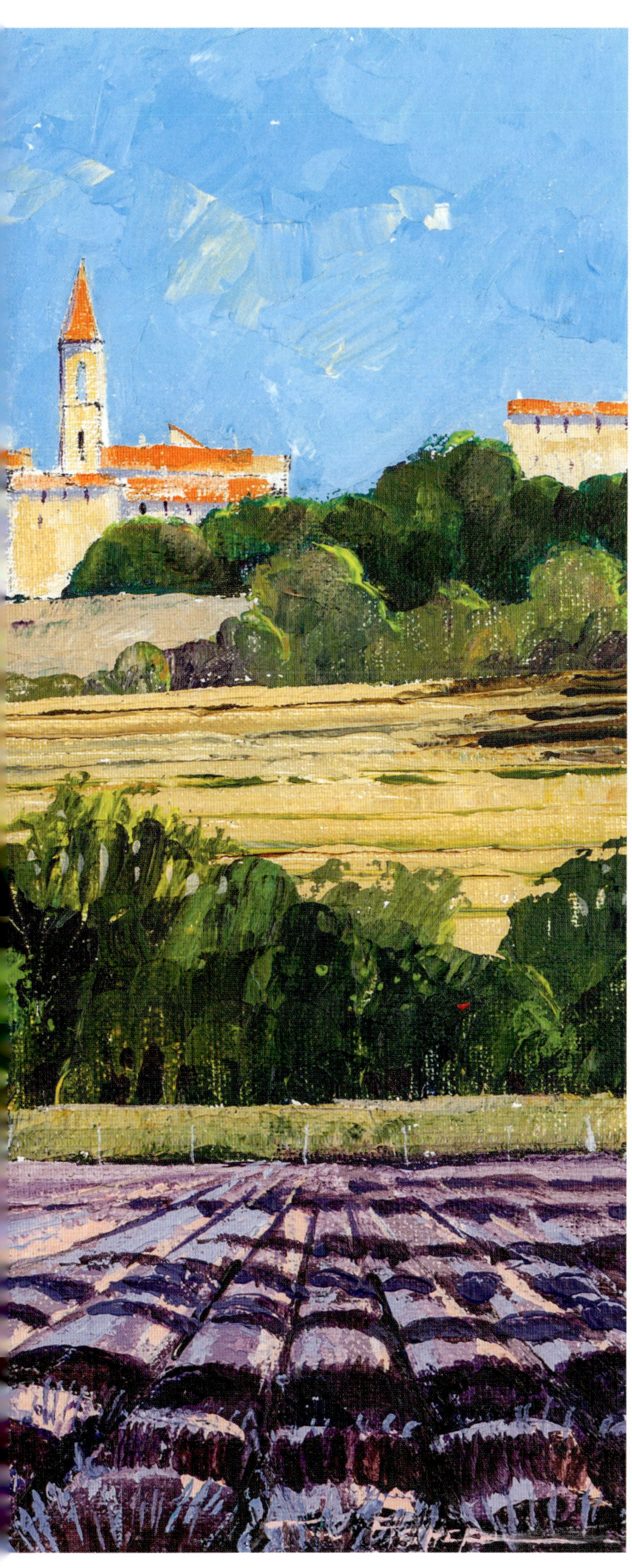

Farmhouse below La Cadière d'Azur, France

40.6 x 30.2cm (16 × 12in)

This is a subject I spotted when running a painting holiday in Provence. The original subject had vines in the foreground, though I thought the colours of lavender enhanced the painting so much more. The farmhouse and outbuildings have been painted with a brush, though I do try to use broken striated mixes of colour here, to fit in with the remainder of the painting, which was completed with knives. The hilltop town is painted entirely with knives, which gives a sense of distance. All the trees and foliage were painted with the small round and marble dust.

Index

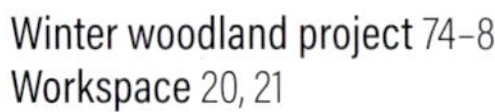
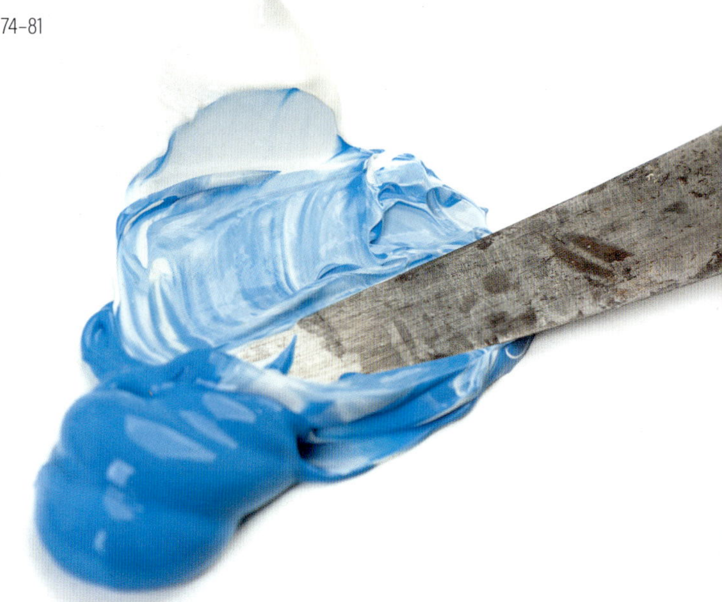